Arm® Helium™ Technology

M-Profile Vector Extension (MVE) for Cortex-M Processors

Arm® Helium™ Technology

M-Profile Vector Extension (MVE) for Cortex-M Processors

Reference Book

JON MARSH

arm Education Media

Contents

4. Data Processing Instructions

5. Memory Access Instructions

Foreword

To declare my interests up front, I have been at Arm for just about 20 years. In that time, the electronics industry, and Arm with it, has changed quite simply beyond belief.

Jon Marsh joined Arm in 1997, a couple of years before I did and I have had the pleasure of knowing and working with him for my entire career at Arm. For the majority of that time I was in charge of Arm's customer training activity and Jon was one of the most capable trainers in the team. He has the rare combination of a deep technical grasp of his subject coupled with the ability to explain complex topics in a clear and accessible way.

When Jon joined Arm, Arm's processors were becoming very popular in the mobile phone industry and were starting to proliferate in other markets. Jon was a key part of the Application Engineering team, providing support and training to a fast-growing worldwide population of silicon and software developers.

Since joining in 1999, I have been fortunate to witness Arm "raising the bar" time and time again. The introduction of the Thumb® instruction set in 1994 was arguably the first and most significant game-changing innovation in the Arm processor family, enabling a step change in performance at the same time as a reduction in memory footprint for constrained processors. The Arm7TDMI was adopted widely in the mobile phone industry and became Arm's first worldwide success story. In the following years, Arm brought out innovative changes at an astonishing rate: the Arm920T with its change to a Harvard bus architecture; the Arm926EJ-S, a fully-synthesizable IP core with hardware Java acceleration; the Arm11 family, with the first implementations of the Thumb-2 instruction set, the TrustZone® security architecture, and Arm's first foray into a multiprocessor extension; then with the switch to the Cortex® brand in 2004, three distinct ranges of processor cores, A, R and M, targeted respectively at high-performance, hard real-time and mass-market microcontrollers.

It is that move into the microcontroller space which has driven the phenomenal growth in shipments of Arm processors for over 15 years. I recently asked one of my embedded industry veteran friends what he thought was the biggest game-changer in the last 50 years of embedded computing. His answer came straight back, "The Cortex-M3," he said. "That put 32-bit computing power into the hands of embedded developers for less than a dollar. And it changed everything." I admit to some bias, but I am with him on this. Go to any embedded industry event, look up the line card of any components distributor and you will find the Cortex-M3 and its descendants everywhere.

The Cortex-M microcontroller revolution didn't stop at the Cortex-M3. With the Cortex-M0 and Cortex-M0+, they got smaller; with the Cortex-M1, they went into FPGA; with the Cortex-M4, they acquired floating-point and DSP capability; with the Cortex-M23 and Cortex-M33, they brought hardware-enforced TrustZone security to microcontrollers for the first time.

Now, with the Cortex-M55, Arm has not just changed the game so much as moved it to an entirely new ballpark in a different city. The Cortex-M55 processor is the first Arm core to implement Helium technology, the M-Profile Vector Extension (MVE). This adds a vector processing instruction set extension which provides a step change in the performance of the core for Digital Signal Processing (DSP) and Machine Learning (ML) workloads.

Why, you might ask, is this happening? And why is it so important that Arm is doing this now? The reason is that we are seeing a change in the way distributed systems are built. Historically, the workloads involved in DSP and ML applications have not been possible on a microcontroller alone, so designers have often added a separate DSP to the device to handle them. This makes the hardware design more complex and the software development significantly more difficult due to the need for multiple tool chains to handle separate applications running on devices with different architectures. The advent of high-speed networking has made it possible to routinely send data to a server to be processed but this, too, has problems as an approach. Not only does it introduce a potentially unacceptable latency into the system, it also comes with increased security risks and increased energy consumption. The most fundamental problem with it is its inherent lack of scalability – neither bandwidth nor server capacity is infinite.

So, the race is on to move as much of this high-performance number crunching closer to the edge of the network, ideally onto a single processor on the endpoint device itself. Put simply, the Cortex-M55 makes this possible.

Earlier Cortex-M microcontroller cores, based on the Armv7-M architecture, rely principally on an integer instruction set for computation. The Cortex-M4 and Cortex-M7 include extensions which provide for floating-point computation and accelerate some DSP operations, making them suitable for a wider range of workloads. The Cortex-M55, based on the Armv8.1-M architecture, goes much further than this with its implementation of the Helium MVE extensions.

These extensions add an entirely new capability to the Cortex-M family – the ability to process vectors of data in simultaneous parallel operations. For certain classes of workload, principally DSP, this allows for a significant increase in throughput, enabling a microcontroller-class device to address, unaided, a much wider range of use cases.

It also rises to the challenge of ever-increasing sophistication in embedded devices, addressing the need for richer and more complex user interfaces, the adoption of touch and voice control, and the need to fuse and interpret data from an ever wider array of sensors.

This new book is a perfect introduction to this new capability. In the early chapters, Jon introduces fundamental concepts at a very basic and accessible level, including single instruction, multiple data (SIMD), vector processing, floating- and fixed-point data representations, and saturation. After an overview of the MVE architecture, the instruction set is broken down into clear groups for discussion, covering subjects like pipeline structure, predication and branch handling, data processing and memory access.

The most practical sections of the book deal with the mechanics of coding for a Helium-capable core such as the Cortex-M55, including compilation, debug and optimization.

Finally, the book concludes with perhaps the most important chapters, on how to implement DSP and ML workloads. Again, we are treated to an excellent introduction to the fundamentals, followed by intensely practical advice on how to code and optimize key algorithms and techniques, such as Fourier transforms, filtering and neural networks.

I am delighted to be able to recommend this book to all software developers looking to extend their knowledge into exciting new fields.

Chris Shore
Director of Product Management, Automotive & IoT Business, Arm
September 2020

Preface

The aim of this book is to introduce Arm's Helium technology, the M-Profile Vector Extension for the Arm Cortex-M processor series. Helium brings exciting new capabilities to microcontrollers, allowing sophisticated digital signal processing or machine learning applications to be run on inexpensive, low-power devices.

The book is intended to be useful to engineers and students who want to learn more about these new features. It is not an introductory text on digital signal processor (DSP) programming, and some prior knowledge of C and Arm assembly language is a prerequisite.

Acknowledgments

I would like to thank Arm Education Media for providing me with the opportunity to write this book and their hard work and help getting it into publication.

Many people have contributed to this book. I would particularly like to thank Fabien Klein and Christophe Favergeon from Arm France, and Salman Arif and Edmund Player from Arm's Application Engineering team for their invaluable help with example code, access to training material, and many suggestions and answers to questions. I would also like to thank François Botman, Sjoerd Meijer and Hanno Becker for their technical expertise and helpful review comments. The book would not have been possible without their assistance.

Jon Marsh, September 2020

Author Biography

Jon Marsh has more than 25 years' industry experience, working both for Arm and its semiconductor partners. He has worked on Arm CPUs from the ARM2 through to today's high-end 64-bit processors. Jon has undertaken consulting work and given training courses on Arm processors at most of the world's top semiconductor and consumer companies and spoken at conferences and universities in Asia, Europe and North America.

Typographical Conventions

Various typographical conventions have been used in this book:

▪ Assembly Language code is shown thus:

```
VADD Q0, Q0, Q1
```

▪ C code is shown similarly:

```
printf("Hello World");
```

▪ Register bits are shown with square brackets, so that Q0[15:0] means bit 15 down to bit 0 of register Q0.

▪ Hexadecimal values are shown preceded by 0x (i.e. 0x10 is decimal 16). Binary values are shown preceded by 0b (for example 0b101).

▪ In syntax descriptions, items in instruction fields are shown enclosed with < >, which must be replaced with appropriate values, as explained. Optional items are enclosed with { }.

▪ C/C++ function names (including Helium intrinsic functions) are shown in lower case.

CHAPTER

Introduction

1

This book is written for software engineers who wish to learn more about Arm's Helium technology, the M-Profile Vector Extension (MVE) for the Arm Cortex-M processor series. It is suitable for engineers who want to migrate to Helium from systems which include a dedicated DSP, existing users of Cortex-M microcontrollers who wish to understand or use the new capabilities of the latest Cortex-M processors, and engineers who want to get started with neural networks and machine learning algorithms for Cortex-M processors.

The text assumes some familiarity with C programming; however, we have tried to make example code easy to follow. We would expect that Helium code will be written in a high-level language, but it is useful for debug and optimization to be familiar with low-level code and so some knowledge of assembly language is also required. Similarly, knowledge of Cortex-M processors and basic DSP theory is also assumed, although we will briefly review those areas where necessary to introduce Helium. Readers may wish to refer to one of Joseph Yiu's excellent books on the Cortex-M family, or to the introductory DSP books published by Arm Education Media.

The book is not a replacement for the Arm Architecture Reference Manual (Arm ARM), which provides the detailed specification for a processor implementation and acts as a reference for software developers to every part of the instruction set architecture (ISA).

In Chapter 1, we will introduce the main new features of Helium and compare it to other Arm single instruction multiple data (SIMD) and DSP options, and look at each of the new features. Chapter 2 looks at SIMD basics, while Chapter 3 covers Helium registers, number formats and other architecture fundamentals. In Chapters 4–6, we will take a detailed look at the instruction set. Chapters 7 and 8 cover the various options for writing code for Helium and measuring performance and optimizing code. At the end of these chapters, there are a small number of questions allowing the reader to check their understanding of the key learning points. Brief answers to these can be found at the back of the book.

The remaining chapters of the book focus on examples. We will review some basic DSP operations and see how they can be implemented on Helium and then look at some specific real-world applications. Finally, we will see how Helium enables interesting and useful machine learning algorithms to be run on Cortex-M microcontrollers.

1.1 Helium Introduction

Arm is the industry's leading supplier of microprocessors, offering a wide range of microprocessor cores to address the performance, power and cost requirements for almost all application markets. The company does not manufacture silicon devices. Instead, Arm creates microprocessor designs, which are licensed to semiconductor companies and OEMs, who then integrate them into system-on-chip (SoC) devices. An ecosystem of more than 1000 companies designs and manufactures silicon and writes development tools and software.

Before introducing Helium, it is useful to understand the distinction Arm makes between architecture and implementations. In order to guarantee compatibility between different processors, Arm defines a series of architecture specifications. These provide a definition as to how CPUs which are compliant must behave. Each processor which implements the Arm architecture conforms to a specific version of the architecture.

Arm processors are used in a very wide range of different applications, with very different performance and price points – from Internet of Things (IoT) sensor nodes to supercomputers. This means that there is a correspondingly wide range of processors to choose from. These are classified in different profiles and conform to different versions of the Arm architecture.

- **Cortex-A** – Application processors. These are used in the most complex/highest performance points, where support for operating systems, such as Linux, Windows or Android, is required.

- **Cortex-R** – These processors are targeted at real-time systems, such as hard drive controllers and mobile phone baseband.

- **Cortex-M** – Microcontroller class processors. These are used in systems where low cost or low power is required, or a more deterministic, fast interrupt response. As of 2019, according to Arm, more than 45 billion Cortex-M based chips have been manufactured.

Arm has adopted the brand name Neoverse to describe its offerings in the infrastructure market space.

Cortex-M processors are very small and can be readily integrated into SoC designs. These processors implement a version of the Arm architecture known as the M-profile. There are several different versions:

- **Armv6-M** – This is implemented by the Cortex-M0, Cortex-M0+, and Cortex-M1 processors. These very popular CPUs are power-efficient and small. (Arm claims an area of 0.0066 mm^2 for the Cortex-M0+ implemented in a foundry 40 nm process, which means that we could fit 150 of these CPUs on a square millimeter of silicon.)

- **Armv7-M** – This version of the architecture is implemented by the Cortex-M3, Cortex-M4 and Cortex-M7 processors, which are at a higher performance point. The Armv7-M ISA provides support for additional addressing modes, conditional execution, bit field processing, and multiply and accumulate (MAC) hardware. Cortex-M4 and Cortex-M7 support 32-bit SIMD operations and an optional floating-point unit (FPU). This may be single precision on Cortex-M4 or Cortex-M7 and can also optionally support double precision on Cortex-M7. Cortex-M7 is superscalar and can support caches and Tightly-Coupled Memory (TCM).

- **Armv8-M** – This version of the architecture adds features, such as TrustZone® security extension support, and is implemented by the newest Cortex-M processors, such as Cortex-M23 and Cortex-M33.

The company also offers the Ethos family of neural processing units (NPUs). The Ethos-U55 microNPU is designed to accelerate machine learning inference performance in area-constrained embedded and IoT devices.

1.2 The Armv8.1-M Architecture

In February 2019, Arm announced the Armv8.1-M architecture. This is an extension of the Armv8-M architecture and includes a range of new features. The new vector ISA, Helium, is the main focus of this text, but there are several additional new features:

- Additional instruction set enhancements for loops and branches (Low Overhead Branch Extension). These will be covered in this book, in Sections 3.3 and 6.1.

- Instructions for half-precision floating-point support. These will be covered in this book in Chapter 4.

- Enhancements in debug including performance monitoring unit (PMU) and additional debug support to focus on signal processing application developments. These latter features include being able to set a breakpoint which triggers (halts code execution and passes control to the debugger) when a certain count value is reached, and being able to set a data watchpoint with a bit mask for data value comparison (for example, for looking for a signal value to be within a certain range). We will look at these in Chapter 8.

There are some additional new features which are not directly related to Helium and which are not covered in this book. Please refer to Arm documentation for more details on these.

- Instruction set enhancement for TrustZone® management of the FPU. This allows for faster context switching between Secure and Non-secure code when both make use of the FPU. When Non-secure code calls a Secure API function, the Secure code is now able to save and restore the Non-secure Floating-Point Status and Control Register (FPSCR) states. This allows the Secure API to use different FPU configurations from Non-secure code, if required.

- Unprivileged debug extension, which allows fine-grained debug access to be granted only to selected unprivileged compartments.

- A new memory attribute, "Privileged eXecute Never" (PXN), is provided in the memory protection unit (MPU). This allows the kernel to prevent arbitrary code, which may have been written into user space, being executed while the CPU is in a privileged mode. This is an important security feature.

- Reliability, availability and serviceability (RAS) extension. This provides a programmer's model and mechanisms for handling CPU hardware faults and to avoid propagation of corrupted data across software contexts (for example, a new Error Synchronization Barrier instruction, ESB).

It is important to note that all existing Armv8-M software can run on Armv8.1-M, to enable easy software migration.

The first implementation of the Armv8.1-M architecture is the Cortex-M55 processor, announced by Arm in February 2020.

The main subject for this book is the Arm Helium technology – MVE for the Arm Cortex-M processor series. It is an extension of the Armv8.1-M architecture and delivers a significant performance uplift for machine learning and digital signal processing (DSP) applications.

With Helium, Arm Cortex-M processors can deliver the computational performance required in many applications. These include areas such as audio, sensor hubs, keyword spotting and voice command control, power electronics, communications (for example, in IoT) and still image processing (in cameras).

Helium provides a SIMD capability for Cortex-M CPUs. This means that a set of 128-bit registers are provided which can be used to hold, for example, 16 separate 8-bit values. A single instruction can operate on each of these values independently (for example, to perform a separate multiply on each of them). It is programmed as an extension to the Arm processor's existing Thumb instruction set.

Helium instructions operate on vectors of elements of the same data type. These data types may be floating-point or integer. Integer elements may be signed or unsigned 8-, 16-, 32- or 64-bit, while floating-point elements may be single (32-bit) or half precision (16-bit). The position of an element within a vector register is referred to as a lane. The instruction set is regular and orthogonal and nearly all instructions perform the same operation in all lanes. This means that most instructions have *n* parallel operations where *n* is the number of lanes that the input vectors are divided into. Each operation is contained within the lane. For most instructions, there is no carry or overflow from one lane to another, although we will see in Chapter 4 that there are some exceptions to this.

Helium does not, in general, perform 64-bit vector operations, although some instructions can produce 64-bit results, or take a 64-bit input, as we'll see later. As the Helium and floating-point register banks are shared, some Armv8-M floating-point extension instructions can act on 64-bit wide data (for example, VLDR.64) and 64-bit double-precision floating-point may optionally be supported in hardware.

The lane width of the operation to be performed is specified by the instruction that is being executed. So, for example, the suffix .S16 indicates that the instruction will operate on signed 16-bit integers within the register(s).

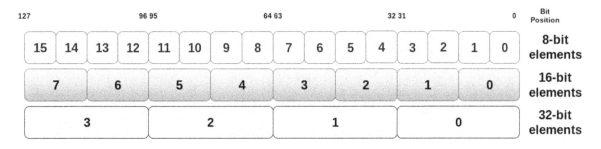

Figure 1.1: Helium vector elements

Figure 1.1 shows that Helium operates on 128-bit wide vectors and these can be made up of elements which are all of the same size. The lanes are numbered as shown.

Helium permits instruction execution to be interleaved. This means that, if the micro-architecture of the CPU supports it, multiple instructions may overlap in the pipeline execute stage. For example, a Vector Load (VLDR) instruction which reads multiple words from memory into a vector register may execute at the same time as a Vector Multiply (VMUL) instruction which uses that data. It is up to the CPU hardware designer to decide how many beats are executed on each clock cycle (or more correctly in Arm architecture terminology, each Architecture tick in a Helium implementation). We will look at this in greater detail later in this book.

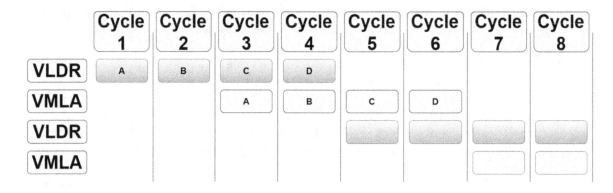

Figure 1.2: Helium instruction overlapping

Figure 1.2 shows how multi-cycle instructions may be able to overlap. Here, we see a vector load and a vector multiply accumulate instruction both being executed during cycles 3 and 4.

A key feature of an efficient vector-based SIMD machine is that the compiler can automatically vectorize loop code, so that multiple operations can be carried out per loop iteration. For example, a simple memory copy routine might be written to copy one word at a time, but the compiler can turn this into a more efficient piece of code which copies one or more vector registers per iteration. However, the number of words to copy might not be an exact multiple of the vector length, and typically there would need to be some tail clean-up code to handle this. Helium removes the need to do this using a technique called loop tail predication. This will be described in detail in Section 3.4.

Helium also makes use of a technique called lane predication, which allows us to apply conditions such that a single instruction may conditionally operate on some lanes but not on others. This allows the compiler to avoid branches and to successfully vectorize code with complex if-then-else type operations. We will look at this in detail in Section 4.4.

The term "predication" may be unfamiliar to some readers. In many computer architectures, conditional control statements are handled by having the program branch to a program location depending upon the result of some comparison or flag. The processor will implement instructions such as conditional branches, conditional calls, returns and perhaps jump tables. Predication is an alternative way to handle such control operations, in which instructions have some "predicate" (a Boolean value) associated with them. The instructions execute but will only modify the state of the processor or memory if the associated predicate condition permits it. This avoids branches over small sections of code, thus avoiding branch penalties caused by the CPU pipeline. As we shall see, Helium makes use of predication to make code smaller, faster and more easily vectorizable by the compiler.

Helium provides interleaving and deinterleaving loads and stores, which let us read and write vector registers to and from memory with strides of two or four. It also includes vector gather-load and vector scatter-store instructions. Scatter-gather refers to the process of gathering data from, or scattering data into, the non-contiguous locations in memory, rather than reading sequentially from a single buffer. These instructions provide memory access to elements in a vector register, using an individual address offset for each element in the vector, which is specified using elements in another vector register. This allows software to efficiently handle arbitrary memory access patterns, for example accessing non-sequential elements in arrays of data. It can be used to emulate special addressing modes like circular addressing, which are often used in DSP. We will look at these instructions in greater detail in Section 5.2.

Finally, Helium adds vector instructions which perform arithmetic operations on complex numbers (with real and imaginary components) and these can be integers or floating-point. It also includes instructions which can use the 128-bit vector registers to support handling of very large integers. There are instructions to perform 128-bit arithmetic and to chain these operations together to support integers of even larger size.

CPU designers have several options for implementing hardware which is compliant with the Armv8.1-M architecture:

- The Helium option can be omitted. This means that there is just the Armv8.1-M integer core, which optionally may include a scalar FPU. Optionally, this FPU may support double-precision floating-point arithmetic.

- The CPU can be implemented with Helium included, but with support for vectored integer instructions only. Again, the implementation may include an optional scalar FPU (and whether this supports double-precision floating-point arithmetic is also optional).

- Helium can be implemented within the CPU with both vector integer and vector floating-point support.

1.3 Comparison with Other Arm SIMD/DSP Options

The Arm architecture has more than 30 years of ongoing development and, during that time, a range of features and extensions have been included to allow SIMD, vector and DSP operations. Here, we will briefly look at these and show how Helium fits into the overall picture.

In 2004, the Arm Cortex-A8 CPU was the first CPU to include the Armv7-A Advanced SIMD extensions, more commonly known by the Arm trademark Neon. The main purpose of adding SIMD extensions was to accelerate media processing algorithms running on the CPU. In Armv8-A, with the move to a 64-bit architecture (AArch64), Neon gained many new features including full IEEE double-precision float, 64-bit integer operations and a larger register file (thirty-two 128-bit vector registers).

Cortex-A CPUs are typically some orders of magnitude larger (in terms of silicon die area and gate count) than the Cortex-M devices covered in this book. They will typically have very wide, fast interfaces to cache memory, allowing 128-bit data to be read (or written) in a single cycle. Cortex-M processors, on the other hand, often do not have a cache and may store data in on-chip SRAM, with only a 32-bit wide path available. Furthermore, multiplier circuits take a relatively large amount of die area and power/energy. To make efficient use of the memory data path and multipliers, the architecture should be designed to keep both as busy as possible. This means that simply adding Neon to Cortex-M processors would not be optimal.

Helium was designed with these constraints in mind, with a goal of achieving efficient signal processing performance in very small processors, at a range of performance points. It provides many new architectural features to allow Cortex-M applications which were not previously possible. Nevertheless, there are many common features between Helium and Neon, as we shall see.

1.3.1 Comparison of Helium with Neon

Neon is an architectural extension for A-Profile processors, including Arm Cortex-A and Neoverse, which provides a high performance SIMD capability. There are many similarities between Helium and Neon. Both Helium and Neon use registers in the FPU as vector registers. Both use 128-bit vectors and many vector processing instructions are common to both architectures.

However, Helium is a completely new design for efficient signal processing performance in small processors. It offers many new architectural features specifically for embedded use cases, as it is optimized for area (cost) and power, bringing Neon-like capabilities (SIMD instructions for Cortex-A) to the M-Profile architecture.

Helium is optimized to make efficient use of all the available hardware in the smaller Cortex-M cores. It has a smaller number of vector registers, and some operations can use both vector registers and a scalar value from the standard R0–R14 set in the integer core. Neon is able to perform vector operations using a scalar, but uses FPU registers for this. When we look at intrinsic functions later in the book, we'll see that both Helium and Neon intrinsics use the '_n_' modifier for this.

Helium provides half-precision floating-point (FP16) support, which is not present in all versions of Neon. (Architecture Armv8.2-A introduces FP16 for the latest Cortex-A processors.) Additionally, it has many extra features, including scatter-gather memory access, support for complex arithmetic (with real and imaginary components), loop predication, lane predication, and many extra scalar and vector instructions.

The key similarities and differences between the two instruction sets are summarized in the table. (Neon for Armv7-A and for Armv8-A have some differences in register numbers and other capabilities.)

	Helium	Neon
Vector Size	128-bit	64- or 128-bit
Vector Registers	8	16 or 32
Half-precision Floating-Point	Yes	In Armv8.2-A onwards
Vector instructions can use R0–R14	Yes	No
Reduction operations across vector	Yes	No
Tail Loop and Lane Predication	Yes	No
Scatter-Gather Memory Access	Yes	No
Complex Arithmetic Instructions	Yes	No
Pairwise Arithmetic (VPADD, VPMAX)	No	Yes
Micro-architecturally complex instructions	No	Yes

Neon has some micro-architecturally complex instructions (for example, VSQRT which calculates square roots) which would require too much silicon area for Helium. Other instructions not supported include VBIT, VCNT, VRECP, VSWP, VTBL, VTRN and VZIP, but Helium allows efficient mimicking of these operations. For example, permutation of data within registers can be done with scatter-gather, and iterative Newton–Raphson methods can be used for fast vector square root/reciprocal implementations.

1.3.2 Comparison of Helium with the Scalable Vector Extension (SVE)

In 2016, Arm announced the Scalable Vector Extension (SVE) for the Armv8-A architecture. This significantly adds to the vector processing capabilities of the architecture in the AArch64 (64-bit) execution state. Hardware implementations can support vector lengths scalable from 128 up to 2048 bits. SVE is complementary to Neon (not a replacement) and is primarily aimed at HPC (High Performance Computing) scientific workloads. Applications such as quantum physics, astronomy, climate science, fluid dynamics and drugs research can make use of enormously powerful computer systems. SVE adds many features which allow vectorizing compilers to do a significantly better job of parallelizing existing code.

SVE allows CPU designers to choose the vector length from 128 bits up to 2048 bits per vector register. It supports a vector-length agnostic (VLA) programming model that can adapt to the available vector length, so that users can compile code for SVE once and then run it at different implementation performance points.

Obviously, supercomputers have very different requirements to the embedded systems that Helium targets, but Helium and SVE have several features in common, including:

- Gather-load and scatter-store.

- Per-lane predication. This allows complex control code to be vectorized and reduces serialization of loop head and tails.

- Predicate-driven loop control and management. This similarly reduces the vectorization overhead.

1.3.3 Comparison with DSP Features of Cortex-M

Cortex-M processors which implement Architecture Armv7-M (or later) include a set of SIMD instructions. This has allowed them to replace a stand-alone DSP in some applications.

The Cortex-M4, Cortex-M7, Cortex-M33 and Cortex-M35P processors provide SIMD instructions that operate on 8- or 16-bit integers. The instructions make use of the standard register bank in the CPU, unlike Helium which uses a separate set of eight 128-bit registers. These standard integer core registers (R0, R1 etc.) are 32-bits wide, but the SIMD instructions operate on two 16-bit values or four 8-bit values within a 32-bit register. This means there is a maximum of four operations per instruction (compared with 16 for Helium).

As we will see in this book, 8- or 16-bit data operations are useful for processing audio or video data which may not require full 32-bit precision. The SIMD instructions in Armv7-M are targeted at specific algorithms, unlike Helium which is highly orthogonal and a good compiler target. Floating-point arithmetic can be accelerated using the optional FPU on these processors, but this does not provide SIMD or vector operation. The table summarizes the differences.

	Helium	Armv7-M SIMD
Vector registers	Yes (8 x 128-bit)	No
Floating-point SIMD	Yes	No
Operations per instruction	Up to 16	Up to 4
Integer SIMD operand sizes	8-, 16- and 32-bit	8- and 16-bit

1.3.4 Comparison of Helium with a Stand-alone DSP

Many current systems use a stand-alone programmable DSP. Before we look at Helium in detail, it is worth reminding ourselves of the main features of a DSP. DSPs are typically designed with the ability to perform computation and memory accesses in parallel (this may require a Harvard-style memory interface with connections to separate instruction and data memories). They will typically provide a single-cycle multiply accumulate (MAC) instruction, zero overhead loops, fractional and saturating arithmetic, support for circular buffers (or circular memory addressing modes) and accumulators with one or more "guard" bits.

The concept of a "guard bit" may not be familiar to all readers. In signal processing and fixed-point arithmetic, they are used to avoid overflow when accumulating.

A system which contains both a CPU and DSP has the advantage that both can run independently. Performance and power can be optimized by providing the DSP subsystem with maximal data throughput. However, a DSP typically needs more specialist programming skills and usually a separate toolchain to the processor. Each DSP family has its own features and so non-portable code will need significant rewriting when moving from one to another.

1.4 Helium Use Cases

There are many systems currently which use a Cortex-M processor in combination with a dedicated programmable DSP. Helium allows such systems to be implemented with just a single processor. This approach provides several advantages.

From a software development viewpoint it allows a single toolchain to be used, rather than separate CPU and DSP compilers and debuggers. It means that the programmer needs to be familiar with just one architecture. It also removes the need for inter-processor communications. This latter point can be quite important, as debugging the real-time interaction between two processors running different software can be difficult and time-consuming. The Cortex-M CPU is easier to program than a dedicated DSP as it is a good target for a vectorizing compiler (and it is also simpler to hand-code in assembly language, if required).

Similarly, at the hardware design level using one processor rather than two can simplify the system and thereby reduce die area (and cost) and speed up design cycle times. For example, only one memory system is required and there is no need to implement shared memory for communication between the CPU and DSP.

Helium provides a significant speedup when compared to regular Cortex-M Thumb code, with performance gains of up to 15 times faster being seen on machine learning code and up to five times faster on DSP algorithms. This can be useful even when an existing Cortex-M system is sufficiently powerful as it allows the CPU to spend more time sleeping and so potentially reduces dynamic power consumption.

Some current systems just have a stand-alone DSP. Here, Helium allows Cortex-M processors to be used as a replacement. They will provide much higher performance for non-DSP workloads and their superior code density may allow for a significant reduction in required memory footprint, leading to reduced overall system costs.

1.5 Questions

1. How many 8-bit integers can be stored in the Helium register bank, in total?

2. Which version of the Arm architecture introduced Helium?

3. Does Helium support double-precision floating-point calculations?

CHAPTER 2

SIMD/Vector Processor Overview

In this chapter, we will cover the basics of SIMD/Vector computer architecture and look at floating- and fixed-point number representations.

2.1 SIMD/Vector Processing

Before we move on to look at the specifics of Helium, a brief review of some computer architecture fundamentals may be useful.

Single instruction, multiple data (SIMD) is a term which describes hardware in which multiple processing elements can perform the same operation on multiple items of data, at the same time. In other words, there are simultaneous parallel calculations being performed, but only a single instruction is executing. This means we are making use of data-level parallelism.

Similarly, a scalar operation is one which is performed on single data items. A vector operation is one which is performed on a one-dimensional array of data.

SIMD operation does not imply a superscalar processor. Superscalar means that the CPU can execute more than one instruction during a clock cycle, by simultaneously dispatching instructions to different execution units within the processor. SIMD should also not be confused with multiple threaded operation (SMT), in which we may have concurrent threads operating in parallel.

Amdahl's law is a formula which gives the theoretical speedup in execution when a system is improved. The law is named after the computer scientist Gene Amdahl, whose career included being the Chief Architect of the influential IBM System-360 mainframe (and reputedly also inventing the marketing term FUD – Fear, Uncertainty, Doubt). In parallel computing, the law is used to show the speedup from using multiple processors or processing elements. For example, if we can parallelize an algorithm, the potential speedup is limited by the parts that cannot be parallelized. In simple terms, if we can parallelize 50% of a piece of code, the maximum speedup is 2×. Amdahl's law is important in the context of SIMD and vector machines. Many of the design decisions for the Helium architecture are informed by Amdahl's law. If we can operate on 16 pieces of data at a time, instead of 1, our potential data throughput is increased by a factor of 16, but only if we are able to avoid, or minimize, pieces of code which must operate in a scalar fashion.

2.2 Floating-Point and Fixed-Point Numbers

All computer software must deal with numbers and therefore needs some method to represent numbers. In this section, we provide a brief introduction to the fundamentals of fixed-point and floating-point arithmetic. Programmers with prior DSP or floating-point experience may find that they can skip over this section.

Several different formats may be used to represent signal data within a DSP system.

Integer
This is a number representation which deals with positive and negative whole numbers.

Fixed-point
This is a number representation which allows real or fractional numbers to be handled, but with a fixed number of digits after (and often before as well) the radix point (the decimal point in base-10 notation, or the binary point in computing). This avoids the overhead of hardware to deal with the complexity of floating-point. Q-format is commonly used in hardware implementations. In this, the number of fractional bits is specified and, optionally, the number of integer bits. For example, a Q31 number has 31 fractional bits; a Q1.14 number has 1 integer bit and 14 fractional bits. Helium provides support for Q15 and Q31 numbers. There is a sign bit to show whether the number is positive or negative, followed by a binary point and then 15 or 31 binary digits. The 16- or 32-bit value is being used to represent the range from −1 to 1. For example, the decimal value 0.75 represented as a signed Q15 value would be the integer value 0x6000. Fixed-point arithmetic allows fractional numbers to be handled using only integer hardware.

In Q15 format we are, in effect, using the 16 bits to represent the range from −1.0 to (almost) +1.0, rather than the normal integer representation of −32768 to +32767. The fixed-point representation is asymmetric, so that the lowest value we can represent is −1.0, but the highest value is one bit smaller than +1.0 (i.e. 32768/32767).

We can convert values from decimal representation to Q15 with a simple multiplication. For example, we can initialize Q15 variables with code like the following, rather than having to calculate what 0.123 looks like in fractional binary.

```
typedef short q15;

q15 a = 0.123 * 32768.0;
```

Floating-point
This is a number representation which allows real values to be handled in a manner similar to scientific notation, so that a number is represented with a mantissa and an exponent (for example, 12345 is stored as 1.2345×10^4) where 1.2345 is the mantissa and 4 is the exponent. Floating-point can handle a wider range of values than fixed-point, giving the ability to deal with both very small numbers and very large numbers, at varying degrees of accuracy. The IEEE-754 standard is normally used to specify representation and handling of floating-point arithmetic.

In addition to the format used, attention must also be paid to the number of bits used to represent a number, with 8-, 16-, 32- and 64-bit values being commonplace, and even larger values being used in some scientific and cryptographic applications.

The IEEE-754 standard is the reference for computer floating-point mathematics implementations, including Arm floating-point systems. The standard defines precisely what result will be produced by each floating-point operation, over the full range of possible input values.

The ANSI/IEEE Std. 754 defines a set of formats for representing floating-point numbers. The main formats described in the original (1985) version of the specification are:

- 32-bit numbers – single-precision

- 64-bit numbers – double-precision

More recent versions of the specification add several further formats, including 16-bit (half-precision) which we'll look at in more detail later in this chapter.

Single-precision – Figure 2.1 shows how the 32 bits in single-precision format are used.

Figure 2.1: Single-precision floating-point number format

- Bit 31 is the sign bit (0 for a positive number, 1 for a negative number)

- Bits 30:23 are the exponent

- Bits 22:0 are the mantissa

The 8-bit exponent field is used to store a value between −127 and 128, using offset binary. In other words, the value stored in the 8-bits has 127 subtracted from it. For example, an exponent value of 0 is stored as 0111 1111 (127).

The mantissa is formed from the 23 bits as a binary fraction. Floating-point numbers are normalized, so that there is only one non-zero digit to the left of the binary point. In other words, we always have an implicit binary "1." in front of the mantissa value.

The real value represented by the 32-bit binary data is therefore:

$(-1)^{Sign} \times 2^{Exponent-127} \times 1.Mantissa$

The IEEE specification uses certain bit patterns to represent some special cases:

- 0 is defined as each of the mantissa and exponent bits being zero.

- A group of very small "de-normalized" numbers is obtained by removing the requirement that the leading digit in the mantissa is a one. Denormal numbers are a special case. If you set the exponent bits to zero, you can represent very small numbers other than zero by setting mantissa bits. Because normal values have an implied leading 1, the closest value to zero you can represent as a normal value is $\pm 2^{-126}$. To get smaller numbers, the 1.m interpretation of the mantissa value is replaced with a 0.m interpretation. Such extremely small numbers are rarely used in real software, and in many applications they are ignored and flushed to zero.

- A set of bit patterns referred to as NaNs (Not a Number).

- A set of bit patterns which represent negative and positive infinity.

Double-precision – this arithmetic simply adds more bits to both the mantissa and exponent, so that bit 63 is the sign bit, bits 62:52 store the exponent (this time with an offset of 1023 rather than 127) and bits 51:0 the mantissa. Helium does not support vector operations on double-precision floating-point numbers.

The IEEE-754 standard now also defines a half-precision floating-point, referred to as binary16, which has 1 sign bit, 5 exponent bits and 10 bits of mantissa. The exponent encoding is with an offset of 15 (i.e. a binary value of 00001 represents −14, a binary value of 11110 represents 15). The encodings 00000 and 11111 have special meanings (zero/subnormal numbers and infinity or NaN, respectively). Figure 2.2 shows the format of half-precision floating-point numbers.

Figure 2.2: Half-precision floating-point number format

Half-precision – requires less memory storage (and bandwidth) than single-precision. As Helium vectors are fixed at 128-bits wide, it also allows twice as many floating-point calculations to be performed per cycle. This provides a significant performance increase. This is achieved at the expense of precision and range and may not be suitable for some algorithms. Furthermore, C compilers do not typically support its use, as the standard C floating-point types (float, double) do not map to half-precision representation.

In many algorithms, the small loss of precision is an acceptable trade-off for the performance gains from doubling the number of floating-point operations per instruction. Half-precision floating-point has recently found favor in neural network applications for this reason. It can also be used in many other signal processing algorithms, for example, running peak detection in spectral analysis.

Errors and Rounding
The IEEE-754 specification describes what a compliant implementation should do with respect to rounding of results that cannot be expressed precisely. A simple example of such a calculation would be 100.0 ÷ 3.0. This would require an infinite number of digits (in both base-10 and binary) to represent precisely. The specification gives different rounding options to cope with this (round toward positive infinity, round toward negative infinity, round toward zero, and round to nearest).

IEEE-754 also specifies the outcome when an exceptional operation occurs:

- **Overflow** – A result that is too large to represent.

- **Underflow** – A result that is so small that precision is lost.

- **Inexact** – A result that cannot be represented without a loss of precision.

- **Invalid** – A calculation which cannot be performed, for example the square root of a negative number.

- **Division by zero**.

The specification also describes what action must be taken when one of these exceptional operations is detected. Possible outcomes include the generation of a NaN result, or denormalized numbers in the case of underflow. In general, DSP and machine learning algorithms do not make use of such values, and DSP hardware does not support their use. Helium vector operations do not check for such exceptional cases. If we want the C compiler to perform vectorization and to generate Helium instructions, we must specify that we don't care about these cases, as we'll see in Chapter 7.

One facet of floating-point representation that may not be immediately obvious is that there can be a loss of precision when converting between a 32-bit int value and a 32-bit float. A 32-bit floating-point number has a 23-bit mantissa and this means that there are a large set of 32-bit int values which if converted to a 32-bit float cannot be represented exactly. If software converts such a value to floating-point and then back to an integer, the result will be a different but nearby value.

2.2.1 Saturating Arithmetic

Arithmetic operations on fixed-point numbers are straightforward. If we multiply two Q15 values using conventional integer arithmetic, the resulting product will be a 30-bit value, with two bits coming from the original sign values. In order to convert this to a Q31 value, it will be necessary to double the result. In fact, it is necessary to double and saturate the result.

If we take the Q15 value 0x8000 (−1) and multiply it by 0x8000 (−1), the result is 0x40000000, which would represent 0.5 in Q31 format. If we double this, we would get 0x80000000, which represents −1, rather than the correct answer of 0x7FFFFFFF (the value closest to +1.0). Saturation prevents this overflow from a large positive value to a large negative value (or vice versa).

Saturation of a signed Q15 calculation means that any result greater than 0x7FFF is set to 0x7FFF and any result smaller than 0x8000 (−1) is saturated to 0x8000.

In order to fit the result of a multiplication into the same representation as its operands, it must be rounded or truncated. The fractional digits lost represent a precision loss, although as we have seen, there is no possibility of an overflow occurring as the result cannot lie outside the range −1 to 1.

However, addition (or subtraction) has the possibility of overflow. If we add two fixed-point numbers together, each of which lies between −1 and 1, it is obvious that the highest possible result is 2, which cannot be represented in Q15 or Q31 format. In some cases, an algorithm may need to flag this as an error and raise some kind of exception. In other cases, we may simply perform a halving operation, or saturate the result, so that any positive overflow results in the largest possible number and a negative overflow results in the largest negative number. The halving operation uses an intermediate extended accumulator allowing non-overflowing operation prior to halving.

2.2.2 Fixed-Point and Floating-Point DSP

When coding DSP software, a decision must often be made about whether to use fixed- or floating-point numbers to represent signals. It is usually simpler for programmers to work with floating-point. Recoding to use fixed-point arithmetic can be demanding and take time. However, floating-point hardware is often more expensive, slower and/or uses more power than the fixed-point equivalent. Fixed-point values may occupy less memory space than floating-point values (although half-precision floating-point on Helium requires only 16-bit values). Fixed-point is often mandated by older speech and audio codecs but, as we shall see later in the book, it is also finding use in neural network algorithms.

The use of floating-point arithmetic gives us a much larger dynamic range, as it allows both small and large numbers to be handled and this can be useful when handling very large datasets, or in situations where the range is unpredictable.

However, it is important to understand the difference between range and precision. With fixed-point notation, the spacing between adjacent numbers that can be represented is always the same. In floating-point notation, adjacent numbers are not uniformly spaced, as the gaps between large numbers are bigger than the gaps between small numbers. When a calculation is performed, the result must be rounded to the nearest value that can be represented in the format in use.

This rounding and/or truncating of numbers during signal processing is a source of quantization error or "noise" – the difference between an analog value and the quantized digital value.

Applications which only need a low level of resolution and which have a low dynamic range requirement might use a fixed-point arithmetic format (for example, Q15 arithmetic).

2.2.3 Floating-Point Formats in Helium

The Armv8.0-M architecture provides support for scalar single-precision (32-bit) and double-precision (64-bit) floating-point and so this also applies to Armv8.1-M. However, Armv8.1-M also provides support for the following:

- scalar half-precision (16-bit) floating-point

- vector half-precision (16-bit) floating-point

- vector single-precision (32-bit) floating-point

Support for these is optional within a CPU.

The advantages of making use of vector operations have already been described. The reasons for adding half-precision floating-point support may be less obvious. It provides two main benefits. One is that (using Helium) the processor can handle double the amount of data in the same time when comparing half-precision with single-precision. We can perform eight half-precision floating-point calculations, or four single-precision calculations in one instruction. The other reason is that half-precision data requires less memory space than single- or double-precision. Areas which need a high dynamic range, but not a high resolution, can use half-precision floating-point. Examples of this might include audio data from a microphone, for spotting keywords or voice commands.

2.2.4 C Data Types and Intrinsics

The Arm C Language Extensions (ACLE) software standard allows C/C++ programmers to exploit the Arm architecture in a standard, portable manner. It includes standard type definitions and intrinsic functions. The specification can be downloaded from:

https://developer.arm.com/architectures/system-architectures/software-standards/acle

Many programmers using Cortex-M CPUs will be familiar with the Cortex Microcontroller Software Interface Standard (CMSIS) (covered in Chapter 7), which encourages the use of a number of C coding standards, in particular MISRA (Motor Industry Software Reliability Association) C. This uses typedefs to ensure that ANSI types are consistently represented, so that, for example, we use `int8_t` rather than signed char, `uint16_t` rather than unsigned short, and so on. We will follow that convention throughout this book.

When writing code in C, we may wish to use intrinsic functions to access Helium instructions. These are pseudo-function calls, which the compiler replaces with an appropriate instruction or instruction sequence. These will be covered in much greater detail later in the book, but it is useful to introduce them here to help you to read the example code that follows.

The Arm Compiler header file arm_mve.h, which is an implementation of the ACLE standard, defines a set of vector types of different sizes, for example:

`float32x4_t` is a vector of four 32-bit floating-point values (which can be held in a single Q register).

We can define a vector using a single register of any of the allowed data types and sizes.

```
(u)int8x16_t, (u)int16x8_t, (u)int32x4_t, (u)int64x2_t, float16x8_t,
float32x4_t
```

And correspondingly, a set of vectors which would require two registers:

```
(u)int8x16x2_t, (u)int16x8x2_t, (u)int32x4x2_t, float16x8x2_t,
float32x4x2_t
```

Or four registers:

```
(u)int8x16x4_t, (u)int16x8x4_t, (u)int32x4x4_t, float16x8x4_t,
float32x4x4_t
```

The compiler allocates vector variables to Helium registers and can pass vector parameters into these registers. The use of generic vector types allows the programmer to interpret vector values however they like. For example, a set of integers in a register may be treated as fixed-point values, complex numbers, polynomials etc.

2.3 Questions

1. What does SIMD mean?

2. If we perform a saturating arithmetic operation on a signed 8-bit value, what is the maximum possible result?

3. What are the advantages of using half-precision floating-point?

CHAPTER

Helium Architecture

3

We will now look at the fundamentals of the Helium ISA, which apply across many or all instructions, ahead of detailed coverage of each instruction in Chapters 4–6.

3.1 Helium Fundamentals

The design of the Helium architecture needed to take some important hardware constraints into consideration.

Cortex-M processors are small and not all of them have a data cache. They often use SRAM as their main external memory for data and this will typically have a 32-bit wide path. This means that a 128-bit wide vector data load might take four cycles to complete.

Additionally, multiplier hardware is relatively large in comparison with the total size of the CPU (and therefore expensive both in terms of silicon area/dollar cost and power). Having four 32-bit wide multipliers in order to perform a 128-bit MAC on every cycle would be prohibitively expensive.

To achieve the best performance at the lowest cost, it is important to keep both the memory and multiplier hardware as busy as possible. For this reason, Helium makes use of the computer architecture concept of "vector chaining."

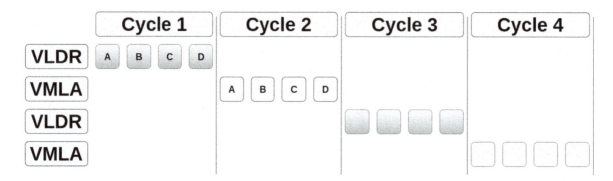

Figure 3.1: Sequence of interleaved VLDR and VMLA instructions without overlapping

Figure 3.1 shows a sequence of Vector Load (VLDR) and Vector Multiply Accumulate (VMLA) instructions. Each operates on a 128-bit wide vector, which is split into four equal-sized 32-bit pieces, which are known as "beats" in Helium. These are labeled A, B, C and D. These beats always perform 32-bits of computation, irrespective of the element size, so a beat could contain one 32-bit, two 16-bit or four 8-bit MACs. In the figure, each instruction executes in a single cycle. In hardware, this could be achieved either by providing 128-bit wide multipliers and data paths for loads (which would require a larger, more expensive processor), or by reusing smaller hardware within the same clock cycle (which could lead to long cycle times and slow clock speeds).

However, as the data load operation and the multiply accumulate make use of separate hardware, it is possible for the CPU to overlap execution of beats of both instructions, as shown in Figure 3.2.

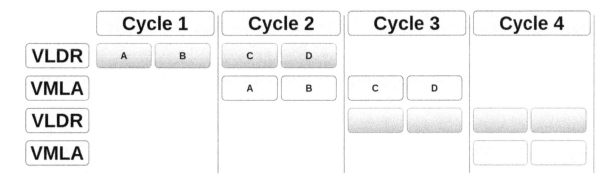

Figure 3.2: VLDR/VMLA *overlapping beats*

Here, we see that the multiply accumulate can start to execute while the previous VLDR continues. The instructions are overlapped. This can happen even if the value loaded by the VLDR is used by the subsequent VMLA. Beat A of the VMLA only has a dependency on beat A of the VLDR. As beat A completed on the previous cycle, overlapping beats A and B with beats C and D does not present a problem. In this example, we are still processing two beats (64-bits) per cycle, which would still require a relatively large amount of hardware in comparison to the smallest Cortex-M microcontrollers.

Figure 3.3 shows how a processor with a 32-bit wide data path and 32-bit multiplier could handle the same instruction sequence.

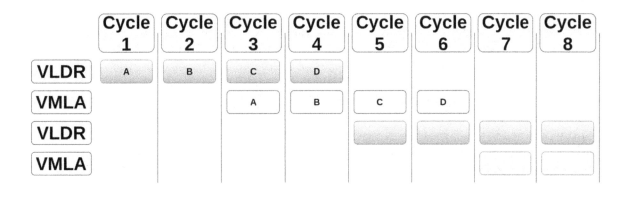

Figure 3.3: Overlapping load/multiply beats with 32-bit wide data path and multiplier

The overlapping of the loads and multipliers enables the CPU to have double the performance of an equivalent single-issue scalar processor (loading and performing MACs on eight 32-bit values in eight cycles), without the area and power penalties of implementing a dual-issue processor.

The concept of "beat-wise" execution enables efficient implementation of multiple performance points. The CPU designer can implement hardware which can perform one, two or four beats per cycle, without any change to the architecture. To ensure that this overlapped execution of instructions works well, the Helium ISA is designed so that every instruction operates on (at most) 64-bits of data per beat and there are no data dependencies across the vector.

Although beat-wise execution provides highly efficient utilization of hardware resources, permitting a significant performance increase versus a scalar processor, it does cause some issues. It means that we can have multiple partially executed instructions at the same time. This can make handling of interrupts and faults during such a sequence more complicated.

In Figure 3.3, beat D of the VLDR happens after beat A of the VMLA has completed. So, if the memory location used for beat D triggers a fault, the processor needs to remember that the following instruction was part executed. It does this by storing a value which shows which beats have already been executed. If, after the exception handler runs, the program returns to this location, the hardware already knows which beats should not be re-executed. (We'll see in Section 7.8.3 of this book that this information is stored in the ECI field of the FPSCR.)

This means that the hardware does not need the ability to undo the effects of a partially executed instruction (which would cost silicon area). It also means that exceptions can be taken without having to wait for currently executing instructions to complete, which is important in providing low interrupt latency.

3.1.1 Helium Registers

Helium makes use of eight 128-bit wide registers. These registers are shared with the Cortex-M Scalar FPU, as shown in Figure 3.4. In the FPU, we have access to 32 single-precision (32-bit) registers named S0–S31. The same hardware registers may also be treated as 16 double-precision (64-bit) registers named D0–D15. This means that D0 is the same hardware register as S0 and S1 etc. In Helium, the eight vector registers are named Q0–Q7. Helium register Q0 is the same physical register as S0–S3 or D0–D1 floating-point registers. Q1 is the same as S4–S7 or D2–D3 in the floating-point register bank and so on. As the Helium registers are effectively shared with the scalar FPU, this means that there is no additional overhead required to save and restore these registers when an exception occurs (and so no effect on interrupt latency).

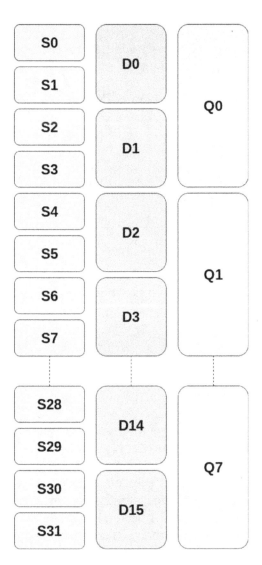

Figure 3.4: Floating-point/Helium register bank

It might be thought that eight registers are not enough to protect the compiler from register pressure and frequent spills from registers to the stack. However, because most instructions can make use of the scalar register file, this is often avoided. Many instructions can be specified in the form "Vector = Vector <operation> Scalar" or "Scalar = Vector <operation> Vector". This means that the compiler (or assembly language programmer) can often use registers from the integer core as part of vectorized code.

In addition to the eight vector registers, architecture Armv8.1-M adds a new special purpose register, the Vector Predication Status and Control Register (VPR). This is automatically saved and restored using the exception stack frame, as part of an exception event. We'll look in detail at this register in Section 4.4 of the book.

3.1.2 Lanes

Each 128-bit register may be divided into lanes of width 8-, 16- or 32-bits. Figure 3.5 shows how this is done.

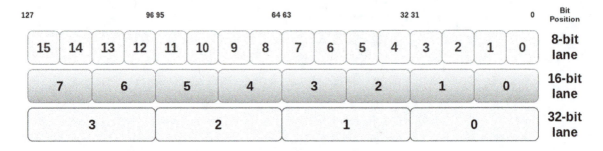

Figure 3.5: Division of Helium register into lanes

Each lane may then be treated by an instruction as one of the following:

- Integer (8-, 16- or 32-bit wide)

- Fixed-point saturating (Q7, Q15, Q31)

- Floating-point (half- or single-precision).

Helium allows conditional execution for each of the lanes in the vector. This is called lane predication. The Vector Predication Status and Control Register (VPR) holds a condition value for each lane. Some vector instructions (for example, Vector Compare, VCMP) change the condition values in the VPR. When these flags have been set appropriately, subsequent code can use the VPT (Vector Predicate Then) instruction to allow conditional execution of instructions in a vector predication block on a per-lane basis. This block may be up to four instructions long. This is analogous to the IF-THEN (IT) instruction block in regular Thumb-2 code, although there are some important differences, as we will see later. The VPST (Vector Predicate Set Then) instruction effectively combines the VCMP and VPT instructions. In Section 4.4, we will look at this in more detail.

3.1.3 Beats and Ticks

In the Armv8.0-M architecture, most instructions are considered "atomic" units for execution. This means that they are either executed, or not executed. A Helium vector instruction, however, executes in four sequential beats, from beat 0 to beat 3.

An architecture tick is defined as an atomic unit of execution (some time period which cannot be further subdivided from the point of view of the instruction set architecture – typically a clock cycle).

It is up to the CPU hardware designer to decide how many beats are executed on each architecture tick in a Helium implementation. (The Architecture Reference Manual calls this "IMPLEMENTATION

DEFINED".) It is not architecturally required that the number of beats per cycle is fixed and in theory it could change at runtime.

- In a single-beat system, one beat might occur for each tick.

- In a dual-beat system, two beats might occur for each tick.

- In a quad-beat system, four beats might occur for each tick.

The permitted lane widths, and lane operations per beat, are:

- For a 32-bit lane size, a beat performs a one-lane operation.

- For a 16-bit lane size, a beat performs a two-lane operation.

- For an 8-bit lane size, a beat performs a four-lane operation.

In the Cortex-M55 processor, there is a "dual-beat per tick" implementation of Helium. This means that there are 64 bits, worth of compute per "tick" (processor cycle). Such an implementation is allowed to overlap instructions as we saw in Section 1.2 and the final two beats of one operation may be executed at the same time as the first two beats of the next vector instruction.

3.1.4 Instruction Example

So far, we have mentioned just two of the Helium instructions, Vector Load (`VLDR`) and `VMLA`. In Chapters 4–6 of this book, we will look at every instruction in detail. However, before introducing some of the key new features of Helium, it is useful to have some understanding of the basic instruction format.

Each of the vector instructions begin with a V followed by some letters which indicate the operation of the instruction. As we will see later, there may also be letters which modify the operation or add some extra option. For some instructions, we also have the option to specify conditional execution. After the instruction mnemonic, we may specify the data type (for example, `.F16` for 16-bit floating-point, `.U32` for 32-bit unsigned integer etc.). We then may specify a destination register for the result and one or two source registers which provide the vectors to be operated upon.

Example:

```
VMUL.F32 Q0, Q1, Q0
```

`VMUL`   – this is a Vector Multiply instruction

`.F32`   – the data in the vector registers is to be treated as 32-bit floating-point values

`Q0,`   – write the results into register Q0

`Q1, Q0`   – the values to be multiplied are in Q1 and Q0.

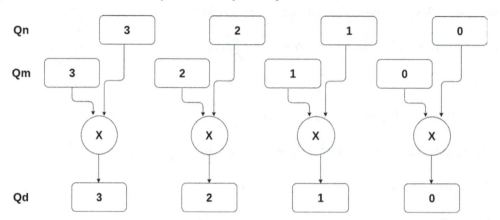

Figure 3.6: VMUL *operation*

The operation of the VMUL instruction is shown in Figure 3.6. It shows four 32-bit elements in each of the source registers Qm and Qn. Each element in Qm is multiplied by the corresponding element in Qn and the results are stored in Qd. Of course, the VMUL instruction can also operate on eight 16-bit elements, or sixteen 8-bit elements.

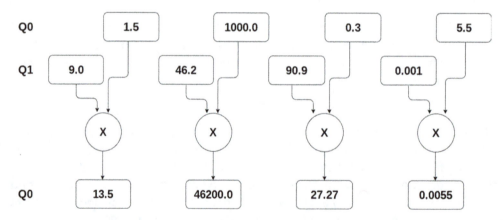

Figure 3.7: VMUL *with floating-point data values*

In Figure 3.7, we see what happens when we insert some real data values and execute the example instruction above, VMUL.F32 Q0, Q1, Q0

3.2 Helium Vector Processing

In this section, we will look at how C code can be vectorized by the compiler and compare the vectorized output with code which does not use Helium.

3.2.1 Code Example Comparing Helium with Scalar Code

Consider the following simple C function. It takes as its inputs two equal-sized arrays of floating-point numbers in memory and a variable indicating the number of items in the array. It multiplies each pair of numbers from the two input arrays and stores the results in a third array.

```
void arm_mult_f32( float32_t * __restrict A, float32_t * __restrict B, float32_t * __
restrict Dst, uint32_t blockSize)
{
  for   (int i = 0; i<blockSize; i++)
        Dst[i] = A[i] * B[i];
}
```

If we compile this code with Arm Compiler 6, using the following flags:

```
-armclang -target arm-armnone-eabi -march=armv8.1m.main+mve.fp+fp.dp
mthumb -mfloat-abi=hard -O3
```

We get the following assembly language code for our inner loop:

```
        .p2align 2
.LBB0_13: @ =>This Inner Loop Header: Depth=1
        VLDRW.U32 Q0, [R1], #16
        VLDRW.U32 Q1, [R0], #16
        VMUL.F32 Q0, Q1, Q0
        VSTRB.8 Q0, [R2], #16
        LE LR, .LBB0_13
```

(Note that the exact output may depend upon compiler version and other factors.)

What is of interest here is that the compiler has been able to automatically vectorize our unmodified C code. It has been able to generate code which uses vector floating-point instructions. The inner loop contains only vector operations. We have two vector loads (VLDRW), each of which reads four 32-bit values from memory, a vector multiply (VMUL) which does four 32-bit floating-point multiplications, and a vector store (VSTRB) which writes four 32-bit results to memory. The registers R0 and R1 point to our source arrays A and B, while R2 points to Dst.

For comparison, if we compile the same source code and use the flag -fno-vectorize so that we continue to use Helium instructions and floating-point hardware, the inner loop is as follows:

```
VLDR          S0, [R1, #4]
VLDR          S2, [R0, #4]
VMUL.F32      S0, S2, S0
VSTR          S0, [R2, #4]
ADDS          R0, #4
ADDS          R1, #4
ADDS          R2, #4
```

Again, we have two VLDR instructions, a VMUL and a VSTR. However, this is floating-point code, rather than Helium vector code. The registers being used (S0, S2) are 32-bits wide and hold a single-precision floating-point value. Only one floating-point multiply per loop iteration is performed. Measuring performance with a model of Cortex-M55, this loop takes eight cycles per iteration in both cases, but the vectorized code performs four times as many multiplies per loop.

3.3 Low Overhead Branch Extension

Modern processor implementations almost always fetch instructions into a pipeline to improve throughput and increase maximum clock speeds. Whenever there is a control flow instruction (a branch), or an exception event such as an interrupt, there is the potential for instructions to be fetched which will not then be executed. This means that the pipeline must be flushed and new instructions fetched from the correct location. This causes a delay of some clock cycles, known as a branch delay or branch penalty. Some processors may attempt to predict (guess) whether a conditional branch is taken or not, and a significant amount of computer architecture research has been done to improve the performance of such branch predictors.

However, not all Cortex-M processors have branch predictors. The sophisticated branch predictors used by very high-performance CPUs can occupy several times more die area than the entire Cortex-M CPU, with a price and power cost to match. This means that every time we execute a branch instruction, there is the possibility of paying the branch penalty cycle count cost.

Most DSP algorithms make extensive use of tightly looped code, so achieving good performance on branches for loops is a key goal.

Consider a simple piece of (non-Helium) code which reads a series of 8-bit values pointed to by R0 and sums them, producing a result in R3. R2 gives the number of values to be added.

```
    MOV R3, #0          // initialize the sum to 0
loopSum:
    LDRB R1, [R0], #1   // read a byte and increment the pointer
    ADD R3, R3, R1      // add the value read onto previous sum
    SUBS R2, R2, #1     // decrement the counter
    BNE  loopSum        // if not at 0, go round the loop again
```

Each loop contains four instructions and processes one byte per iteration. Helium allows us to parallelize the load and add operations, so that a very significant speedup can be obtained. Nevertheless, the decrement of R2 (the loop iteration counter) and the conditional branch to the top of the loop account for two of the four instructions in the loop. The existence of a branch penalty means that the cycle overhead of the loop handling code is likely to be greater than 50%.

A technique that a compiler can use to mitigate this effect is to unroll loops, so that the overhead of loop handling is shared over a higher number of instructions. Loop unrolling also helps the compiler to perform auto-vectorization, as we shall see later.

One way that programmable DSPs address this is to have hardware support for zero overhead loops. A common way to do this is to implement a REPEAT instruction, which tells the processor to repeat the following instructions a certain number of times. Arm does not actually have a repeat assembly language instruction, but conceptually it would look as follows:

```
REPEAT R2, #2          // Repeat the next 2 instructions R2 times
   LDRB    R1, [R0], #1
   ADD R3, R3, R1
```

This requires the hardware to keep track of several variables. It must record the address of the first instruction in the loop, how many instructions are still to be repeated before the next iteration, and the number of iterations left. To avoid having to save and restore these non-programmer visible registers when an interrupt or other exception occurs, many programmable DSPs simply (implicitly) disable interrupts while the loop is in progress. This can have a severe effect on interrupt latency and real-time determinism. This approach also makes precise fault handling impossible (if the load instructions hit an area of memory which generates an abort, we would be unable to fix the problem and attempt to retry).

For these reasons, Helium takes a different approach and introduces a pair of loop instructions. A loop begins with a While Loop Start (WLS) or Do Loop Start (DLS) instruction and finishes with a LE (Loop End) instruction.

In each case, the loop start instruction copies the iteration count to the integer core LR register. For WLS, it also performs a check to see whether the iteration count is zero and, if so, causes execution to branch to the end of the loop. DLS is used for a loop where there will always be at least one iteration and so does not need this step. The LE instruction checks LR to see whether another iteration is required and, if so, it branches back to the start.

Now, this does not sound like it will save us many cycles. We still have what is effectively a comparison and branch at the end of our loop. However, the processor can locally store the start and end addresses of the loop and so it can start fetching instructions from the start location without even needing to fetch the LE instruction.

Our code now looks like this (this is still non-vectorized code):

```
        MOV      R3, #0
        WLS      LR, R2, loopEnd
loopStart:
        LDRB     R1, [R0], #1
        ADD      R3, R3, R1
        LE       LR, loopStart
loopEnd:
```

On the first iteration of the loop, the instructions are executed linearly, as follows:

```
        MOV      R3, #0
        WLS      LR, R2, loopEnd
        LDRB     R1, [R0], #1
        ADD      R3, R3, R1
        LE       LR, loopStart
```

However, when the `LE LR, loopStart` instruction is executed, our loop cache now knows where to fetch the next instruction from. We do not need to re-execute the `WLS` and `LE` instructions, so that subsequent loops simply execute the two instructions of the loop until the counter reaches zero.

```
        LDRB        R1, [R0], #1
        ADD         R3, R3, R1
        LDRB        R1, [R0], #1
        ADD         R3, R3, R1
        LDRB        R1, [R0], #1
        ADD         R3, R3, R1
etc.
```

If something happens which breaks us out of the loop (for example, an interrupt), then the cached loop information is flushed. If execution returns into the loop, the re-execution of the `LE` instruction is sufficient to repopulate the cache. In other words, executing loops in this way does not need any changes to our interrupt handling.

Apart from on the first iteration (or the first iteration after an interrupt return), the processor is spending every cycle performing the loading and adding. The pipeline flush/branch penalty is eliminated. Furthermore, it is common for such loops to contain Vector Load (`VLDR`) instructions interspersed with data processing operations (for example, a Vector Multiply Accumulate, `VMLA`). In processor implementations of Helium which support overlapping of such instructions (where beat-wise execution means we can load one value on the same cycle as performing the multiply on the previously loaded data), it is possible to overlap such instructions even from the end of one iteration of the loop to the start of the next.

The Low Overhead Branch Extension is a mandatory part of the Armv8.1-M architecture (i.e. it is still present even when Helium is not implemented).

3.4 Tail Predication

In the previous section, our code performed an operation on a single byte per loop. Helium allows us to easily vectorize this kind of code.

We can look at some example memory copy code:

```
void memcpy(char * __restrict dest, char * __restrict src, int bytes)
    {
    for (int i = 0; i< bytes; i++)
        dest[i] = src[i];
    }
```

Arm Compiler 6 produces the following assembly code:

```
        DLSTP.8         LR, R2
.LBB0_1:
        VLDRB.U8        Q0, [R1], #16
        VSTRB.8         Q0, [R0], #16
        LETP            LR, .LBB0_1
```

This code is straightforward to understand. R1 points to the source memory, R0 points to the destination memory and R2 holds the number of bytes to copy. We have a DLS instruction at the start, a vector load, vector store and then a LE. However, this instruction has TP on the end. This stands for tail predication.

The instructions in the loop read and write 16 bytes per iteration (because that is what a 128-bit vector can contain). Normally, a vectorizing compiler would have to make sure that the number of bytes in the block to be copied in the vectorized loop was a multiple of 16. Any remaining bytes that needed to be copied would be done in a separate block of non-vectorized epilogue code at the end. For example, consider the case where we ask the memcpy() function to copy a buffer which is from address 0 to (decimal) address 42.

Figure 3.8 illustrates the problem. The vectorized code reads and writes 16 bytes in a vector register. However, in this example, our input buffer contains 43 bytes, which is not a multiple of 16, so that we need to find a way of dealing with the final 11 bytes. This is done by a scalar tail loop.

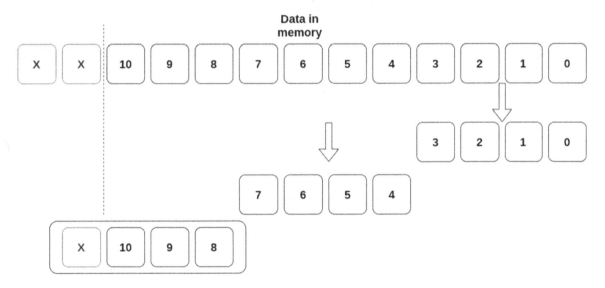

Figure 3.8: Tail loop handling problem

In pseudocode, we would have something like the following:

```
for (int i=0; i < 32; i+=16)
{   // the vectorized code which copies 16 bytes per iteration }
for (int i=32; i < 42; i++)
{   // the tail loop code which copies 1 byte per iteration }
```

The tail loop is, in effect, the original unvectorized loop, except that it now starts at 32, rather than 0.

Although we have been able to achieve a speedup by vectorizing the code, there is a cost. Having both the vector and the tail loop increases the size of our code and means that we have to execute two loops.

Tail predication solves these problems and allows the execution of loops that process multiple data elements in one single vector loop that are not an exact multiple of the number of elements that fit in a vector. By including the TP suffix on our loop, Helium lets us avoid the necessity for such tail epilogue code.

Let's look again at the assembly code output. The instruction `DLSTP.8 LR, R2` sets up a tail-predicated loop, where register LR contains the number of elements to be processed, with its initial value coming from R2. The `LETP LR, .LBB0_1` Loop End instruction branches back to the label LBB0_1 and decrements the number of elements to be processed in LR.

The processor uses the size field (.8 or .32, for example) and the number of elements to calculate the correct number of loop iterations to perform. On the last loop, if the number of remaining elements is less than the vector length, the appropriate number of elements at the end of the vector are disabled. This means that all parts of the memory copy can be executed in parallel, and the non-vector tail code can be eliminated. This makes for simpler (and smaller) code, as well as speeding things up. In Arm Compiler 6, tail-predicated loops can be generated from source code or intrinsics.

3.5 Helium Instruction Set

In Chapters 4–6, we will look at each of the instructions available within Helium. As most people will code in C or a high-level language, rather than directly in assembly language, it might be thought unnecessary to learn about this. However, it can be useful for a variety of reasons:

■ Using intrinsic functions may allow us to produce significantly faster code, or to save power consumption. This requires understanding of the instruction set. Intrinsics are function calls that the compiler replaces with appropriate assembly language instructions. This allows access to the Helium instructions from high-level code. In some of the examples in this chapter and the ones which follow, we'll use intrinsic functions, but we'll have a much more detailed look at them in Chapter 7.

■ When optimizing C code, it can be useful to be able to inspect the compiler output, in order to determine whether it is vectorizing fully, and some familiarity with the instruction set is useful here.

■ When debugging code which is not working, it can be invaluable to be able to read the disassembly of the code and to understand what is happening on each line.

3.5.1 Instruction Set Basics
The basic construction of Helium instructions is similar to that used for the VFP (floating-point) instructions found on other Cortex-M processors. It is important to be aware that many of the instructions have the same mnemonics, and that, for example, VADD might be a scalar floating-point addition (using the floating-point extension), or a vector addition (using Helium).

The basic format of an instruction is:

```
V{<mod>}<op>{<shape>}{<extra>}{<cond>}{<.dt>} {<dst>}, src1, src2,
{<rot>}
```

This means that each instruction begins with the letter V and is then followed by:

- `<mod>` – This is a modifier for the instruction. There may be no modifier, or it can be one of Q (saturating), H (halving), D (doubling), or R (rounding).

- `<op>` – This specifies the operation: for example, ADD, SUB, CMP etc.

- `<shape>` – For some instructions, we can optionally specify either L (long) or N (narrow).

- `<extra>` – Some instructions have their own instruction-specific modifier, which may be one of T (top), B (bottom), A (accumulate), X (exchange) or V (across).

- `<cond>` – This field specifies a condition and is only available inside a VPT (Predication) block and may be either T (Then) or E (Else).

- `<dst>` – Destination register(s), which may be General Purpose (R) and/or Quad Vector (Q). Destination registers are typically shown as Qd or Rd in the syntax descriptions which follow. For multiply-accumulate instructions, they may be shown as Qda, or Rda/Rdb.

- `<src>` – Source register(s), which may be General Purpose (R) and/or Quad Vector (Q). Source registers are typically shown as Qm, Qn and/or Rm, Rn in the syntax descriptions which follow.

- `<.dt>` – Data type – which may be Float (F), Integer (I), Signed (S), Unsigned (U), 8, 16, 32 or 64. For some instructions, only the size is required, for others both a type and a size are needed.

- `<rot>` – Rotation. This is used for certain instructions which operate on complex numbers.

Some examples will make this clearer.

```
VLDRW.U32 Q0, [R0]
```

Here, we have the initial V, which tells us that this is a Helium (or Neon or floating-point) instruction. The LDR tells us that this is a register load from memory and W means we are operating on words. The modifier, shape and extra fields are empty. The data type is U32, unsigned 32-bit. The destination for the load is the 128-bit register Q0 and the source is the memory address pointed to by the scalar register R0. The instruction will load four 32-bit words from the address held in R0.

```
VQRDMLADHX.S32 Q2, Q1, Q0
```

Again, we have the initial V. This time it is followed by a Q, which specifies a saturating math operation, R (rounding) and D (doubling). We will look at what those options do in detail in the next section. MLA means this is a multiply-accumulate instruction. The D (dual) and H (return high half) are instruction-specific options and X is exchange. The data type (S32) is a signed 32-bit integer. The operation writes its results into Q2 and performs the multiply-accumulate on data in registers Q1 and Q0.

Some instructions allow us to specify immediate values. It is not possible to encode an arbitrary 32-bit constant in an opcode which is at most 32-bits wide. Many instructions permit a 12-bit immediate value to be encoded, arranged as an 8-bit value which can be rotated by an even number of places to the desired position within a 32-bit word. Obviously, a floating-point constant cannot be encoded within an instruction. Helium instructions which include a constant will sometimes have a limited range of values (for example, most of the shifts described in this chapter allow a shift value of 1 to 32 bits) and these will be noted in the instruction description.

In the chapters which follow, we will look at each instruction in turn. The syntax from the Architecture Reference Manual is adopted. Optional components are enclosed in curly brackets {}.

Syntax descriptions of Helium vector instructions will typically be followed by <v>. This indicates that a T (Then) or E (Else) may be present, associated with lane predication resulting from a VPT or VPST instruction, explained in Section 4.4. Some instructions may instead have <c> indicating a standard Arm condition code (for example, GE greater than or equals etc.) The <.dt> field represents the data type, as already explained.

The notation Q after certain Helium instructions allows us to optionally specify the use of one of the following instruction qualifiers.

- .N means the assembler must use a 16-bit encoding for the instruction. If this is not possible, an assembler error is produced.

- .W means the assembler must use a 32-bit encoding for the instruction. If this is not possible, an assembler error is produced.

If neither .W nor .N is specified, the assembler can select either a 16-bit or 32-bit encoding.

For some instructions, we'll also show examples of the operation of the instruction. We'll show input and output registers inside square brackets, with the element values separated by commas. The least significant value is written first. For example, a vector of eight 16-bit integers can be written as Q2 = [7, 6, 5, 4, 3, 2, 1, 0].

3.5.2 Instruction Modifiers
There are four optional instruction modifiers:

- Q – This specifies a saturating operation. Saturating instructions which saturate cause the "Cumulative Saturation" (QC) flag to be set, in the FPSCR. This flag is "sticky," so that once set, it remains set until explicitly cleared. The VMRS and VMSR instructions can be used to read and write the FPSCR.

▨ H – This modifier causes the instruction to halve the result and is only available for addition and subtraction instructions (VHADD, VHSUB and VRHADD). As we have seen, this can be useful for saturating arithmetic, or for calculation of a mean value.

▨ D – This specifies a "Doubling" operation and is only available for saturating variants of long and "high half" multiplies, VQDMLALH, VQDMLSDH, VDQMULDH and VQRDMULH. For example, VQRDMULH multiplies the corresponding elements in two vectors, doubles the results, and places the most significant half of the result in the destination vector register. If any of the results would overflow, they are saturated and the QC flag is set. The second operand may be a scalar register rather than a vector. As we saw in Section 2.2, a doubling multiply is useful in saturating arithmetic.

▨ R – This forces the instruction to always "Round to Nearest". This rounding can be thought of as an addition of $2^{(N-1)}$, prior to truncation, where N is number of bits to be discarded during the operation. This value of N is the shift amount in the case of right-shift instructions, one for halving operations, or the destination word size for narrowing instructions.

Certain instructions have extra specifiers, such as T (Top) or B (Bottom). We will look at all of these as we go through the individual instructions. Some instructions may only read part of the input vectors. For example, the vector-multiply-long instructions:

```
VMULLB.S16  Qd,  Qn,  Qm
```

```
VMULLT.S16  Qd,  Qn,  Qm
```

These read the even (bottom) or odd (top) elements of each signed 16-bit input vector, multiply them, and write to a double-width 32-bit vector.

3.5.3 Instruction Shapes
Certain instructions may use two modifiers which relate to their "shape."

▨ L – Long. This means that input elements are promoted before the operation. An 8-bit element may be promoted to 16- or 32-bits, or a 16-bit element to 32-bits.

▨ N – Narrow. This means that input elements are demoted before the operation.

Some instructions may only write part of the results. For example, the Vector Shift Right and Narrow (VSHRN) instruction will read in a double-width input vector and write to the even or odd elements of the single-width result vector, depending upon whether bottom (even) or top (odd) is specified.

For example, the instruction:

```
VSHRNB.I16  Q0,  Q1,  #4
```

will take each of the eight 16-bit integer elements from Q1, shift them right by four places, narrow them to eight bits and write them to the even elements of Q0 (which holds sixteen 8-bit integers).

The values in the odd elements are left unchanged. This means that we could use a VSHRNB/VSHRNT pair to convert two vectors of 16-bit values into one of 8-bit values, with some amount of shifting for scaling. Figure 3.9 shows the above VSHRNB instruction, with Q1 at the top and Q0 at the bottom.

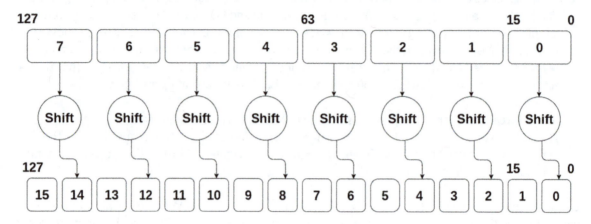

Figure 3.9: Operation of Vector Shift Right and Narrow Bottom instruction (VSHRNB)

Note that (unlike Neon), there is no "W" wide option in Helium. (In Neon, this operates on a double-word vector and a quad-word vector.)

3.6 Questions

1. Which FPU registers correspond to Helium register Q1?

2. How many 8-bit operations are performed in a single beat?

3. What does TP stand for in the instruction LETP?

4. In the instruction VLDRW.U32 Q0, [R0], what does .U32 mean?

CHAPTER

Data Processing
Instructions

4

In this chapter, we describe the various data processing operations which can be carried out by Helium instructions. Nearly all instructions are, in effect, SIMD versions of scalar instructions, performing four, eight or sixteen times the number of operations, in parallel. Helium does not typically have algorithm-specific instructions which perform different operations in different lanes. These can be difficult for the compiler (and the programmer) to make effective use of, as they rely on being able to recognize an intent across multiple lines of code.

However, in many cases, instructions are provided which perform a vector "reduction," where the same operation is performed across a vector, with the result being placed in a scalar register. This is often the last step when an algorithm has been vectorized. Scalar code will perform a series of the same operations and produce an output. Vectorized code will do this across a vector and a final step of "reducing" those vector values to one final result is needed.

4.1 Arithmetic Operations

This section covers standard arithmetic and logical operations, such as addition, subtraction, shifts and Boolean operations. It also includes less-common instructions including those for bit counting and reversal, and conversions between data types.

4.1.1 Addition and Subtraction

The ISA includes several different forms of addition and subtraction.

VADD – Vector Add. Add the value of the elements in the first source vector register to either the respective elements in the second source vector register or a general-purpose register. The result is then written to the destination vector register. It can be performed on floating-point values (which means that the <.dt> field below would be F16 or F32) or integers (8-, 16- or 32-bit sized elements, i.e. I8, S8, U8, I16, S16, U16, I32, S32 or U32) stored in 128-bit vector registers (see Section 3.1.4 for a description of the <.dt> field).

Syntax:
```
VADD<v><.dt> Qd, Qn, Qm
VADD<v><.dt> Qd, Qn, Rm
```

Example:

Initial Conditions:
```
Q2 = [ 1, 2, 3, 4, 5, 6, 7, 8]
Q1 = [ 10, 0, 10, 0, 10, 0, 10, 0]
```

Instruction:
```
VADD.I16 Q3, Q2, Q1
```

Result:
```
Q3 = [ 11, 2, 13, 4, 15, 6, 17, 8]
```

Example:

Initial Conditions:

        Q0 = [10, -20, -30, 40]
        R0 = 100

Instruction: `VADD.I32 Q5, Q0, R0`

Result:

        Q5 = [110, 80, 70, 140]

VSUB – Vector Subtract. Subtracts the value of the elements in the second source-vector register from either the respective elements in the first source-vector register or a general-purpose register. The result is then written to the destination-vector register.

Syntax: `VSUB<v><.dt> Qd, Qn, Qm`
                 `VSUB<v><.dt> Qd, Qn, Rm`

VADC, VSBC – Vector Add (or Subtract) with Carry. This can only be used on 32-bit integer arithmetic. Carry is across beats, with carry in at the bottom from the FPSCR.C bit (and carry out at the top to that bit). The variants VADCI and VSBCI allow the initial value of the FPSCR.C bit to be forced to 0 or 1. If lane predication means that some beats are disabled, FPSCR will not be updated for those beats. The FPSCR.N, V and Z bits are zeroed.

Syntax: `VADC{I}<v>.I32 Qd, Qn, Qm`
                 `VSBC{I}<v>.I32 Qd, Qn, Qm`

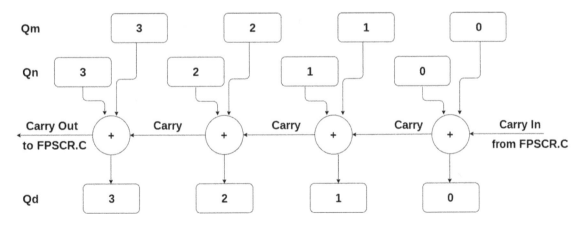

Figure 4.1: VADC *instruction*

Figure 4.1 shows the VADC instruction in operation. If lane predication means that all beats are enabled, the overall effect is to synthesize a 128-bit addition. These instructions find use in large-integer arithmetic (for example, in cryptographic code), as explained in Chapter 11.

Example:

Initial Conditions:
       FPSCR.C=1 (input carry is SET)
       Q0 = [0x4000000, 0x30000000, 0x20000000, 0x10000000]
       Q1 = [0x1000000, 0x05000000, 0x0F000000, 0xEFFFFFFFF]

Instruction: VADC.I32 Q2, Q0, Q1

Result:
       Q2 = [0x50000000, 0x35000000, 0x2F000001, 0x00000000]

VADDV, VADDVA – Vector Add Across Vector, Vector Add Across Vector Accumulate. Add across the elements of a vector register, accumulating the result into a scalar. It can be performed on integer values stored in 128-bit vector registers. The VADDVA variant adds the initial value of the destination registers to the result.

Syntax: VADDV<v><.dt> Rda, Qm
                 VADDVA<v><.dt> Rda, Qm

Example:

Initial Conditions:
       Q0 = [0x1000, 0x2000, 0x4000, 0x8000]

Instruction: VADDV.U32 R0, Q0

Result:
       R0 = 0xF000

VADDLV, VADDLVA – Vector Add Long Across Vector, Vector Add Long Across Vector Accumulate. Add across the elements of a vector register, accumulating the result into a scalar. The 64-bit result is stored across two general-purpose registers, with the upper half in an odd-numbered register and the lower half in an even-numbered register. It can be performed on 32-bit integer values (S32 or U32) stored in 128-bit vector registers. The VADDLVA variant adds the initial value of the destination registers to the result.

Syntax: VADDLV<v><.dt> RdaLo, RdaHi, Qm
                 VADDLVA<v><.dt> RdaLo, RdaHi, Qm

VNEG – Vector Negate. Negates the value of each element in a vector register. Obviously, this can only be done on signed integer or floating-point elements.

Syntax: VNEG<v><.dt> Qd, Qn, Qm

VQADD, VQSUB – Vector Saturating Add, Vector Saturating Subtract. These are saturating addition and subtraction instructions, which can only be applied to integer elements (i.e. the data type cannot be .F16 or .F32). They add (or subtract) the value of the elements in the first source-vector register to either the respective elements in the second source-vector register or a general-purpose register. The result is saturated before being written to the destination-vector register.

Syntax: VQADD<v><.dt> Qd, Qn, Qm
                 VQADD<v><.dt> Qd, Qn, Rm

                 VQSUB<v><.dt> Qd, Qn, Qm
                 VQSUB<v><.dt> Qd, Qn, Rm

VHADD, VHSUB – Vector Halving Add (or Subtract). Add (or subtract) the value of the elements in the first source-vector register to either the respective elements in the second source-vector register or a general-purpose register. The result is halved before being written to the destination-vector register. These instructions can only be applied to integer results.

Syntax: VHADD<v><.dt> Qd, Qn, Qm
                 VHADD<v><.dt> Qd, Qn, Rm

                 VHSUB<v><.dt> Qd, Qn, Qm
                 VHSUB<v><.dt> Qd, Qn, Rm

Example:

Initial Conditions:
        R0 = 500
        Q0 = [-32768, 12288, -20480, 28672, 28672, -20480, 12288, 32767]

Instruction: VHADD.S16 Q2, Q0, R0

Result:
        Q2 = [-16134, 6394, -9990, 14586, 14586, -9990, 6394, 16633]

VRHADD – Vector Rounding Halving Add. This is a variant of VHADD which performs rounding. It adds the value of the elements in the first source-vector register to the respective elements in the second source-vector register. The result is rounded and halved before being written to the destination-vector register.

Syntax: VRHADD<v><.dt> Qd, Qn, Qm

4.1.2 Absolute Values
There are instructions related to finding the absolute value of a signed number.

VABS – Vector Absolute Value. This returns the absolute value of each element. It takes a signed integer (or floating-point) value and produces an unsigned output.

Syntax: VABS<v><.dt> Qd, Qm

Example:

Initial Conditions:
          Q1 = [55, -40, 36, 23, 11, -9, 0, 10]

Instruction: VABS.S16 Q0, Q1

Result:
          Q0 = [55, 40, 36, 23, 11, 9, 0, 10]

VABD – Vector Absolute Difference. Subtract the elements of the second source-vector register from the corresponding elements of the first source-vector register and place the absolute values of the results in the elements of the destination-vector register.

Syntax: VABD<v><.dt> Qd, Qn, Qm

Example:

Initial Conditions:
          Q1 = [0.0, 1.0, 2.0, 3.0]
          Q2 = [100.0, 99.0, 98.0, 97.0]

Instruction: VABD.F32 Q0, Q1, Q2

Result:
          Q0 = [100.0, 98.0, 96.0, 94.0]

VABAV – Vector Absolute Difference and Accumulate Across Vector. Subtract the elements of the second source-vector register from the corresponding elements of the first source vector and accumulate the absolute values of the results. The initial value of the general-purpose destination register is added to the result. It is, in effect, a variant of the above VABD instruction.

Syntax: VABAV<v><.dt> Rda, Qn, Qm

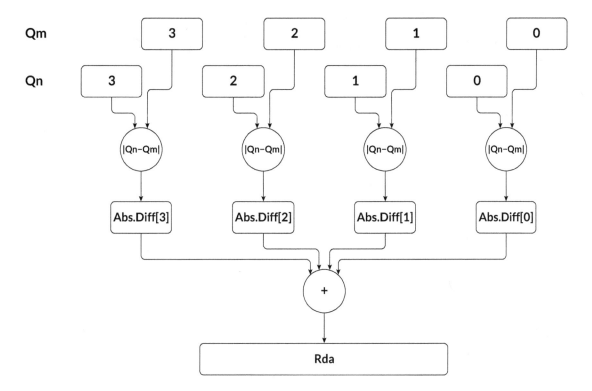

Figure 4.2: VABAV *instruction operation*

Figure 4.2 shows the VABAV instruction operating on two vectors of 32-bit elements. The absolute difference between the elements in each vector is calculated by subtraction (the sign of the result is disregarded) and the sum of the differences is accumulated into a scalar register.

Example:

Initial Conditions:
      R2 = 500
      Q0 = [0, 1, 2, 4, 8, 16, 32, 64]
      Q1 = [6, 7, 8, 9, 10, 11, 12, 13]

Instruction: VABAV.S16 R2, Q0, Q1

Result:
      R2 = 500 + |-6| + |-6| + |-6| + |-5| + |-2| + |5| + |20| + |51| = 601

4.1.3 Shifts

In this section, the vector right shift, left shift and shift insert operations are described.

Right Shift Instructions

Helium provides a set of right shift instructions. Right shift instructions only support an immediate value as the second operand (as we'll see, right shifts with a value from a register are achieved by performing a left shift with a negative value). The range of this immediate value depends upon the instruction. For simple shifts, it may be anywhere from 1 up to the size of the data element (obviously, only integer values can be shifted). For the instructions with the N (Narrow) option, the allowable range is from 1 to half of the data element size.

VSHR – Vector Shift Right. Shifts each element of a vector register to the right by the immediate value. The operation can only be performed on integer data types.

Syntax: `VSHR<v><.dt> Qd, Qm, #<imm>`

VSHRN – Vector Shift Right and Narrow. This can only be performed on 16- or 32-bit integer values in a vector. Performs an element-wise narrowing to half-width, with shift, writing the result to either the top half (T variant) or bottom half (B variant) of the result element. The other half of the destination-vector element retains its previous value.

Syntax: `VSHRNT<v><.dt> Qd, Qm, #<imm>`
                 `VSHRNB<v><.dt> Qd, Qm, #<imm>`

VRSHR – Vector Rounding Shift Right. Shift each element right and round.

Syntax: `VRSHR<v><.dt> Qd, Qm, #<imm>`

Normally, when we shift an integer quantity right, the least significant bits will be discarded. For example, if we have the integer value 9, and we want to perform division by 4, we can do a right shift of two places. This would produce the answer 2, which is the integer closest to the exact answer of 2.25. However, when we consider division with negative numbers, there are several possible options, including rounding toward zero, always rounding down (toward negative infinity, as Python does), or round to nearest. This instruction achieves a round to nearest by adding the value of 2^{N-1} before performing the shift (where N is the number of bits being shifted).

VRSHRN – Vector Rounding Shift Right and Narrow. This can only be performed on 16- or 32-bit integer values in a vector. It performs an element-wise narrowing to half-width (see Section 3.5.3), with shift, writing the rounded result to either the top half (T variant) or bottom half (B variant) of the result element. The other half of the destination-vector element retains its previous value.

Syntax: `VRSHRNT<v><.dt> Qd, Qm, #<imm>`
                 `VRSHRNB<v><.dt> Qd, Qm, #<imm>`

There are also saturating versions of these shift instructions.

VQSHRN – Vector Saturating Shift Right and Narrow. Performs an element-wise saturation narrowing to half-width (see Section 3.5.3), with shift, writing the result to either the top half (T variant) or bottom half (B variant) of the result element. The other half of the destination-vector element retains its previous value. The allowable data types are .S16, .S32, .U16 and .U32.

Syntax: VQSHRNT<v><.dt> Qd, Qm, #<imm>
               VQSHRNB<v><.dt> Qd, Qm, #<imm>

This instruction shifts right each element by a certain number of bits and then reduces the width of the result to the desired size (for example, from 16 to 8, or from 32 to 16). Depending upon the data and the size of the shift applied, it would be possible (without saturation) for the result to overflow. The saturation ensures that if the result of the shift is larger than the highest possible in the destination-vector element, it will be clipped to that value and if the result of the shift is smaller than the lowest possible value in the destination-vector element, it will be clipped to that lowest value. Usually, these instructions will be executed as a pair. Figure 4.3 shows a VQSHRNB instruction.

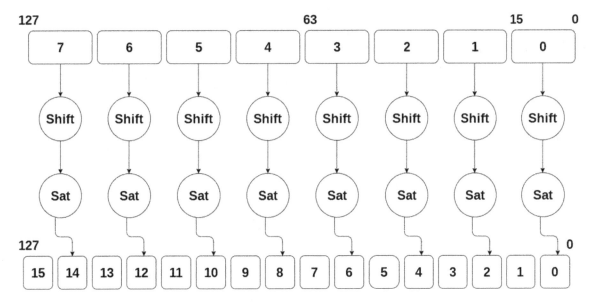

Figure 4.3: VQSHRNB instruction – Shift right, saturate and narrow operation (bottom)

VQSHRUN – Vector Saturating Shift Right Unsigned and Narrow. Performs an element-wise saturation narrowing to half-width, with shift, writing the result to either the top half (T variant) or bottom half (B variant) of the result element. The other half of the destination-vector element retains its previous value.

Syntax: VQSHRUNT<v><.dt> Qd, Qm, #<imm>
               VQSHRUNB<v><.dt> Qd, Qm, #<imm>

VQRSHRN – Vector Saturating Rounding Shift Right and Narrow. Performs an element-wise saturation narrowing to half-width, with shift, writing the rounded result to either the top half (T variant) or bottom half (B variant) of the result element. The other half of the destination-vector element retains its previous value.

Syntax:

```
VQRSHRNT<v><.dt> Qd, Qm, #<imm>
VQRSHRNB<v><.dt> Qd, Qm, #<imm>
```

VQRSHRUN – Vector Saturating Rounding Shift Right Unsigned and Narrow. Performs an element-wise saturation narrowing to half-width, with shift, writing the rounded result to either the top half (T variant) or bottom half (B variant) of the result element. The other half of the destination-vector element retains its previous value.

Syntax:

```
VQRSHRUNT<v><.dt> Qd, Qm, #<imm>
VQRSHRUNB<v><.dt> Qd, Qm, #<imm>
```

Left Shift Instructions
There are corresponding left shift instructions. Left shift instructions support a scalar/vector register or an immediate value as the second operand. The variants which use an immediate value shift each element of a vector register to the left by the immediate value. The variants which shift by a scalar register value use only the least significant byte (LSB) (and this can be negative, i.e. perform a shift to the right). The vector variant shifts each element of the first vector by a value from the least significant byte of the corresponding element of the second vector and places the results in the destination vector.

VSHL – Vector Shift Left. Shifts each element of a vector register to the left, either by an immediate value, or by the value specified in the LSB of a scalar source register. The vector variant shifts each element of the first vector by a value from the least significant byte of the corresponding element of the second vector and places the results in the destination vector.

```
Syntax: VSHL<v><.dt> Qd, Qm, #<imm> // immediate value
        VSHL<v><.dt> Qda, Rm         // specified in lsb of scalar register
        VSHL<v><.dt> Qd, Qm, Qn      // vector variant
```

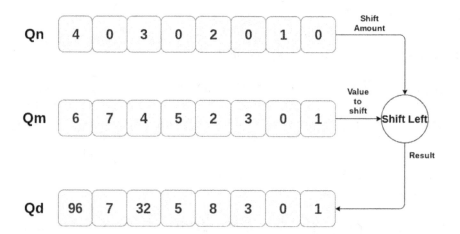

Figure 4.4: Example of VSHL *vector variant*

Figure 4.4 shows a simple example of VSHL where the shift amount is specified in a vector. From the left-hand side, we see that the value of 6 shifted left by four places gives a result of 96, the value of 7 shifted left by zero places gives a result of 7, and so forth.

VSHLC – Whole Vector Shift Left with Carry. A logical shift left by 1–32 bits, with carry across elements, carry in from a scalar register, and carry out to the same general-purpose register. In effect, this allows a 128-bit vector register to be treated as a single 128-bit scalar. The carry in is from the lower bits of the general-purpose register (i.e. if a shift of five bits is specified, the five least significant bits of the scalar register will be shifted into the vector register). As the instruction treats the register as a single 128-bit entity, there is no data type specified. Applications which require large-integer arithmetic (for example, computation of mathematical constants, rendering of fractal images, or cryptography) may use this instruction. It can also be used for moving elements within a vector.

The operation of the instruction is shown in Figure 4.5.

Syntax: VSHLC<v> Qda, Rdm, #<imm>

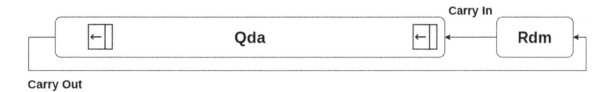

Figure 4.5: VSHLC *instruction*

VSHLL – Vector Shift Left Long. Selects an element of 8- or 16-bits from either the top half (T variant) or bottom half (B variant) of each source element, performs a left shift by an immediate value, performs a signed or unsigned left shift by an immediate value and places the 16- or 32-bit results in the destination vector. The permitted data types are .S8, .S16, .U8 and .U16.

Syntax: VSHLLT<v><.dt> Qd, Qm, #<imm>
               VSHLLB<v><.dt> Qd, Qm, #<imm>

VRSHL – Vector Rounding Shift Left. The vector variant shifts each element of the first vector by a value from the least significant byte of the corresponding element of the second vector and places the results in the destination vector. The register variant shifts each element of a vector register by the value specified in a source register.

Syntax: VRSHL<v><.dt> Qda, Rm   // specified in lsb of scalar register
               VRSHL<v><.dt> Qd, Qm, Qn // vector variant

There are equivalent saturating left shifts.

VQSHL – Vector Saturating Shift Left. The register variant shifts each element of a vector register by the value specified in a source register. The immediate variant shifts each element of a vector register to the left by the immediate value. The vector variant shifts each element of the first vector by a value from the least significant byte of the corresponding element of the second vector and places the results in the destination vector.

Syntax: VQSHL<v><.dt> Qda, Rm
                 VQSHL<v><.dt> Qd, Qm, Qn
                 VQSHL<v><.dt> Qd, Qm, #<Imm>

VQSHLU – Vector Saturating Shift Left Unsigned. The unsigned variant produces unsigned results, although the operands are signed.

Syntax: VQSHLU<v><.dt> Qd, Qm, #<Imm>

VQRSHL – Vector Saturating Rounding Shift Left. The vector variant shifts each element of the first vector by a value from the least significant byte of the corresponding element of the second vector and places the results in the destination vector. The register variant shifts each element of a vector register by the value specified in a source register.

Syntax: VQRSHL<v><.dt> Qda, Rm
                 VQRSHL<v><.dt> Qd, Qm, Qn

Shift Insert Instructions
The shift insert instructions shift all elements by an immediate value and insert the result into the destination register at the specified position. The "vacated" bits are unchanged. The instruction does not distinguish between different types of data. This can be useful for packing data into elements. For example, a common format for 16-bit pixel data is 565 RGB (5 bits of red data, 6 bits of green data, 5 bits of blue data). The shift insert instruction allows easy selection of the relevant number of bits of data from (for example) pixel data stored as separate red, green and blue bytes.

The available instructions are:

VSLI – Vector Shift Left and Insert. This takes each element in the operand vector, left shifts them by an immediate value, and inserts the results in the destination vector. Bits shifted out of the left of each element are lost.

Syntax: VSLI<v><.dt> Qd, Qm, #<Imm>

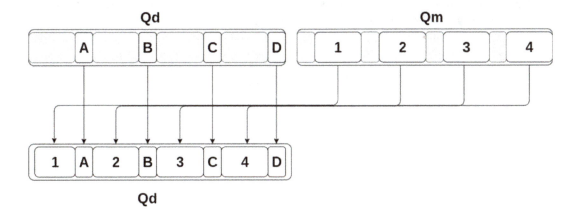

Figure 4.6: VSLI *instruction*

Figure 4.6 shows the VSLI instruction operating on 32-bit elements. The four elements in Qm are left shifted by the specified amount and inserted into register Qd.

VSRI – Vector Shift Right and Insert. This takes each element in the operand vector, right shifts them by an immediate value, and inserts the results in the destination vector. Bits shifted out of the right of each element are lost.

Syntax: VSRI<v><.dt> Qd, Qm, #<Imm>

Example:

Initial Conditions:
        Q0 = [0x11111111, 0x22222222, 0x33333333, 0x44444444]
        Q1 = [0xABABABAB, 0x55555555, 0x66666672, 0x17777799]

Instruction: VSRI.32 Q0, Q1, #8

Result:
        Q0[i] = Q1[i] >> 8 | Q0[i] & 0xFF000000 for i={0..3}
        Q0= [0x11ABABAB, 0x22555555, 0x33666666, 0x44177777]

4.1.4 Logical Operations
Helium provides a full range of logical operators. As these operate on a bitwise basis, they apply to the full 128-bit register and there is no need to specify the size or type of data.

VAND – Vector And. This instruction performs a bitwise AND of one vector register with another vector register. A data type may be specified, but is ignored, as this is a bitwise operation.

Syntax: VAND<v>{<.dt>} Qd, Qn, Qm

VBIC – Vector Bit Clear. This instruction does a bitwise AND of a vector register and the complement of another vector register. This allows the programmer to clear specific bits more easily than by using AND. There is also an immediate version, which performs a bitwise AND of a vector register and the complement of an immediate value. This allows an immediate version of VAND to be synthesized by the assembler (it performs VBIC, but with the specified immediate value inverted).

Syntax:
```
VBIC<v>{<.dt>} Qd, Qn, Qm
VBIC<v>{<.dt>} Qda, #<imm>
```

Example:

Initial Conditions:
        Q3 = [0x11, 0x12, 0x13, 0x14, 0x15, 0x16, 0x17, 0x18]

Instruction: VBIC.I16 Q3, #3

Result:
        Q3 = [0x10, 0x10, 0x10, 0x14, 0x14, 0x14, 0x14, 0x18]

VORR – Vector Or. This does a bitwise OR of a vector register with another vector register. There is also an immediate variant, which performs a bitwise OR of a vector register with the immediate operand value.

Syntax:
```
VORR<v>{<.dt>} Qd, Qn, Qm
VORR<v>{<.dt>} Qda, #<imm>
```

VORN – Vector Or Not. This computes a bitwise OR NOT of a vector register with another vector register. Again, the assembler can implement a pseudo-instruction of VORN with an immediate value by using VORR with the complement of the specified immediate value.

Syntax:
```
VORN<v>{<.dt>} Qd, Qn, Qm
```

VEOR – Vector Exclusive Or. This instruction does a bitwise EOR of one vector register with another vector register.

Syntax:
```
VEOR<v>{<.dt>} Qd, Qn, Qm
```

4.1.5 Minimum and Maximum
Helium provides instructions to find the Maximum or Minimum values. In the instruction variants which look for the maximum or minimum value across a vector, and store the result in a general-purpose register, the upper half of the general-purpose register is cleared when dealing with half-precision input data.

VMAX, VMIN – Vector Maximum/Minimum. Find the maximum/minimum value of the elements in the source operands and store the result in the corresponding destination elements.

Syntax: `VMAX<v>{<.dt>} Qd, Qn, Qm`
                     `VMIN<v>{<.dt>} Qd, Qn, Qm`

Example:

Initial Conditions:
        Q0 = [0, 1, 2, 3, 4, 5, 6, 7]
        Q1 = [1, 0, -3, 0, 1, 0, -1, 0]

Instruction: `VMAX.U16 Q2, Q1, Q0`

Result:
        Q2= [1, 1, 2, 3, 4, 5, 6, 7]

`VMAXA`, `VMINA` – Vector Maximum/Minimum Absolute. The absolute variant takes the elements from the destination vector, treating them as unsigned, and compares them to the absolute values of the corresponding elements in the source vector. The larger/smaller values are stored back into the destination vector.

Syntax: `VMAXA<v>{<.dt>} Qda, Qm`
                     `VMINA<v>{<.dt>} Qda, Qm`

Example:

Initial Conditions:
        Q0 = [0, 1, 2, 3, 4, 5, 6, 7]
        Q1 = [1, 0, -3, 0, 1, 0, -1, 0]

Instruction: `VMAXA.S16 Q2, Q1, Q0`

Result:
        Q2= [1, 1, 3, 3, 4, 5, 6, 7]

`VMAXV`, `VMINV` – Vector Maximum/Minimum Across Vector. Find the maximum/minimum value of the elements in a vector register. Store the maximum/minimum value in the general-purpose destination register only if it is larger/smaller than the starting value of the general-purpose destination register. The general-purpose register is read as the same width as the vector elements. The result of the operation is sign-extended to 32 bits before being stored back.

Syntax: `VMAXV<v>{<.dt>} Rda, Qm`
                     `VMINV<v>{<.dt>} Rda, Qm`

`VMAXAV`, `VMINAV` – Vector Maximum/Minimum Absolute Across Vector. The absolute variant of the instruction compares the absolute value of signed vector elements and treats the value in the general-purpose register as unsigned.

Syntax:
```
VMAXAV<v>{<.dt>} Rda, Qm
VMINAV<v>{<.dt>} Rda, Qm
```

Example:

Initial Conditions:
QO = [0, -1, 2, -3, 4, -5, 6, -7]

Instruction: `VMAXAV.S16 R1, Q0`

Result:
R1=7

VMAXNM, VMAXNMA, VMAXNMV, VMAXNMAV, VMINNM, VMINNMA, VMINNMV, VMINNMAV – There
are floating-point variants of each of the above instructions. These can operate on half-precision
(.F16) or single-precision (.F32) values. They handle NaN values as specified by the IEEE754-2008
specification, and when one operand is a number and the other is a quiet NaN, they return the number.

Syntax:
```
VMAXNM<v><.dt> Qd, Qn, Qm
VMAXNMA<v{<.dt>} Qda, Qm
VMAXNMV<v><.dt> Rda, Qm
VMAXNMAV<v{<.dt>} Rda, Qm

VMINNM<v><.dt> Qd, Qn, Qm
VMINNMA<v{<.dt>} Qda, Qm
VMINNMV<v><.dt> Rda, Qm
VMINNMAV<v{<.dt>} Rda, Qm
```

4.1.6 Format Conversion and Rounding

This section describes two instructions, VCVT and VRINT. VCVT is unusual in that it requires two data
types to be specified. The first is the output data type, the second the input data type.

VCVT – Vector Convert. This instruction has a range of options. It can perform conversion between:

▪ Integer to floating-point

▪ Floating-point to integer

▪ Floating-point to fixed-point

▪ Fixed-point to floating-point

▪ Floating-point precisions (.F32.F16 and .F16.F32)

Conversions between types need to use the same number of bits. For example, a signed or unsigned 32-bit integer can be converted to `.F32` (single-precision floating-point). It cannot be converted directly to a half-precision floating-point (`.F16`) value.

When converting between single-precision and half-precision floating-point values, the suffixes `T` or `B` are used to select the top or bottom half of the `.F16` input vector.

For conversions involving fixed-point values, the instruction must specify the number of fraction bits (which will be in the range 1–16 or 1–32 depending upon the element size).

Conversion from floating-point to integer requires some rounding to be applied. The suffixes A, N, P or M are added to the instruction to specify one of four RM (Rounding Mode) values:

- A (RM = 00) – round to nearest with ties to away

- N (RM = 01) – round to nearest with ties to even

- P (RM = 10) – round toward plus infinity

- M (RM = 11) – round toward minus infinity

```
Syntax: VCVT<v><.dt> Qd, Qm, #<fbits> // Floating-point to fixed-point
        VCVT<v><.dt> Qd, Qm                // Integer to floating-point
        VCVT<T><v><.dt> Qd, Qm             // Between single-precision and
                                           //    double-precision float
        VCVT<ANPM><v><.dt> Qd, Qm          // Floating-point to integer
```

Example:

Initial Conditions:
Q0 = [0, 1, 2, 3]

Instruction: `VCVT.F32.S32 Q1, Q0`

Result:
Q1 = [0.0, 1.0, 2.0, 3.0]

Similarly, `VCVTN.S16.F16 Q5, Q7` converts the half-precision floating-point data in register Q7, rounds to nearest (with ties to even) and stores the result in Q5.

Example:

Initial Conditions:
Q7 = [0.7, 0.6, 0.5, 0.4, 0.3, 0.2, 0.1, 0.0]

Instruction: `VCVTB.F32.F16 Q5, Q7`

Comment: This converts the half-precision floating-point data in the bottom half of Q7 to single-precision floating-point and stores the result in Q5. Note that some of the values shown in the initial conditions cannot be represented without some loss of precision in half-precision floating-point. The output is an approximation of [0.7, 0.5, 0.3, 0.1].

Result:
Q5 = [0.700195, 0.5, 0.300049, 0.099976]

`VRINT` – Vector Round Integer. This instruction does not perform a conversion. It rounds a floating-point value to an integer value, leaving the result in floating-point format.

Syntax: `VRINT<op><v><.dt> Qd, Qm`

There are six different rounding modes available, specified by the <op> suffix:

- A – round to nearest with ties to away

- N – round to nearest with ties to even

- P – round toward plus infinity

- M – round toward minus infinity

- Z – round toward zero

- X – round to nearest, with ties to even, raising inexact exception if the result is not numerically equal to the input

Example:

Initial Conditions:
Q0 = [0.3, 0.4, 0.8, 0.99, 1.1, 1.4, 1.7, 1.9]

Instruction: `VRINTZ.F16 Q1, Q0`   `// Round toward zero`

Result:
Q1 = [0.0, 0.0, 0.0, 0.0, 1.0, 1.0, 1.0, 1.0]

4.1.7 Bit Counting
There are a pair of instructions which count leading zeros and sign bits. These can be useful in a range of algorithms, including normalization and Newton–Raphson division (or finding roots).

VCLS – Vector Count Leading Sign bits. Returns the number of bits that match the topmost bit (i.e. the sign bit in a signed integer). The count does not include the topmost bit. This instruction can, of course, only be used with signed integer data.

Syntax: VCLS<v><.dt> Qd, Qm

VCLZ – Vector Count Leading Zeros. Returns the number of zeros starting at the most significant bit. It supports 8-, 16- or 32-bit size integer value inputs.

Syntax: VCLZ<v><.dt> Qd, Qm

Example:

If we want to normalize a set of unsigned 32-bit integers in a vector, we could use the following instruction sequence:

```
VCLZ.S32       Q1, Q0
MOV            R0, #32
VMINV.S32      R0, Q1
VSHL.S32       Q0, R0
```

If we start with:
        Q0 = [0x0, 0x30, 0x70, 0xFF]

the VCLZ instruction will produce
        Q1 = [32, 26, 25, 24]

The VMINV instruction (covered in section 4.1.5) will find the minimum value within the vector if it is lower than the initial value in R0. We therefore precede this with a MOV to set the initial value to the maximum permitted shift of 32. VMINV sets R0 to 24, the lowest value within the vector.

Finally, VSHL shifts our original vector in Q0 24 places left, so that:
        Q0 = [0x0, 0x30000000, 0x70000000, 0xFF000000]

4.1.8 Element Reversal
Helium provides instructions which can be used to reorder elements within a vector.

VREV16 – Vector Reverse in Half-words. Reverses the order of 8-bit elements in each half-word of the vector.

Syntax: VREV16<v><.8> Qd, Qm

`VREV32` – Vector Reverse in Words. Reverses the order of 8-bit or 16-bit elements in each word of the vector. The size field in the instruction must be either 8 or 16.

Syntax: `VREV32<v><.size> Qd, Qm`

Figure 4.7 shows the execution of a `VREV32.16` instruction. The 128-bit vector register contains eight 16-bit elements. The instruction reverses the order of those 16-bit elements within each 32-bit word.

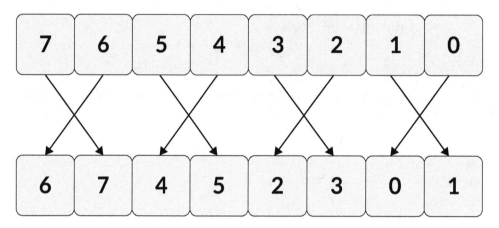

Figure 4.7: `VREV32.16` *instruction*

`VREV64` – Vector Reverse in Double-Words. Reverses the order of 8-bit, 16-bit, or 32-bit elements in each double-word of the vector.

Syntax: `VREV64<v><.size> Qd, Qm`

Figure 4.8 shows the execution of a `VREV64.16` instruction. The 128-bit vector register contains eight 16-bit elements. The instruction reverses the order of those 16-bit elements within each 64-bit double-word.

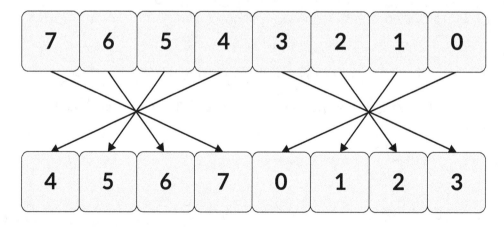

Figure 4.8: `VREV64.16` *instruction*

VBRSR – Vector Bit Reverse and Shift Right. This instruction reverses the specified number of least significant bits in each element of a vector register and sets the other bits to zero. The number of bits to reverse is specified in the bottom byte of a scalar register and must lie within the range from 0 to the element size. As we will see later, this instruction can be useful in an optimized fast Fourier transform (FFT) implementation.

Syntax: `VBRSR<v><.size> Qd, Qn, Rm`

Example: The following code would simply reverse each of the bits within each 32-bit element in Q0.

```
MOVS R0, #32
VBRSR.32 Q0, Q0, R0
```

In Chapter 9, we'll look again at this instruction and its role within an efficient implementation of the FFT.

4.2 Multiplication

There are numerous multiplication instructions provided in Helium. In addition to the saturating and doubling variants that we saw with the add and subtract operations, we also have some instructions which use the fact that multiplication produces an answer which is larger (more bits) than the values being multiplied. For example, multiplication of two 16-bit integers produces a 32-bit result. We therefore have instructions which select part or all of the result.

- An instruction which outputs the least significant (low) half of the result:

  □ VMUL

- Instructions which output the most significant (high) half of the result:

  □ VMULH (and the rounding version, VRMULH)

  □ VQDMULH (and the rounding version, VQDRMULH)

- Instructions which output all of the result. As these require a double-width element to store the output, they can only operate on the top or bottom half of the inputs:

  □ VMULL

  □ VQDMULL

4.2.1 Multiply Instructions

VMUL – Vector Multiply. Multiply the value of the elements in the first source-vector register by either the respective elements in the second source-vector register or a general-purpose register. The least significant part of the result is then written to the destination vector register. For example, if we multiply two 32-bit elements, the result will be the least significant 32-bits of the 64-bit result.

Syntax: VMUL<v><.dt> Qd, Qn, Qm
              VMUL<v><.dt> Qd, Qn, Rm

Section 3.1.4 contains an example of the VMUL instruction execution.

VMULH, VRMULH – Vector Multiply Returning High Half, Vector Rounding Multiply Returning High Half. Multiply each element in a vector register by its respective element in another vector register and return the high half of the result. The result is optionally rounded before the high half is selected.

Syntax: VMULH<v><.dt> Qd, Qn, Qm
              VRMULH<v><.dt> Qd, Qn, Qm

VQDMULH, VQRDMULH – Vector Saturating Doubling Multiply Returning High Half, Vector Saturating Rounding Doubling Multiply Returning High Half. Multiply a general-purpose register value by each element of a vector register to produce a vector of results or multiply each element of a vector register by its corresponding element in another vector register, double the results, and place the most significant half of the final results in the destination vector. The results are optionally rounded before being saturated.

Syntax: VQDMULLH<v><.dt> Qd, Qn, Qm
              VQRDMULLH<v><.dt> Qd, Qn, Qm

VMULL – Vector Multiply Long. Performs an element-wise integer multiplication of two single-width source operand elements. These are selected from either the top half (T variant) or bottom half (B variant) of double-width source-vector register elements. The operation produces a double-width result. When the input type is 32-bit, this means that the output will be a vector of two 64-bit integers, making this one of the few Helium instructions which produces 64-bit results.

Syntax: VMULL<T><v><.dt> Qd, Qn, Qm

Example: VMULLT.S8 Q0, Q1, Q2
              VMULLB.S8 Q0, Q1, Q2

Figure 4.9 shows the VMULLT instruction with the "top" 8-bit wide input elements from Qm and Qn being multiplied and the 16-bit results being stored in Qd.

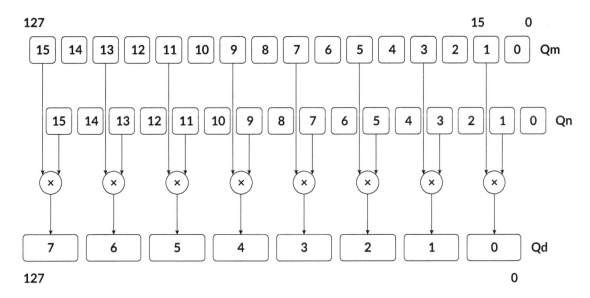

Figure 4.9: VMULLT.S8 *instruction*

VMULL – Vector Multiply Long. This is a variant of the above, which performs an element-wise *polynomial* multiplication of two single-width source operand elements. These are selected from either the top half (T variant) or bottom half (B variant) of double-width source-vector register elements. The operation produces a double-width result. Two options are available. Setting <.dt> to .P8 specifies an 8 × 8 ->16 and .P16 specifies a 16 × 16 ->32 polynomial multiplication.

Syntax: VMULL<T><v><.dt> Qd, Qn, Qm

Example: VMULLT.P8 Q0, Q1, Q2

Polynomial multiplication may be unfamiliar to some readers. In computer arithmetic, we normally view a string of binary digits as representing a single number. However, we could also view it as a polynomial in x whose coefficients are either 0 or 1. This is useful in a part of number theory called field arithmetic. The Boolean operators AND, OR, XOR and NOT can act as arithmetic operators in a binary finite field. The simplest of these is called GF(2), where GF stands for Galois Field and two is the number of elements (0 and 1). By using shift instructions, you can extend this to larger Galois fields. This has applications in cryptography, cyclic redundancy checks and Error Correction Codes (ECCs), such as Reed–Solomon. In each of these, the bits in the binary string are interpreted as coefficients on a polynomial in a finite field.

A polynomial multiplication uses XOR to sum up rows, when regular binary multiplication would use ADD. When we perform an addition, there is potentially a carry from one row to the next. This does not happen when we use XOR alone.

Normal Multiplication

```
    1   1   0   1
        1   0   0   1
    ─────────────────
       (1)  1   0   1
    0   0   0   0
0   0   0   0
1   1   0  (1)              +
   (1)              ←──Carry
────────────────────────
1   1   1   0   1   0   1
```

Polynomial Multiplication

```
    1   1   0   1
        1   0   0   1
    ─────────────────
        1   1   0   1
    0   0   0   0
0   0   0   0
1   1   0   1              +
────────────────────────
1   1   0   0   1   0   1
```

The example shows the difference between normal and polynomial multiplication. In each case, the result is obtained by repeated shifts and addition. In the normal case, there is a column where two 1 values (denoted with a circle) are added and produce a carry. In the polynomial case, there is no carry and so a different result is obtained.

Illustrating the connection to polynomial multiplication, the operation above could be thought of in terms of multiplying two polynomial functions, where each bit represents a power. So:

1101 represents $x^3 + x^2 + 0 + 1$
1001 represents $x^3 + 0 + 0 + 1$.

In Chapter 11, we will see how this instruction can be used to synthesize much longer polynomial multiplication, which can be required in cryptography.

VQDMULL – Vector Saturating Doubling Multiply Long. Performs an element-wise integer multiplication of two single-width source operand elements. These are selected from either the top half (T variant) or bottom half (B variant) of double-width source-vector register elements or the lower single-width portion of the general-purpose register. The product of the multiplication is doubled and saturated to produce a double-width product that is written back to the destination-vector register. Like VMULL, this instruction produces a 64-bit result if the input type is .S32.

Syntax:
```
VQDMULL<T><v><.dt> Qd, Qn, Qm
VQDMULL<T><v><.dt> Qd, Qn, Rm
```

4.2.2 Multiply Accumulate (MAC)

We now look at the multiply accumulate instructions. At first glance, it may seem like there are a lot of different instructions. However, we can broadly divide them into two classes:

▪ MAC operations producing vector results:

☐ VFMA/VFMS (Vector * Vector + Vector, Floating-point only)

☐ VMLA (Vector * Scalar + Vector, Integer only)

☐ VFMAS (Vector * Vector + Scalar, Floating-point only)

☐ VMLAS (Vector * Vector + Scalar, Integer only)

☐ VQ[R]DMLAH (saturation / doubling / rounding variants of VMLA)

☐ VQ[R]DMLASH (saturation / doubling / rounding variants of VMLAS)

- MAC instructions producing scalar results:

☐ VMLADAV/VMLAV, VMLSDAV

☐ VMLALDAV, VMLALV, VMLSLDAV

☐ VRMLALDAVH/VRMLALVH, VRMLSLDAVH

In many instructions, we can also use the A and/or X suffixes. An A specifies "accumulate" (i.e. accumulate on to the existing value in the scalar register, as opposed to overwriting it). An X specifies "exchange" which means that we exchange adjacent pairs of values in Qm when performing the multiplies.

In Helium, floating-point multiply-add/subtract operations are always fused. This is a floating-point multiply-add operation performed in a single step, with rounding happening at the end. In an unfused multiply-add, we would calculate the multiplication, round it to a certain number of significant bits, add the result to the accumulator, and round again. A fused multiply-add computes the entire multiply and add expression to its full precision before rounding the result. This can improve the accuracy of calculations that involve the accumulation of products, such as matrix multiplication, convolution etc.

VFMA, VFMS – Vector Fused Multiply Accumulate, Vector Fused Multiply Subtract. Multiply each element of the first source vector by the respective element in the second vector register. Each result is then added to (or subtracted from) the respective element in the destination vector. The result of each multiply is not rounded before the addition or subtraction (as explained above). This instruction only permits .F16 and .F32 data types.

Syntax: VFMA<.dt> Qda, Qn, Qm
             VFMS<.dt> Qda, Qn, Qm

Example: VFMA.F32 Q2, Q1, Q0

VMLA – Vector Multiply Accumulate. Multiply each element in the source vector by a scalar value and add to the respective element from the destination vector. Store the result in the destination register.

This instruction multiplies a vector by scalar and accumulates into a vector. This means that the same value is being used for each of the multiplications.

Syntax: VMLA<.dt> Qda, Qn, Rm

Example:

Initial Conditions:
          Q0 = [0x1000, 0x2000, 0x4000, 0x6000]
          Q2 = [0x10, 0x20, 0x40, 0x60]
          R3 = 2

Instruction: VMLA.S32 Q2, Q0, R3

Result:
          Q2 = [0x2010, 0x4020, 0x8040, 0xC060]

The Vector Multiply Accumulate instruction works in the following manner. The elements stored in the vector register Qn are each multiplied by the value in the scalar register Rm. The resulting values are added to the elements stored in the vector register Qda, and the result is written into Qda. The accumulator value is fixed at 32-bits, regardless of input element size. Figure 4.10 shows this.

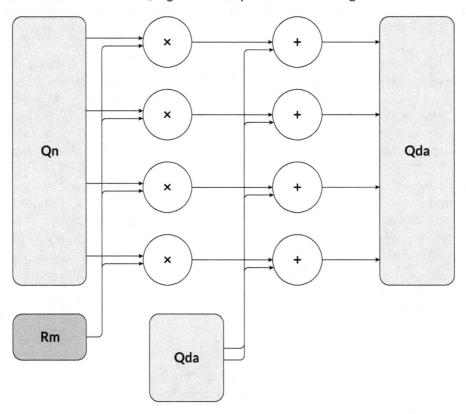

Figure 4.10: VMLA *instruction*

VMLAS – Vector Multiply Accumulate Scalar. Multiply each element in the source vector by the respective element from the destination vector and add to a scalar value. Store the result in the destination register.

This instruction can only operate on integer data types.

Syntax: VMLAS<v><.dt>   Qda, Qn, Rm

VFMAS – Vector Fused Multiply Accumulate Scalar. Multiply each element in the source vector by the respective element from the destination vector and add to a scalar value. Store the result in the destination register. The result of each multiply is not rounded before the addition.

This instruction can only operate on floating-point data types.

Syntax: VFMAS<v><.dt>   Qda, Qn, Rm

Example:

Initial Conditions:
          R0 = 0x3800 (= 0.5 in half-precision floating-point format)
          Q0 = [0.0, 1.0, 2.0, 3.0, 0.0, 1.0, 2.0, 3.0]
          Q1 = [19.5, 19.0, 20.0, 18.0, 18.0, 19.5, 21.0, 20.0]

Instruction: VFMAS.F16 Q0, Q1, R0

Result:
          Q0 = [0.5, 19.5, 40.5, 54.5, 0.5, 20.0, 42.5, 60.5]

VMLADAV{A}{X} – Vector Multiply Add Dual Accumulate Across Vector. The elements of the vector registers are handled in pairs. In the base variant, corresponding elements from the two source registers are multiplied together, whereas the exchange variant swaps the values in each pair of values read from the first source register, before multiplying them with the values from the second source register. The results of the pairs of multiply operations are combined by adding them together. At the end of each beat these results are accumulated and the lower 32 bits written back to the general-purpose destination register. The initial value of the general-purpose destination register can optionally be added to the result.

If A is added to the instruction (for example, VMLADAVA), it means accumulate with existing register contents. Adding an X to the instruction means exchange adjacent pairs of values in Qm.

Syntax: VMLADAV{A}{X}<v><.dt> Rda, Qn, Qm

Figure 4.11 shows an example of the VMLADAVA.S32 instruction.

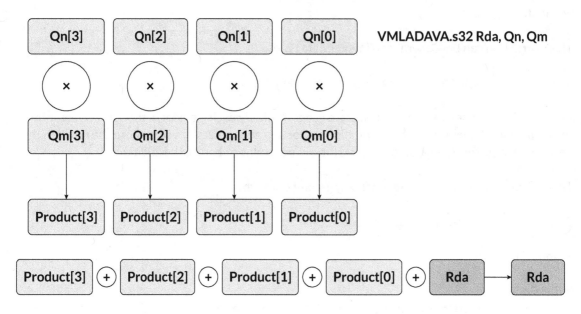

VMLADAVA.s32 Rda, Qn, Qm

Figure 4.11: VMLADAVA.S32 *instruction*

VMLAV – Vector Multiply Accumulate Across Vector. This is an alias of VMLADAV without exchange.

Syntax: VMLAV{A}<.dt> Rd, Qn, Qm

This operation produces a 32-bit scalar result in a general-purpose register. The "A" variant accumulates onto the existing value of Rd. The VMLAV instruction does a MAC operation across the vector. This means that it multiplies each vector element in Qn with the corresponding element in Qm. It then adds together all of the results. In the VMLAVA variant, it then adds that result to the value that was already in the scalar register Rd.

VMLALDAV(H){A}{X} – Vector Multiply Add Long Dual Accumulate Across Vector. The elements of the vector registers are handled in pairs. In the base variant, corresponding elements from the two source registers are multiplied together, whereas the exchange variant swaps the values in each pair of values read from the first source register, before multiplying them with the values from the second source register. The results of the pairs of multiply operations are combined by adding them together. At the end of each beat these results are accumulated. The 64-bit result is stored across two registers, the upper half is stored in an odd-numbered register and the lower half is stored in an even-numbered register. The initial value of the general-purpose destination registers can optionally be added to the result. Again, if A is added to the instruction, it means accumulate with existing register contents. Adding an X to the instruction means exchange adjacent pairs of values in Qm. The instruction only supports 16-bit and 32-bit integer inputs. The 64-bit accumulator provides a greater dynamic range where necessary.

Syntax: VMLALDAV{A}{X}<v><.dt> Rda, Qn, Qm

`VMLALV` – Vector Multiply Accumulate Long Across Vector. This is an alias of VMLALDAV without exchange.

Syntax: `VMLALV{A}<.dt> RdaLo, RdaHi, Qn, Qm`

A key point to notice here is that the accumulator register(s) for these instructions come from the general-purpose integer register file and not the vector registers. This reduces the pressure on the vector registers (of which there are only eight). It also allows the architecture to avoid a potential problem with an exception occurring during the execution of overlapping instructions, one of which crosses the boundary of beats. An instruction like `VMLALVA`, which multiplies a vector of 32-bit values and produces a 64-bit result to be accumulated needs to preserve the full 64-bit multiplier output. It would be difficult for the hardware to handle this without using general-purpose registers to hold the output.

When vectorizing a multiply accumulate operation, there is normally a "reduction" operation, in which the intermediate sums are added together. This is easily accomplished by the `VMLAL` group of instructions. However, these are only available for integer operands. For floating-point MACs, we may still need to perform this final reduction step using several instructions.

`VRMLALDAVH` – Vector Rounding Multiply Add Long Dual Accumulate Across Vector Returning High 64 bits. The elements of the vector registers are handled in pairs. In the base variant, corresponding elements from the two source registers are multiplied together, whereas the exchange variant swaps the values in each pair of values read from the first source register, before multiplying them with the values from the second source register. The results of the pairs of multiply operations are combined by adding them together. At the end of each beat these results are accumulated. The upper 64 bits of a 72-bit accumulator value are selected and stored across two registers, the top 32 bits are stored in an even-numbered register and the lower 32 bits are stored in an odd-numbered register. The initial value of the general-purpose destination registers can optionally be shifted up by eight bits and added to the result. The result is rounded before the top 64 bits are selected.

Syntax: `VRMLALDAVH{A}{X}<v><.dt> RdaLo, RdaHi, Qn, Qm`

In the following C code, we can see the `VRMLALDAVHA` instruction being used to compute the dot product of two Q31 vectors. The `vldrwq_s32` intrinsic is used to load two vectors (each containing four Q31 elements). The `vrmlaldavhaq_s32` intrinsic then multiplies together the corresponding pairs in each vector and accumulates the result into sum. The code comes from CMSIS, which we'll look at in detail later in the book, and can be found here:

https://github.com/ARM-software/CMSIS_5/blob/develop/CMSIS/DSP/Source/BasicMathFunctions/arm_dot_prod_q31.c

```
#include "arm_helium_utils.h"
void arm_dot_prod_q31(    const q31_t * pSrcA,    const q31_t * pSrcB,    uint32_t
blockSize,    q63_t * result)
{
    uint32_t  blkCnt;              /* loop counters */
    q31x4_t vecA;
    q31x4_t vecB;
    q63_t       sum = 0LL;
    /* Compute 4 outputs at a time */
    blkCnt = blockSize >> 2;
    while (blkCnt > 0U)
    {
        /*            * C = A[0]* B[0] + A[1]* B[1] + A[2]* B[2] + .....+ A[blockSize-1]*
B[blockSize1]
         * Calculate dot product and then store the result in a temporary buffer.
         */

        vecA = vld1q(pSrcA);
        vecB = vld1q(pSrcB);
        sum = vrmlaldavhaq(sum, vecA, vecB);

        /*
         * Decrement the blockSize loop counter
         */

        blkCnt--;

        /*
         * advance vector source and destination pointers
         */

        pSrcA += 4;
        pSrcB += 4;
    }
}
```

VRMLALVH{A} – Vector Rounding Multiply Accumulate Long Across Vector Returning High 64 bits. This is an alias of VRMLALDAVH without exchange. It takes 32-bit inputs only and returns the top 64 bits of a 72-bit accumulator.

Syntax: VRMLALVH{A}<v><.dt> RdaLo, RdaHi, Qn, Qm

VMLSDAV{A}{X} – Vector Multiply Subtract Dual Accumulate Across Vector. The elements of the vector registers are handled in pairs. In the base variant, corresponding elements from the two source registers are multiplied together, whereas the exchange variant (specified by appending X to the instruction) swaps the values in each pair of values read from the first source register, before multiplying them with the values from the second source register. The results of the pairs of multiply operations are combined by subtracting one from the other. At the end of each beat these results are accumulated and the lower 32 bits written back to the general-purpose destination register. The initial value of the general-purpose destination register can optionally be added to the result (this is specified by adding A to the instruction). Only signed integer (.S8, .S16 or .S32) data types can be used.

Syntax: `VMLSDAV{A}{X}<v><.dt> Rda, Qn, Qm`

`VMLSLDAV(H){A}{X}` – Vector Multiply Subtract Long Dual Accumulate Across Vector. The elements of the vector registers are handled in pairs. In the base variant, corresponding elements from the two source registers are multiplied together, whereas the exchange variant swaps the values in each pair of values read from the first source register, before multiplying them with the values from the second source register. The results of the pairs of multiply operations are combined by subtracting one from the other. At the end of each beat these results are accumulated. The 64-bit result is stored across two registers, the upper half is stored in an odd-numbered register and the lower half is stored in an even-numbered register. The initial value of the general-purpose destination registers can optionally be added to the result.

Syntax: `VMLSLDAVH{A}{X}<v>.S32 Rda, Qn, Qm`

`VRMLSLDAVH{A}{X}` – Vector Rounding Multiply Subtract Long Dual Accumulate Across Vector Returning High 64 bits. The elements of the vector registers are handled in pairs. In the base variant, corresponding elements from the two source registers are multiplied together, whereas the exchange variant swaps the values in each pair of values read from the first source register, before multiplying them with the values from the second source register. The results of the pairs of multiply operations are combined by subtracting one from the other. At the end of each beat these results are accumulated. The upper 64 bits of a 72-bit accumulator value are selected and stored across two registers, the top 32 bits are stored in an even-numbered register and the lower 32 bits are stored in an odd-numbered register. The initial value of the general-purpose destination registers can optionally be shifted up by eight bits and added to the result. The result is rounded before the top 64 bits are selected. This instruction can only be used with `.S32` data.

Syntax: `VRMLSLDAVH{A}{X}<v>.S32 Rda, Qn, Qm`

`VQDMLADH{X}`, `VQRDMLADH{X}` – Vector Saturating Doubling Multiply Add Dual Returning High Half, Vector Saturating Rounding Doubling Multiply Add Dual Returning High Half. The elements of the vector registers are handled in pairs. In the base variant, corresponding elements from the two source registers are multiplied together, whereas the exchange variant swaps the values in each pair of values read from the first source register, before multiplying them with the values from the second source register. The results of the pairs of multiply operations are combined by adding them together and doubling the result. The high halves of the resulting values are selected as the results. The base variant writes the results into the lower element of each pair of elements in the destination register, whereas the exchange variant writes to the upper element in each pair. The results are optionally rounded before the high half is selected and saturated. The data type must be `.S8`, `.S16` or `.S32`.

Syntax: `VQDMLADH{X}<v><.dt> Qd, Qn, Qm`
               `VQRDMLADH{X}<v><.dt> Qd, Qn, Qm`

`VQDMLASH`, `VQRDMLASH` – (vector by vector plus scalar) Vector Saturating Doubling Multiply Accumulate Scalar High Half, Vector Saturating Rounding Doubling Multiply Accumulate Scalar High

Half. Multiply each element in the source vector by the respective element from the destination vector, double the result and add to a scalar value. Store the high half of each result in the destination register. The result is optionally rounded before the high half is selected and saturated (the VQRDMLASH variant).

Syntax: VQDMLASH<v><.dt> Qda, Qn, Rm
               VQRDMLASH<v><.dt> Qda, Qn, Rm

VQDMLSDH{X}, VQRDMLSDH{X} – Vector Saturating Doubling Multiply Subtract Dual Returning High Half, Vector Saturating Rounding Doubling Multiply Subtract Dual Returning High Half. The elements of the vector registers are handled in pairs. In the base variant, corresponding elements from the two source registers are multiplied together, whereas the exchange variant swaps the values in each pair of values read from the first source register, before multiplying them with the values from the second source register. The results of the pairs of multiply operations are combined by subtracting one from the other and doubling the result. The high halves of the resulting values are selected as the results. The base variant writes the results into the lower element of each pair of elements in the destination register, whereas the exchange variant writes to the upper element in each pair. The results are optionally rounded before the high half is selected and saturated.

Syntax: VQDMLSDH{X}<v><.dt> Qd, Qn, Qm
               VQRDMLSDH{X}<v><.dt> Qd, Qn, Qm

4.2.3 Complex Mathematics Instructions

Many DSP algorithms make use of complex numbers, for example, FFT and filters. It is common to store such numbers as interleaved real/imaginary components in the same vector. Helium has a set of instructions which allows this to be handled natively, including VCADD, VCMLA and VCMUL. Even and odd elements of the source vectors are interpreted to be the real and imaginary components, respectively, of a complex number. Having the ability to do complex multiplication and addition in vector registers reduces the register pressure associated with higher-radix FFTs, making better performance possible.

Multiplication of two complex numbers needs two multiplies and two add/subtracts. If we have $(a + bi) \times (x + yi)$, the result will be $(ax - by) + (ay + bx)i$.

VCADD, VHCADD – Vector Complex Add with Rotate, Vector Halving Complex Add with Rotate. This instruction performs a complex addition of the first operand with the second operand rotated in the complex plane by the specified amount. A 90-degree rotation of this operand corresponds to a multiplication by a positive imaginary unit, while a 270-degree rotation corresponds to a multiplication by a negative imaginary unit. (The result is halved for VHCADD.) This instruction can only be used with data types .F16, .F32, .I8, .I16 or .I32. The value of rotate must be either 90 or 270.

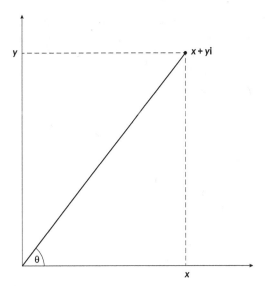

Figure 4.12: An Argand diagram

An Argand diagram is a plot of complex numbers as points in the complex plane using the x-axis as the real axis and the y-axis as the imaginary axis. Figure 4.12 is an example. If we begin with a complex number x + yi and rotate it counter-clockwise by 90 degrees, we obtain -y + xi (a 90-degree rotation is effectively a multiplication by i).

Syntax: VCADD<v><.dt> Qd, Qn, Qm, #<rotate>

Example:

Initial Conditions:
        Q3 = [10+20i, 30+40i] (the actual register value is [10, 20, 30, 40])
        Q4 = [60+70i, 80+90i] (is [60, 70, 80, 90])

Instruction: VCADD.I32   Q2, Q3, Q4, #90

Comment: The #90 means this is effectively performing a complex add where the second operand is multiplied by i.

Result:
        Q2 = [10+20i, 30+40i] + i * [60+70i, 80+90i]
           = [10+20i, 30+40i] + [60i-70, 80i-90]
           = [-60+80i, -60+120i] (is [-60, 80, -60, 120])

VCMUL – Vector Complex Multiply. The instruction performs the computation on the corresponding complex number element pairs from the two source registers and the destination register. Considering the complex number from the second source register on an Argand diagram, the number is rotated counterclockwise by 0, 90, 180, or 270 degrees. If the transformation was a rotation by 0 or 180 degrees, the two elements of the transformed complex number are multiplied by the real element of the first source register. If the transformation was a rotation by 90 or 270 degrees, the two elements are multiplied by the imaginary element of the complex number from the first source register. The only permissible datatypes are .F16 and .F32.

Syntax: VCMUL<v><.dt> Qd, Qn, Qm, #<rotate>

The following tables give an example of how the rotate options work. We can store four 32-bit floating-point values in a 128-bit register, which means we can have a pair of complex floating-point numbers. Here, we label those values as A0 and A1 in register Qn and B0 and B1 in register Qm, with the imaginary components in words 0 and 2 and the real components in words 1 and 3.

Bit position	127:96	95:64	63:32	31:0
Qn	A0 (Re)	A0 (Im)	A1 (Re)	A1 (Im)
Qm	B0 (Re)	B0 (Im)	B1 (Re)	B1 (Im)

If we execute the instruction VCMUL.F32 Qd, Qn, Qm, #Rotate, then the corresponding set of results in Qd will be as follows:

Qd	127:96	95:64	63:32	31:0
Rotation 0	A0(Re).B0(Re)	A0(Re).B0(Im)	A1(Re).B1(Re)	A1(Re).B1(Im)
Rotation 90	−A0(Im).B0(Im)	A0(Im).B0(Re)	−A1(Im).B1(Im)	A1(Im).B1(Re)
Rotation 180	−A0(Re).B0(Re)	−A0(Re).B0(Im)	−A1(Re).B1(Re)	−A1(Re).B1(Im)
Rotation 270	A0(Im).B0(Im)	−A0(Im).B0(Re)	A1(Im).B1(Im)	−A1(Im).B1(Re)

VCMLA – Vector Complex Multiply Accumulate. This performs a multiply in the same way as VCMUL. Again, only floating-point data types are allowed. The result of the multiplication is added on to the existing value in the destination-vector register. The multiplication and addition operations are fused and the result is not rounded.

Syntax: VCMLA<v><.dt> Qda, Qn, Qm, #<rotate>

Example:

Initial Conditions:
        Q0 = [0+I, 0+2i, 2+I, 10+5i]
        Q1 = [10+11i, 14+15i, 10+12i, 12+8i]

Instructions: VCMUL.F16   Q2, Q0, Q1, #0
                VCMLA.F16   Q2, Q0, Q1, #270

Comment: We can perform four half-precision floating-point multiplies. The instruction sequence performs a vector complex conjugate of Q0 multiplied by Q1. The conjugate of the first vector is multiplied by the second vector with this sequence:

Result:
        Q2 = [11-10i, 30-28i, 32+14i, 160+20i]

A further example which uses VCMUL and VCMLA is given in Section 8.5 of this book.

4.2.4 Fixed-Point Complex Multiply

The above instructions operate only on floating-point elements. If we wish to perform a fixed-point complex multiply, then the instructions VQDMLA and VQDMLS, Vector Saturating Doubling Multiply Add/Subtract, must be used. (Recall that we saw earlier that doubling is necessary when multiplying fixed-point numbers because of the sign bit and saturation to prevent overflow.) Typically, to keep the result at the same size as the inputs, we would use the Returning High Half variant (H suffix). These instructions are described earlier in this chapter. The base variant of these instructions writes its results into the lower of each pair of elements. The exchange variant (X suffix) writes to the upper element in each pair. For a complex multiply, we simply use the pairing VQDMLSH and VQDMLAHX. However, we can create conjugate variants as the table shows. The value produced in Qd in each case is shown. A hyphen shows where the value is left unchanged by the instruction. The table assumes 32-bit elements, but the same principles can be applied to using these instructions with 16- or 8-bit elements.

Bit position	127–96	95–64	63–32	31–0
Qn	A0 (Re)	A0 (Im)	A1 (Re)	A1 (Im)
Qm	B0 (Re)	B0 (Im)	B1 (Re)	B1 (Im)
VQDMLSDH	A0(Re).B0(Re) – A0(Im).B0(Im)	-	A1(Re).B1(Re) – A1(Im).B1(Im)	-
VQDMLSDHX	-	A0(Im).B0(Re) – A0(Re).B0(Im)	-	A1(Im).B1(Re) – A1(Re).B1(Im)
VQDMLADH	A0(Re).B0(Re) + A0(Im).B0(Im)	-	A1(Re).B1(Re) + A1(Im).B1(Im)	-
VQDMLADHX	-	A0(Im).B0(Re) + A0(Re).B0(Im)	-	A1(Im).B1(Re) + A1(Re).B1(Im)

4.3 Data Moves

Helium provides instructions which allow us to move values between vector and scalar registers.

VMOV – Vector Move. An instruction set obviously needs to have a method to load immediate values into registers and to transfer data between registers. In Helium, we also need to be able to move values between general-purpose scalar registers and the vector registers. The VMOV instruction does this. There are a variety of options:

- Copy the value of one vector register to another vector register (implemented as an alias of VORR `Qd, Qm, Qm`).

- Copy two 32-bit vector lanes to two general-purpose registers.

- Copy two general-purpose registers to two 32-bit vector lanes.

- Copy the value of one vector lane to a general-purpose register.

- Copy the value of a general-purpose register to a vector lane.

- Set each element of a vector register to an immediate operand value.

Syntax:

```
VMOV<c><.dt>  Qd[idx], Rt      // scalar register to vector lane
VMOV<c><.dt>  Qd, #Imm         // set each lane to immediate value
VMOV<c><.dt>  Qd, Qm           // move one vector reg to another
VMOV<c> Rt, Qd[idx]            // vector lanes to scalar register

VMOV<c> Rt, Rt2, Qd[idx], Qd[idx2]  // 2 vector lanes to 2 scalar regs
VMOV<c> Qd[idx], Qd[idx2], Rt, Rt2  // 2 scalar registers to 2 vector
lanes
```

Examples:

```
VMOV Q3[2], R4           // Set element 2 of vector register Q3 equal to
                         //  the contents of scalar register R4
VMOV Q0, #0              // Set all elements of Q0 equal to 0
```

The floating-point extension to the Armv8-M architecture provides forms of the VMOV instruction which allow one or two single-precision register(s) (S0–S31) to be copied to or from one or two general-purpose register(s) and between a double-precision register (D0–D15) and a general-purpose integer register. There are also instructions to copy values between single-precision registers and between double-precision registers. As Helium and the FPU share a set of registers, these instructions may also be used to copy parts of the Helium registers Q0–Q7, although they do not execute in a beat-wise fashion and so may not be optimal when interleaved with other Helium instructions.

```
Syntax: VMOV<c><q> Rt, Sn            // Single-precision float register to
                                     //  integer reg
        VMOV<c><q> Sn, Rt
        VMOV<c><q> Rt, Rt2, Sm, Sm1
        VMOV<c><q> Sm, Sm1, Rt, Rt2  // 2 integer regs to 2 single-precision
                                     //  float regs
        VMOV<c><q> Rt, Rt2, Dm
```

```
VMOV<c><q> Dm, Rt, Rt2
VMOV<c><q>.F32 Sd,Sm          // One single-precision register to
                                 another
VMOV<c><q>.F64 Dd,Dm
```

4.3.1 Move Variants

There are also some instructions which combine a move with another operation.

VMVN – Vector Bitwise Not. This sets each element of a vector register to the bitwise inverse of an immediate operand value, or the bitwise inverse of the value of another vector register.

Syntax: `VMVN<v><.dt>   Qd, Qm`
                `VMVN<v><.dt>   Qd, #Imm`

VMOVL – Vector Move and Long. This instruction selects an element of 8- or 16-bits from either the top half (T variant) or bottom half (B variant) of each source element, sign or zero-extends, performs a signed or unsigned left shift by an immediate value and places the 16- or 32-bit results in the destination vector.

Syntax: `VMOVL<T><v><.dt>   Qd, Qm`

Example:

Initial Conditions:
        Q0 = [700, 600, 500, 400, 300, 200, 100, 0] // 16-bit integers
        // Recall that 700 is the least significant value

Instructions: `VMOVLT.S16 Q1, Q0`
                `VMOVLB.S16 Q2, Q0`

Result:
        Q1 = [600, 400, 200, 0]   // 32-bit integers
        Q2 = [700, 500, 300, 100]

VMOVN – Vector Move and Narrow. Performs an element-wise narrowing to half-width, writing the result to either the top half (T variant) or bottom half (B variant) of the result element. The other half of the destination-vector element retains its previous value.

Syntax: `VMOVN<T><v><.dt> Qd, Qm`

Example:

Initial Conditions:
        Q1 = [600, 400, 200, 0]   // 32-bit integers
        Q2 = [700, 500, 300, 100]

Instructions: VMOVNT.I32 Q0, Q1
                    VMOVNB.I32 Q0, Q2

Result:
        Q0 = [700, 600, 500, 400, 300, 200, 100, 0] // 16-bit integers

VQMOVN – Vector Saturating Move and Narrow. Performs an element-wise saturation to half-width, writing the result to either the top half (T variant) or bottom half (B variant) of the result element. The other half of the destination vector element retains its previous value.

Syntax: VQMOVN<T><v><.dt> Qd, Qm

VQMOVUN – Vector Saturating Move Unsigned and Narrow. Performs an element-wise saturation to half-width, writing the result to either the top half (T variant) or bottom half (B variant) of the result element. The other half of the destination vector element retains its previous value. The result is saturated to an unsigned value.

Syntax: VQMOVUN<T><v><.dt> Qd, Qm

Figure 4.13 shows a VQMOVUNT.S16 instruction, narrowing from 16-bit to 8-bit elements. Each of the eight input elements from Qm is saturated to 8-bits and then written into the corresponding top (odd-numbered) lane in Qd.

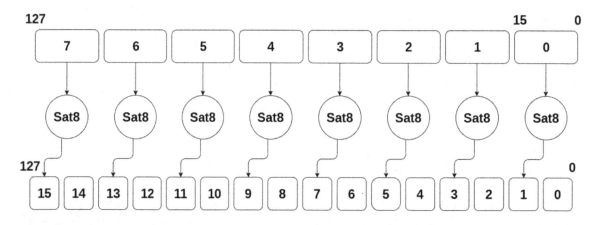

Figure 4.13: VQMOVUNT.S16 *instruction*

We have some instructions which set each element within a vector (either with values from a general-purpose register, or with a specified pattern).

VDUP – Vector Duplicate. This copies the value of a general-purpose register into each element of a vector register.

Syntax: VDUP<v><.size> Qd, Rt

Figure 4.14 shows the VDUP instruction being used to copy a value from R0 into the four 32-bit lanes in register Q0.

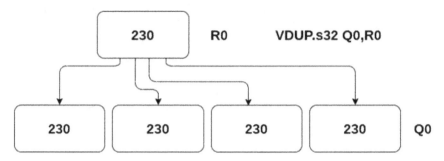

Figure 4.14: VDUP.S32 *instruction*

VDDUP, VIDUP, VDWDUP, VIWDUP – Vector Decrement/Increment and Duplicate, Vector Decrement/ Increment with Wrap and Duplicate. These instructions fill a vector with elements of successively decrementing or incrementing values, starting at an offset specified in a scalar register. This value is decremented or incremented by a specified immediate value (which can only be one of 1, 2, 4 or 8). In all variants, the updated start offset is written back to Rn. For the wrapping variant, the operation wraps so that the values written to the vector register elements are in the range [0, Rm]. If Rn and Rm are not a multiple of the immediate value, or if Rn was greater than or equal to Rm, the resulting values of Rn and Qd will be unknown.

Syntax:
```
VDDUP<v><.size>   Qd, Rn,     #<imm>
VDWDUP<v><.size>  Qd, Rn, Rm, #<imm>
VIDUP<v><.size>   Qd, Rn,     #<imm>
VIWDUP<v><.size>  Qd, Rn, Rm, #<imm>
```

Figure 4.15 shows the VIDUP instruction in operation. The initial value of 9 is taken from R0 and placed in the bottom lane of Q0. Each successive lane is filled with incrementing values (10, 11, 12) with the increment value coming from the #1 in the instruction. At the end of the instruction, R0 is updated to point to the next value (13).

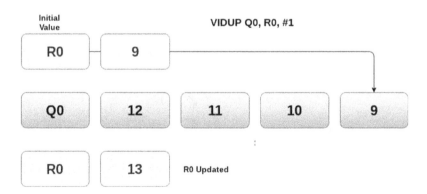

Figure 4.15: VIDUP *instruction*

A further example using the VIWDUP instruction is included in Section 5.2.1.

Finally, the Armv8.1-M floating-point extension adds the VINS instruction. While this is not a vector operation, it is a new data move instruction which can be useful for Helium code.

VINS – Floating-Point Move Insertion. This instruction copies the lower 16 bits of a single-precision floating-point source register into the upper 16 bits of a single-precision floating-point destination register, leaving the other bits unchanged.

Syntax: VINS<v>.F16 <Sd>, <Sm>

This allows us to move 16-bit values from one lane of a Helium vector to another.

4.4 Comparison and Predication

The IF-THEN (IT) instruction is very common in standard Thumb code on Cortex-M processors. It provides a way to conditionally execute instructions while avoiding the use of conditional branches (and therefore avoid paying branch penalty cycles). As we will see, the IT instruction is not suitable for vectorized code, because we would like to be able to operate on each element in a vector individually. Most Helium instructions are therefore not able to be used inside IT blocks. However, the mechanism used in Helium (the VPT or VPST instruction) works in a very similar way to the IT instruction, so we will start with a quick reminder.

When our code has some kind of conditional execution (an "if" or "switch" statement, for example), the compiler has a choice. It can either handle this with conditional branches (for example, BNE, Branch Not Equals), or it can use an IT instruction. The IT instruction allows up to four of the subsequent instructions to be conditionally executed, depending upon the state of the Application Program Status Register (APSR) bits (zero, carry etc.) and the condition specified in the IT instruction. The conditionally executed instructions may be arithmetic logic unit (ALU) or memory operations. The final instruction of the block is allowed to be a conditional branch.

The IT instruction has the IT opcode followed by up to three suffix letters, each of which may be T (THEN) or E (ELSE), and the condition code to use, so that the actual encoding of the instruction might be IT, ITT, ITE, ITET, ITEEE etc.

So, we might see something like this:

```
CMP     R0, #100
ITE     EQ       // the E specifies the 2nd following instruction is "Else"
MOVEQ R1, #1 // set R1 to 1 if it was equal
MOVNE   R1, #2 // set R1 to 2 if it was not equal
```

Note that the EQ and NE conditions attached to the MOV instruction are actually encoded in the IT instruction.

When we vectorize code, we might have multiple values to be compared rather than one. So, we need to use a vector compare instruction (for example, VCMP). Instead of simply executing or not executing an instruction, we need the ability to conditionally operate on individual lanes, so that a THEN condition can be applied to some elements and an ELSE condition to others.

The Vector Predication Status and Control Register (VPR) bits 15:0 contain a 16-bit field (VPR.P0), that is one predication bit per 8-bit lane. Each group of four bits determines the predication of each of the four bytes within the corresponding beat, regardless of instruction data type. If the value of a bit is 0, the corresponding vector lane will be masked. If it is 1, the corresponding vector lane will be active. The VPR.P0 fields are set by VCMP and VPT instructions, as we will see.

Figure 4.16 shows how this lane predication operates. The VADD instruction only operates on the true predicated lanes. The lanes in Q2 shown with a "-" retain their previous values and are not written by the instruction. In this case, we are dealing with 16-bit integer lanes, and so there are two VPR bits for each lane.

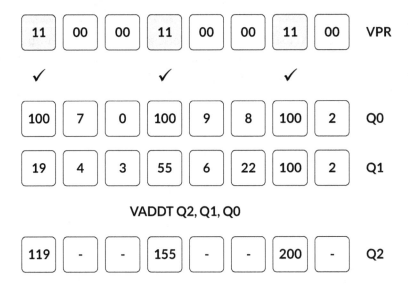

Figure 4.16: Lane-based predication

So, instead of using IT, we must use the VPT instruction. The VPT instruction allows predication based on the result of a comparison. It allows a "vector predication block" of up to four instructions following a VPT (or VPST) instruction to be defined. Each of these instructions is subject to the predication condition held in the VPR register.

Figure 4.17 shows the effect of a VPT instruction on VPR.P0. In this case, the comparison is between vector register Q0 and scalar register, with the EQ (Equals) condition. The associated VPR bits are set to 1 if the comparison is true and 0 otherwise. In the example, there are two bits per comparison because we have specified 16-bit elements. This operates in a similar way to VCMP. However, the VPT instruction also sets the VPR mask bits and uses these to allow up to four following instructions to be predicated on a then or else basis (i.e. some lanes may be updated based on the THEN condition instructions and others on the ELSE condition). The state of the bits is inverted when moving from the then to the else section of a VPT block.

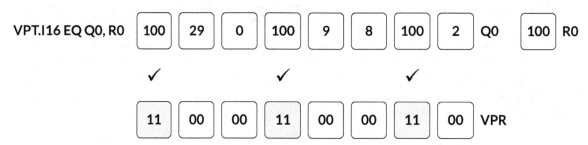

Figure 4.17: VPT instruction effect on VPR.P0

The mechanism by which this is achieved is as follows. The VPR also contains the VPR . MASKn bits, which operate in a similar way to the ITSTATE mask bits. The value of VPR.MASK01 affects bits [7:0] of VPR.P0 and the value of VPR.MASK23 affects bits [15:8] of VPR.P0. The MASK fields encode both the number of instructions outstanding in the current VPT block and whether these instructions are subject to the THEN or ELSE condition. The VPR mask bits cause the VPR predication bits to be inverted if the mask bit is set to 1. In other words, they act as a "toggle current predication condition." The VPR predication bits are not inverted after executing the last instruction in a VPT block. Figure 4.18 shows the VPR and its bit fields.

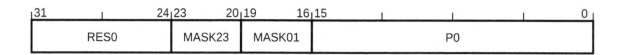

Figure 4.18: The VPR bit fields

A VCMP instruction can be placed inside a vector predication block. This can be a comparison of a vector, or of a floating-point value. VCMP instructions update the predication flag and so can affect the following instructions in the block. These instructions are therefore subject to both the initial block predicate and the update caused by the VCMP instruction. This allows complex predication conditions to be constructed, such as nested-IF statements.

As we have seen, there are some similarities between VPT and the standard Thumb IT instruction but also some important differences.

▪ IT applies the effect of a previous comparison to 1–4 following instructions. VPT performs a comparison itself and applies the result to the following instruction(s) – making it like a vector compare combined with an IF-THEN.

▪ The VPR mask fields are similar to ITSTATE[3:0]. They record the number of instructions in the current VPT block and whether the THEN or ELSE condition applies to them. The mask fields are also able to handle partial instruction execution caused by an interrupt or other exception occurring during the execution of overlapping instructions.

So far, we have looked at how the comparison and predication instructions work. Next, we will look at their operation and syntax and see some examples.

VCMP – Vector Compare. Perform a lane-wise comparison between each element in the first source-vector register and either the respective elements in the second source-vector register or the value of a general-purpose register. The resulting Boolean conditions are placed in VPR.P0. The VPR.P0 flags for predicated lanes are zeroed. The <fc> fields in the syntax are the standard Arm conditions (EQ, NE etc.).

Syntax:
```
VCMP<v><.dt> <fc>, Qn, Qm
VCMP<v><.dt> <fc>, Qn, Rm
```

VCTP – Vector Create Tail Predicate. Creates a predicate pattern in VPR.P0 such that any element numbered with the value of Rn or greater is predicated. Any element numbered lower than the value of Rn is not predicated. If placed within a VPT block and a lane is predicated, the corresponding VPR.P0 pattern will also be predicated. The generated VPR.P0 pattern can be used by an ensuing predication instruction to apply tail predication on a vector register.

Syntax:
```
VCTP<v><.dt> Rn
```

Tail predication was introduced in Section 3.4. Figure 4.19 shows an example of a VCTP instruction executing.

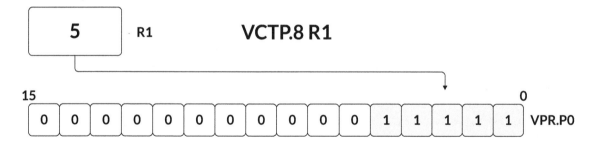

Figure 4.19: VCTP.8 instruction

Example loop tail handling code:

```
VCTP.32 R3               // R3 contains remaining count
VPSTTTT
VLDRWT.F32 Q0, [R0]      // R0 points to SrcA
VLDRWT.F32 Q1, [R1]      // R1 points to SrcB
VMULT.F32     Q2, Q0, Q1
VSTRWT.F32 Q2, [R2]      // R2 is Dst
```

The code uses the VCTP instruction to set the VPR.P0 flags so that only the correct number of remaining elements in the array will be loaded, multiplied and stored.

VPNOT – Vector Predicate NOT. Inverts the predicate condition in VPR.P0. The VPR.P0 flags for predicated lanes are zeroed.

Syntax: VPNOT<v>

Example:

Initial Conditions:
          Q0 = [0, 1, 2, 3]
          Q1 = [4, 3, 2, 1]
          Q2 = [99, 99, 99, 99]
          Q3 = [1, 2, 3, 4]

Instructions:
```
VCMP.S32     LE, Q0, Q1   // set VPR.P0 on Q0[i] <= Q1[i] (i=0..3)
VPNOT                     // invert current predicate conditions in VPR.P0
VPSEL        Q2, Q2, Q3   // selection based on inverted condition
```

Result:
          Q2 = [1, 2, 3, 99]

VPSEL – Vector Predicated Select. Compute a byte-wise conditional select of a vector register with another vector register, based on the VPR predicate bits. Note that although it is possible to specify a data type in the assembly language syntax, it is ignored and not encoded in the instruction.

Syntax: VPSEL<v>{<.dt>} Qd, Qn, Qm

VPT{x{y{z}}} – Vector Predicate Then. Predicates the following instructions, up to a maximum of four instructions, by masking the operation of instructions on a per-lane basis based on the VPR.P0 predicate values. The predicated instructions are referred to as the Vector Predication Block or simply the VPT block. The VPR.P0 predicate values may be inverted after each instruction in the VPT block based on the mask fields. The value of <x> specifies the condition for an optional second instruction in the VPT block, showing whether the condition is the same as for the first instruction (T) or its inverse (E). The values of <y> and <z> specify the conditions for optional third and fourth instructions.

Syntax: VPT{x{y{z}}} <.dt> <fc>, Qn, Qm
                 VPT{x{y{z}}} <.dt> <fc>, Qn, Rm

We can look at some example code. If we have some simple C code which iterates through an array and if it finds any values greater than "CLIP" it sets that value to CLIP:

```
        for (int i = 0; i < LEN; i++) {
            if (data[i] > CLIP) data[i] = CLIP;
        }
```

We can generate some Helium code which performs the same function:

```
        VDUP.32 Q1, R0                          // R0 = CLIP VALUE
        WLSTP.32        LR, R1, loopEnd         // R1 = LEN
loopStart:
        VLDRW.32        Q0, [R2]                // R2 = data pointer
        VPT.S32         GT, Q0, R0              // Compare each lane with R0
        VSTRWT.32       Q1, [R2], #16           // Lane predicated VSTR
        LETP            LR, loopStart
loopEnd:
```

The vector register Q1 is pre-initialized, using the VDUP instruction, so that each lane is set to R0 (the CLIP value). The WLSTP and LETP instructions set up a tail-predicated While loop. In the body of the loop, we simply load a vector of data and compare each lane of the vector with the CLIP value. The store instruction then writes only to the lanes which passed the GT condition, so that the CLIP value is only written to those lanes in memory. Note that although the T (or E) conditions for subsequent instructions are encoded in the VPT opcode, for ease of reading assembly code, they are appended to the instruction they apply to (i.e. the VSTRW becomes VSTRWT here). The vectorizing C compiler is able to generate code which uses these predication features. Note that we have predication occurring as a result of the tail predicated loop (if LENGTH is not a multiple of 4, we will only operate on 1, 2 or 3 words on the final iteration). We also have predication occurring as a result of the VPT instruction. We can also create nested conditions, such as if x then if y, using VPT. Note that the VPT instruction does not have a direct representation as an intrinsic function, as we'll see in Section 7.5.

The final VSTRWT instruction has a scalar effect, in addition to its potential vector operation. It is a post-incremented store and when the instruction completes, the value of R2 will have increased by 16. This occurs unconditionally, even if all vector elements are false predicated, and for most algorithms is the desired behavior.

However, care is sometimes needed with scalar side-effects. For example, consider the following case:

```
    VPTE.S32            GE, Q2, R0
    VMLALDAVAT.S32      %Q[SUM], %R[SUM], Q0, Q1
    VMLALDAVE.S32       %Q[SUM], %R[SUM], Q0, Q1
```

The VMLALDAV instruction multiplies the corresponding pairs of elements in Q0 and Q1 and adds the results together, storing the 64-bit result in a pair of general-purpose registers. The VMLALDAVA variant accumulates the result with the existing register contents. The intent of the code is to use the accumulating variant on the then condition and the non-accumulating variant on the else condition. However, the result will simply be that of the non-accumulating instruction, which will simply over-write the scalar general-purpose registers.

VPST{x{y{z}}} – Vector Predicate Set Then. This predicates the following instructions, up to a maximum of four instructions. It is similar to the VPT instruction. However, no comparison is performed and instead the current value of VPR.P0 is used as the predicate condition.

Syntax: VPST{X{Y{Z}}}

Example:
We start with Q0 = [30, 20, 10, 0] and execute the following instruction sequence:

```
MOVS    R0, 0XFF        // 2 first 32-bit lanes mask
VMSR    P0, R0          // set predicate, VPR=0x000000ff
MOV     R2, #5
VPSTT       // activate predication for next 2 instructions
            // VPR=0x004400ff
VNEGT.S32       Q0, Q0          // negate only active lanes
VMULT.S32       Q0, Q0, R2      // multiply only active lanes by 5
```

As only two lanes are active, and the VPSTT instruction predicates the two instructions which follow it, the effect is that the VNEG and VMUL instructions operate only on those two lanes and the other values are unchanged. The final output is:
        Q0 = [30, 20, –50, 0]

4.5 Questions

1. What instruction is used for vector addition in Helium?

2. What is the difference between the VFMA and VMLA multiply accumulate instructions?

3. Why do we need to use VPT for vector code rather than IT?

CHAPTER

Memory Access Instructions

Helium adds some new load and store instructions to those which already exist in the standard M-profile architecture and these also support the same set of indexing features, including pre- or post-incrementing and pointer writeback.

Helium provides three classes of memory access instructions, which are used for different forms of memory transfers:

▪ Vector Load/Store instructions

▪ Vector Scatter-Gather Load/Store instructions

▪ Vector Deinterleaving/Interleaving Load/Store instructions

Each of these instructions uses the same address space and memory mapping, accesses a single contiguous block of memory and is coherent with the CPU data-side memory.

5.1 Vector Load/Store

VLDR – Vector Load. Load consecutive elements from memory into a destination vector register. Each element loaded will be the zero- or sign-extended representation of the value in memory. In indexed mode, the target address is calculated from a base register offset by an immediate value. Otherwise, the base register address is used directly. The sum of the base register and the immediate value can optionally be written back to the base register. Predicated lanes are zeroed instead of retaining their previous values. The letters B, H and W are used to specify byte, half-word or word loads. This allows us to perform widening operations as part of a load.

Syntax: VLDR{B|H|W}<.dt> Qd, [Rn{, #+/-<imm>}]

Examples:

```
VLDRB.S8     Q0, [R0, #16]    //load with a pre-index offset of 16
VLDRB.S16    Q0, [R0]         //load + widen bytes into 16-bit vector
VLDR.S32     Q0, [R0, #32]!   //load, pre-index by 32+ writeback
VLDR.U32     Q0, [R0], #8     //load, post-increment R0 by 8
VLDRH.S32    Q0, [R0]         //load + widen half words into 32-bit
                                 vector
```

VSTR – Vector Store. Store consecutive elements to memory from a vector register. In indexed mode, the target address is calculated from a base register offset by an immediate value. Otherwise, the base register address is used directly. The sum of the base register and the immediate value can optionally be written back to the base register.

Syntax: VSTR{B|H|W}<.dt> Qd, [Rn{, #+/-<imm>}]

The VSTRB and VSTRH options write bytes and half-words respectively. So, for example, if we had a vector of four Q31 values, performed a right shift of 16 bits and then executed a VSTRH.S32 instruction to write the vector to memory, we would have performed a narrowing operation to convert to Q15 format. Predicated lanes are not written, and the corresponding memory address will retain its previous value.

VLDR and VSTR may also be used to read and write Helium system registers to or from memory, by specifying FPSCR, VPR or P0 as the register.

VLDM, VSTM – Vector Load Multiple/Vector Store Multiple. The VLDM and VSTM instructions, which load or store multiple registers from the FPU to or from memory, are not strictly part of Helium, as they are present in the Armv8-M floating-point extension to the ISA. However, it is useful to know about these instructions, as they are often used by functions to preserve and restore Helium registers, through their aliases VPUSH and VPOP. VPUSH {reglist} is an alias for VSTMDB SP!,{reglist} and VPOP {reglist} is an alias for VLDMIA SP!, {reglist}.

Syntax:
```
VLDMDB {<c>}{<q>}{<.size>} <Rn>!, {reglist}
VLDM {<c>}{<q>}{<.size>} <Rn>{!}, {reglist}
VLDMIA {<c>}{<q>}{<.size>} <Rn>{!}, {reglist}
VSTMDB {<c>}{<q>}{<.size>} <Rn>!, {reglist}
VSTM {<c>}{<q>}{<.size>} <Rn>{!}, {reglist}
VSTMIA {<c>}{<q>}{<.size>} <Rn>{!}, {reglist}
```

VLDMDB and VSTMDB will always update the base register (i.e. the ! is not optional).

5.2 Scatter-Gather

Sometimes, it is necessary to load a set of data into a vector register from addresses which are not contiguous (or conversely to store a vector in non-contiguous memory addresses). In some architectures, this can make it difficult or impossible for code to be vectorized. Helium provides scatter-gather operations to help with this. In this, a Helium register which holds a vector of offset values allows multiple non-contiguous addresses to be accessed with a single instruction.

VLDR – Vector Gather Load. Load byte, half-word, word, or double-word from memory. Each element loaded will be the zero- or sign-extended representation of the value in memory. The result is written back into the corresponding element in the destination vector register Qd. Predicated lanes are zeroed instead of retaining their previous values. The instruction is not permitted in an IT block but may be used within a VPT block.

Syntax:
```
VLDR{B|H|W|D}<.dt> Qd, [Rn, Qm]
```

The instruction exists in two main variants. In the first variant, the addresses used to load or store each element of Qd are given by each element of Qm plus a base address stored in Rn. They are also able to extend or truncate the data being accessed. We can either choose to use the offset contained in each element of Qm directly, or it can be scaled by the element size. Note that the VLDRD.64 instruction produces a vector with two 64-bit results and takes a 64-bit base address.

The offset size matches the size of the load.

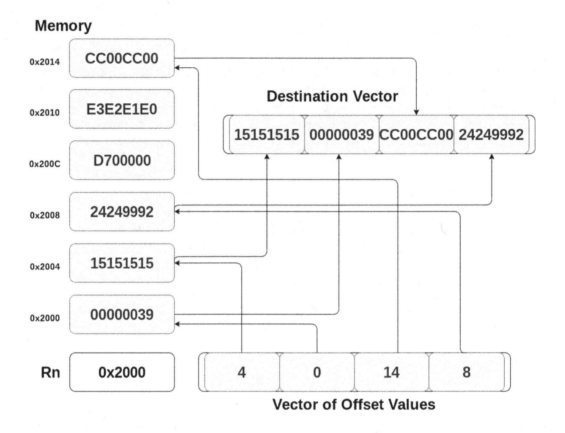

Figure 5.1: Gather-load

Figure 5.1 shows the results of a gather-load VLDRW instruction. The scalar register Rn holds the base address (0x2000 in the figure). The register Qm holds four offset values. The gather-load operation loads four words into the destination vector Qd. The four addresses used for those loads are calculated from the base address added to each of the offset values in Qm.

There is a variant of the load-gather/store-scatter instructions which can sometimes be useful in vectorizing code. Instead of using a base address stored in a general-purpose register, we perform a load from addresses given by each element of Qm plus, optionally, an immediate offset. The base element can optionally be written back, irrespective of predication, with its original value incremented by the immediate or by the immediate scaled by the memory element size.

Syntax: VLDR{B|H|W|D}<.dt> Qd, [Qm{, #+/-<imm>}]

VSTR – Vector Scatter Store. This instruction stores data from elements of Qd into a memory byte, half-word, word, or double-word at the address contained in either a base register Rn plus an offset contained in each element of Qm, optionally shifted by the element size, or each element of Qm plus an immediate offset. The base element can optionally be written back, irrespective of predication, with that value incremented by the immediate or by the immediate scaled by the memory element size (this can be useful for pointer handling).

Syntax:
```
VSTR{B|H|W|D}<.dt> Qd, [Rn, Qm]
VSTR{B|H|W|D}<.dt> Qd, [Qm{, #+/-<imm>}]
```

Scatter-gather operations are powerful, flexible instructions. In Chapter 9, we will look in detail at the implementation of FFT code. The algorithm requires that the memory accesses for the first or final phases are performed with bit-reversed addressing. On some CPUs, this would mean writing code to laboriously reverse the order of data. Helium has a dedicated bit-reversal instruction (VBRSR) which produces a bit-reversed addressing pattern which can then be used by the scatter-gather instructions. Scatter-gather can also be very useful when dealing with sparse matrices – data structures where most of the elements are zero.

It is important to note that contiguous vector accesses will be significantly faster than scatter-gather operations. A gather-load operation, for example, must perform a separate access for each distinct element. So, a gather-load of 32-bit wide data may result in four memory accesses and there could be 16 separate accesses for a load of 8-bit data.

Scatter-gather offsets are unsigned. However, variants which allow a 32-bit offset can generate negative offsets by making use of the fact that addresses wrap at the 32-bit boundary in the Armv8-M architecture. Offsets are limited to the range of the vector type. This means that for the .s8 type, the range is only 0–255, which can be limiting (for example, if dealing with a large array of byte values). One way to work around this is to use the widening/narrowing variants. For example, VLDRB.S16 will load a vector with byte values, but with a 64K (16-bit) offset range. Again, VSTRD.64 writes 64-bit values and may require 64-bit base or offset values.

5.2.1 Circular Buffer Support

A common hardware feature provided on almost all programmable DSPs is the circular buffer. In this section, we will look at what a circular buffer is, and why traditional DSPs use them. We will then look at how this would be implemented on a non-Helium Cortex-M CPU. Finally, we will explain the very flexible and efficient implementation achieved by Helium.

A circular buffer is a memory structure that holds a set of data values accessed by a read pointer. The pointer will iterate through successive values in the buffer. Unlike a normal memory buffer, when the pointer reaches the end, it automatically wraps around to the beginning of the buffer.

Circular buffers can be used for things like finite impulse response (FIR) filters (where we need to operate on the most recent N data values), but they can also be used in inter-process communication where reads and writes may be interleaved.

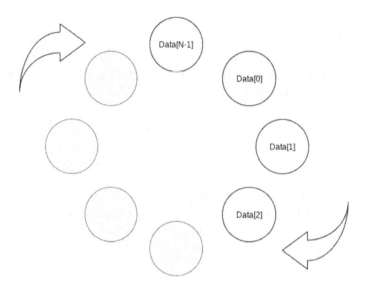

Figure 5.2: Circular buffer

Figure 5.2 shows the basic concept of a circular buffer. It holds N data items, shown here as Data[0], Data[1] ... Data[N−1]. When a new data item is added, it becomes Data[0], the old Data[0] becomes Data[1] and so forth, with the oldest item, Data[N−1], being discarded.

Programmable DSPs typically provide a method of accessing memory called circular addressing, which allows these circular buffers to be supported. Data within the buffer can be accessed in sequence up to its configured size, after which accesses wrap around to the first element, as shown in Figure 5.3.

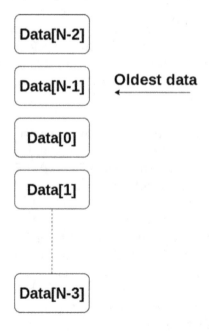

Figure 5.3: Circular addressing

Circular buffers must usually be initialized by the programmer with parameters specifying the desired characteristics. There may be special registers which hold the start location of the buffer in memory, the length (or position of the end location) and the size of items stored in the memory (one, two or four bytes, for example). In some cases, there may be complex hardware which looks at the value of a pointer every time it is incremented and wraps it back to the start if it goes past the end address. This may mean that the number of such buffers is limited (and if it is necessary to preserve the state of such registers during interrupts, there can be a significant effect on interrupt latency). For this reason, some DSPs impose some limitations on circular buffers. For example, the start address may have certain alignment requirements, the length may need to be a power-of-2 value – 8, 16, 32, 64 etc. This allows much simpler hardware, which can implement the circular buffer simply by masking the appropriate bit(s) within the pointer with a bitmask. However, this can make such buffers difficult to access through high-level code.

Nearly all DSP algorithms will be implemented with a loop. For example, in a filter we may have a set of coefficients stored in memory and the loop may iterate through them, using a pointer to the coefficient value currently being operated on. At the end of the loop, the coefficient pointer will need to be updated to point back to the beginning. If a circular buffer is used this step becomes unnecessary, thus saving time.

A common example where circular buffers are useful is when an algorithm is required to operate on only the last N input values. This is a common occurrence in DSP applications. For example, a FIR filter might need access to the N most recent input values in order to calculate an output. It multiplies each one of those values by the corresponding filter coefficient. Each time a new data value arrives, we need to discard the oldest value and shift the $N-1$ older values up one place in the buffer. With a circular buffer, we simply replace the oldest value in the buffer with the newest and move the pointer one address ahead. Instead of the effort to copy each sample to the correct location we simply perform a write to replace the oldest input value with the new data.

Although it is possible to implement a circular buffer on non-Helium Cortex-M processors, memory was treated as a flat linear address space. Instead of a circular buffer, DSP code would typically use a FIFO and shift the data in the FIFO once per block of data. This is more efficient than moving the data each time round an inner loop, but less efficient than a hardware-implemented circular buffer.

Helium provides a solution which allows circular buffers to be used with fully flexible buffer size and placement, and without the need for complicated additional hardware.

It does this with a circular buffer generating instruction, VIWDUP. This creates a vector containing a sequence of incrementing offsets that wrap when an end position is reached.

An example instruction looks like this:

```
VIWDUP.U32 Q0, R0, R1, #2
```

This instruction will load the vector register Q0 with a sequence of U32 (32-bit integer) values, starting at the address given by R0 and wrapping when the value of R1 is reached. At completion, it will update R0 with the new start offset. The immediate value specifies by how much the offsets increment. The #2 in our example means that the offset value will increase by two, each time. The increment (or decrement) value can be 1, 2, 4 or 8. This means Helium can support circular buffers without limits on number, size, or direction.

Figure 5.4 shows the above instruction executing with R1 set to 16 (i.e. wrapping at offset 16) and R0 set to 12. The first value (in the bottom word of Q0) is the value 12, from R0. The instruction specifies an increment of 2, so the next value is 14. The next increment would take us to 16, which is the value in R1 (the point at which we wrap) and so the third value is 0 and the final value in Q0 is 2. R0 is then updated to point to the next starting point, which is 4 in this case.

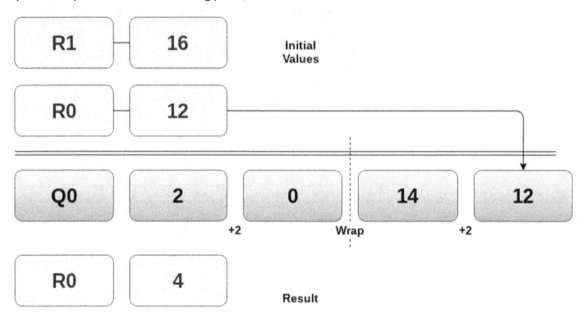

Figure 5.4: Example operation of the sequence-generating instruction VIWDUP

Normally, this instruction which generates an offset vector will be immediately followed by a scatter-gather operation which loads the data. (Recall that the gather-load operation in Helium allows us to load the individual elements in a vector register from a set of non-contiguous memory addresses, whose offsets from a base address are given in another vector register.) This means that the register (Q0 in our example) is available for reuse by other instructions. Note that the ANSI C language does not implicitly support circular buffers or addressing, as there is no construct to describe them. This means that most C compilers can't generate code to use them even if the necessary hardware exists. It will typically be necessary to use intrinsics or library functions to make use of this functionality.

Also, as the VIWDUP instruction knows where the memory access will be wrapped, a hardware implementation may be able to use this information as a performance-boosting "hint" that the data access may be performed as one or two contiguous accesses rather than using scatter-gather. Of course, if an interrupt occurs between the VIWDUP and the following load, the hint is forgotten, but the load will still execute correctly.

5.3 Interleaving and Deinterleaving Loads and Stores

There is also a set of dedicated vector (de)interleaving load/store instructions. Data streams can be interleaved and deinterleaved with strides of two and four, using the instructions VLD2 or VLD4 and VST2 or VST4.

VLD2x, VLD4x – Vector (De)interleaving Load – Stride 2/4. These two sets of instructions load two 64-bit contiguous blocks of data from memory and write them to parts of two or four destination registers. The parts of the destination registers written to, and the offsets from the base address register, are determined by the pat parameter (i.e. VLD20, VLD21, VLD40, VDL41, VLD42, VLD43). If the instruction is executed two (or four) times with the same base address and destination registers, but with different pat values, the effect is to load data from memory and to deinterleave it into the specified registers with a stride of two or four. The base address register can optionally be incremented by 32/64 at the end of the instruction. For example, stereo audio data may consist of interleaved left and right channel data, and the VLD2 and VST2 instructions can be used to interleave and deinterleave this data.

Syntax:
```
VLD2<pat><.size> {Qd, Qd+1}, [Rn]
VLD2<pat><.size> {Qd, Qd+1}, [Rn]!   // with writeback of Rn
VLD4<pat><.size> {Qd, Qd+1, Qd+2, Qd+3}, [Rn]
VLD4<pat><.size> {Qd, Qd+1, Qd+2, Qd+3}, [Rn]!
```

Example:
```
VLD20.32 Q0, Q1, [R5]
VLD21.32 Q0, Q1, [R5]    // Normally executed as VLD20,
                            VLD21 pair
```

VST2x, VST4x–Vector (De)interleaving Store – Stride 2/4. This writes two 64-bit contiguous blocks of data to memory collected from multiple elements from two or four source registers. The parts of the source registers written to, and the offsets from the base address register, are determined by the pat parameter (VST20, VST21, VST40 etc.). If the instruction is executed two (or four) times with the same base address and source registers, but with different pat values, the effect is to interleave the specified registers with a stride of two/four and to save the data to memory. The base address register can optionally be incremented by 32/64.

Syntax:
```
VST2<pat><.size> {Qd, Qd+1}, [Rn]
VST2<pat><.size> {Qd, Qd+1}, [Rn]!   // with writeback of Rn
VST4<pat><.size> {Qd, Qd+1, Qd+2, Qd+3}, [Rn]
VST4<pat><.size> {Qd, Qd+1, Qd+2, Qd+3}, [Rn]!
```

It is worth spending some time understanding the purpose of these instructions and how they work. DSP algorithms are often required to take input data in one format and transform it into another before it can be processed efficiently. Very often, a similar process will need to be followed on the output, too. For example, image data may be stored as red, green, blue (and sometimes alpha) pixel values interleaved in memory. The algorithm may need to have each of the red pixels in one vector, each of the green pixels in another vector and so forth. When we have finished processing this data, we may need to write it back in the same format as it was originally, as shown in Figure 5.5. In the figure, register Q3 holds a set of alpha values for pixels and Q2–Q0 hold RGB data. Using the VST4 instructions, we can write the data out to memory (shown at the bottom of the figure) in an interleaved fashion.

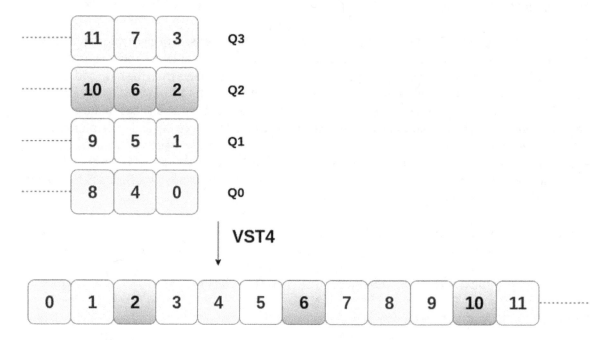

Figure 5.5: Interleaving of pixel data using VST4

The VST4 set of instructions allow us to interleave four 128-bit registers, storing a total of 512-bits of data. However, remember that one of the key features of the Helium architecture is that we have beat-wise execution of instructions that allows memory and ALU/multiplier instructions to be overlapped by the CPU. This imposes the constraint that each instruction must operate on 128-bits of data. Therefore, this four-way interleaving is done with four separate instructions called VST40, VST41, VST42 and VST43.

An obvious way to implement this would be, for example, for one instruction to read (or write) each of the red values, another to handle the green values and so on. However, pixel data is typically byte-sized, and this would produce an inefficient set of non-contiguous memory accesses, making these instructions relatively slow. Instead, the instructions make use of existing hardware in the CPU which can read bytes from both rows and columns within the register bank and swap and reverse the order of these. In other words, the hardware which connects to the CPU memory port is not only able to read the full set of bytes within a register; it can also read 8-, 16- and 32-bit wide values from the same positions in different registers. This allows the architecture to provide interleaving and deinterleaving loads and stores that produce efficient memory accesses, which are always a pair of contiguous 64-bit accesses. The register locations used for these accesses follow a "twisting" pattern.

Figure 5.6 shows the execution of a pair of VST2n.S32 instructions, with 32-bit values (S32) being read from vector registers Q0 and Q1 and being interleaved by two (for example, for left and right audio channels).

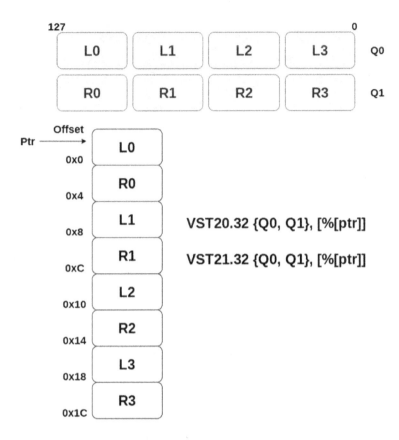

Figure 5.6: Pair of VST2 instructions interleaving data to memory

Figure 5.7 shows the operation of VST instructions in a different fashion. Here, we have a set of VST4x.S32 instructions. The four instructions will write four 128-bit values to memory, representing 64 bytes in total. The figure shows how the .S32 elements in the registers Q0–Q3 are written to various memory offset addresses. So, the top four bytes of Q3 are written to the offset addresses [63:60], the next four bytes of Q3 are written to addresses [47:44] and so on. The gray tones represent the different instructions. So, for example, VST41 will read the bottom word from each of Q3 and Q2 and write them to memory offsets [15:12] and [11:8] and the top word from each of Q1 and Q0 and write them to memory offsets [55:52] and [51:48], respectively.

A consequence of this is that there are no circumstances in which it makes sense to use just one of the interleave instructions. For example, we would always use VLD20 and VLD21 together, rather than just one of them. It might be thought that one extracts even elements and the other odd elements, but this is not the case.

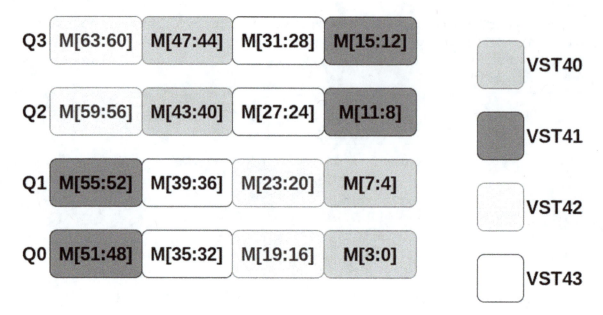

Figure 5.7: VST4x *instruction operation*

5.4 Questions

1. Does the instruction VSTRB.32 narrow or widen the data?

2. If R0 contains 0x1000 at the start of the instruction VLDR.S32 Q0, [R0, #0x40]!, what value will it contain after execution completes?

3. How does a scatter-gather load differ from a standard VLDR instruction?

CHAPTER

Helium Branch, Scalar
and Other Instructions

6

In this chapter, we look at non-vector instructions. This includes the low overhead branch extension and some new scalar instructions and other changes to the instruction set.

6.1 Low Overhead Branch Extension

In Section 3.3, we looked in detail at the low overhead branch extension. Here, we will summarize the various instructions and look at their syntax.

`WLS, DLS, WLSTP, DLSTP` – While Loop Start, Do Loop Start, While Loop Start with Tail Predication, Do Loop Start with Tail Predication. These instructions partially set up a loop. There are two base instructions (`WLS` and `DLS`) which set LR to the number of loop iterations to be performed. For a Do loop (`DLS/DLSTP`), there will always be at least one iteration. When using `WLS` or `WLSTP`, if the number of iterations required is zero, then these instructions will cause a branch to the specified label and the loop body will not be executed. Each loop start instruction is normally used with a matching `LE` or `LETP` instruction.

The TP variants of this instruction set LR to the number of vector elements that must be processed. If the number of elements required is not a multiple of the vector length, then the appropriate number of vector elements will automatically be predicated on the last iteration of the loop.

Syntax:
```
WLS LR, Rn, <label>
WLSTP<.size> LR, Rn, <label>
DLS LR, Rn, <label>
DLSTP<.size> LR, Rn
```

`LE, LETP` – Loop End, Loop End with Tail Predication. This instruction causes a branch back to `<label>` if further iterations of a loop are required. It also stores the loop information in the loop info cache so that future iterations of the loop will branch back to the start just before the `LE` instruction is encountered. One variant of the `LE` instruction checks a loop iteration counter (stored in LR) to check whether additional iterations are required. It also decrements the counter ready for the next iteration. Another variant does not use an iteration count and always triggers another iteration of the loop.

The `LETP` instruction checks the loop iteration counter to determine if additional iterations are required. However, the counter is decremented by the number of elements in a vector. In other words, LR holds the number of elements to operate upon, not the number of loop iterations. The number of elements in a vector is taken from the FPSCR.LTPSIZE field.

Syntax:
```
LE   LR, <label>
LE   <label> // don't check or decrement loop counter
LETP LR, <label>
```

`LCTP` – Loop Clear with Tail Predication. This exits loop mode and clears any tail predication being applied.

Syntax: LCTP<c>

Here, we show an example of a tail-predicated Do loop with the DLSTP instruction used to set up the loop and LETP showing the end of the loop. For some reason, the program needs to break out of the loop early if the sum becomes equal to 126, and the CMP and BEQ instructions are used to do that. It is still necessary to use the LCTP instruction to ensure that tail predication isn't applied to following operations. If this was not done, tail predication might mean that not all lanes were updated by following vector instructions.

```
        MOV        R1, #10
        DLSTP.8    LR, R1        // Loop + Tail predication start
1:
        VLDR       Q0, [R3], #64
        VADDVA.S8  R0, Q0        // r0 = r0 + q0[0...7]
        CMP        R0, #126
        ITT        EQ
        MOVEQ      LR, #0        // clear loop elements counter
        BEQ        #2f           // jump out of the loop
        LETP       LR, #1b       // Loop + Tail predication end
2:
        LCTP
```

6.1.1 Branch Future Instruction

This section of the book describes a class of instructions which form part of the Armv8.1-M architecture, but which may be treated as NOPs (No Operation) by a CPU implementation. Arm Compiler 6 does not generate these instructions and Cortex-M55 implements them as a NOP, taking one cycle to do so. Therefore, this description is included only for the sake of completeness.

Many programmable DSPs (and some older RISC CPUs) have a "branch delay" slot. Essentially, this means that the instructions which are fetched after a branch do not get flushed; they are instead executed. This can be useful to save some cycles which would otherwise be wasted in the form of a branch penalty.

Armv8.1-M provides instructions which allow the compiler to specify the number of branch delay slots it can usefully use for a specific branch. In effect this provides a variable length branch delay slot, which does not depend on the micro-architecture or pipeline length. This gives the benefits of the branch delay slots found on a DSP without any of the complications and without extra hardware being required.

BF, BFX, BFL, BFLX – Branch Future, Branch Future and Exchange, Branch Future with Link, Branch Future with Link and Exchange. This hints to the processor about an upcoming branch to <label> so that the branch will be taken instead of fetching and executing the instruction at <b_label>, reducing any performance penalty associated with execution of a branch. The processor is allowed to treat this instruction as a NOP and so the fallback code at <b_label> must still be present. For the BFL variant, the link register is updated when the branch is performed. The value written is offset from the branch point by four bytes, corresponding to the address of the instruction after the `BL` immediate instruction in the fallback code, which is four bytes long. For the `BFLX` instruction, the value written into the LR is offset by two bytes, the length of the `BLX` instruction of the fallback code.

Syntax:
```
BF<c> <b_label>, <label>        //pc-relative branch
BFX<c> <b_label>, Rn            //branch address in a register
BFL<c> <b_label>, <label>
BFLX<c> <b_label>, Rn
```

Example:

```
BFL <1>, Function1
[code which does something]
[...]
1:      BL Function1
```

`BFCSEL` – Branch Future Conditional Select. The instruction creates a future branch to `<label>` if the condition code passes. If the condition code fails this variant does not behave as a NOP. Instead it creates a future branch to the instruction specified by `<ba_label>` if there is no other active Branch Future entry in the loop and branch cache.

Syntax:
```
BFCSEL <b_label>, <label>, <ba_label>, <cond>
```

Example:

```
start:
        [code which does something]
        [...]
CMP     R2, R1
        BFCSEL switch, start, end, EQ
        [more code]
switch:
        BEQ   start
end:
```

In the example, the `BFCSEL` instruction says that there is a conditional branch at the label `<switch>`. If the condition `EQ` is true it sets up a future branch to `<start>`, otherwise it sets up a future branch to `<end>`. Note that at the location `<switch>` we still have a `BEQ` instruction.

6.2 Armv8.1-M Scalar Instructions

The Armv8.1-M architecture introduces a set of new scalar instructions. These are not part of the Helium vector extension, but are described briefly here as they may be useful in DSP and machine learning algorithms. They mainly comprise a set of conditional execution instructions and a set of new 64-bit shift operations, but there are a small number of other instructions. In addition, some instructions now permit the use of a zero register (ZR) as a scalar source operand.

6.2.1 Conditional Execution

Armv8.1-M introduces a set of conditional execution instructions. Like most of the vector instructions, none of these instructions can be used within an IT block.

CSEL – Conditional Select. This returns, in the destination register, the value of the first source register if the condition is TRUE, and otherwise returns the value of the second source register.

Syntax:
```
CSEL Rd, Rn, Rm, <condition code>
```

Example:
```
CMP R0, #8
CSEL R0, R1, R2, LT
```

This will make R0 = R1 if the result of the previous comparison (R0 with 8) was "less than", else it will make R0 = R2. This would be equivalent to the C ternary if operator. R0 = (R0 < 8) ? R1 : R2 .

CSINC – Conditional Select Increment. Returns, in the destination register, the value of the first source register if the condition is TRUE, and otherwise returns the value of the second source register incremented by 1.

Syntax:
```
CSINC Rd, Rn, Rm, <condition code>
```

Example:
```
MOV        R0, #100
MOV        R1, #10
MOV        R2, #50
CMP        R0, #100
CSINC      R3, R2, R1, NE // R3 = (COND == NE)? R2 : R1+1
                          // So R3 = 11
CSINC      R4, R2, R1, EQ // R4 =(COND == EQ)? R2 : R1+1
                          // So R4 = 50
```

A further two new assembly language instructions are aliases of CSINC.

CSET – Conditional Set. Sets the destination register to 1 if the condition is TRUE, and otherwise sets it to 0. This is an alias of CSINC, equivalent to CSINC Rd, Zr, Zr, (inverted condition code).

Syntax:
```
CSET Rd, <condition code>
```

Example:
```
CMP R0, #100
CSET R0, GT
```

This would set R0 to 1 if it was greater than or equal to 100, otherwise it would make R0 = 0. In C, this could be written as `R0 = (R0 > 100)`.

`CINC` – Conditional Increment. Returns, in the destination register, the value of the source register incremented by 1 if the condition is TRUE. Otherwise returns the value of the source register. So, `CINC Rd, Rn, cond` is an alias of `CSINC Rd, Rn, Rn, inverted (condition code)`.

Syntax: `CINC Rd, Rn, <condition code>`

Example:

```
MOV    R0, #0x55
CMP    R0, R1
CINC   R2, R0, NE // R2 = R0 + 1 if true, R2=0x56
CINC   R3, R0, EQ // R3 = R0 if false, R3=0x55
```

`CSINV` – Conditional Select Invert. Returns, in the destination register, the value of the first source register if the condition is TRUE, otherwise returns the value of the second source register, bitwise inverted.

Syntax: `CSINV Rd, Rn, Rm, <condition code>`

Example:

```
MOV         R0, #100
MOV         R1, #10
MOV         R2, #50
CMP         R0, #100
CSINV       R3, R2, R1, NE // R3 = (COND == NE) ? R2 : ~R1
                           // So R3 = 0xFFFFFFEF
CSINV       R4, R2, R1, EQ // R4 =(COND == EQ) ? R2 : ~R1
                           // So R4 = 50
```

Two new assembly language instructions are aliases of `CSINV`.

`CSETM` – Conditional Set Mask. Sets all bits of the destination register to 1 if the condition is TRUE. Otherwise sets all bits to 0. This is an alias of `CSINV`, equivalent to `CSINV Rd, Zr, Zr, (inverted condition code)`.

Syntax: `CSETM Rd, <condition code>`

Example:

```
MOV         R0, #0xAA
MOV         R1, #0x55
CMP         R0, R1
CSETM       R2, NE // R2 = 0XFFFFFFFF because true
CSETM       R3, EQ // R3 = 0 because EQ is false
```

CINV – Conditional Invert. Returns, in the destination register, the bitwise inversion of the value of the source register if the condition is TRUE, otherwise returns the value of the source register. So `CINV Rd, Rn, cond` is an alias of `CSINV Rd, Rn, Rn, inverted (condition code)`.

Syntax: `CINV Rd, Rn, <condition code>`

Example:
```
MOV   R0, #0x100
MOV   R1, #0xAA
CMP   R0, R1
CINV  R2, R0, NE // R2 = ~R0 if true, so R2=0xFFFFFEFF
CINV  R3, R0, EQ // R3 = R0 if false, so R3=0x100
```

CSNEG – Conditional Select Negation. Returns, in the destination register, the value of the first source register if the condition is TRUE, otherwise returns the value of the second source register negated.

Syntax: `CSNEG Rd, Rn, Rm, <condition code>`

The instruction `CNEG` is an alias of `CSNEG`.

CNEG – Conditional Negate. Returns, in the destination register, the negated value of the source register if the condition is TRUE, otherwise returns the value of the source register. This is an alias of `CSNEG` with Rn equal to Rm.

Syntax: `CNEG Rd, Rn, <condition code>`

Example:
```
MOV   R0, #100
MOV   R1, #99
CMP   R0, R1
CNEG  R2, R0, NE // R2 = -R0 if true, so R2=-100
CNEG  R3, R0, EQ // R3 = R0 if true, so R3=100
```

6.2.2 General-Purpose Register Shifts

ASRL – Arithmetic Shift Right Long. Arithmetic shift right by 1 to 32 bits of a 64-bit value stored in two general-purpose registers. The amount to be shifted may be specified as an immediate value, or in the bottom byte of a general-purpose register. In the register variant, if the shift amount is negative, the shift will be to the left.

Syntax: `ASRL<cond> RdaLo, RdaHi, #Imm`
               `ASRL<cond> RdaLo, RdaHi, Rm`

Example:
```
MOVW R0, #0
MOVT R0, #0x5000   // R0 = 0x50000000
```

```
MOV R1, R0          // R1 = 0x50000000
MOV R2, #-1 // Negative Shift amount
ASRL R0, R1, R2    //R0, R1 = 0xA0000000, 0xA0000000
```

LSRL – Logical Shift Right Long. Logical shift right by 1 to 32 bits of a 64-bit value stored in two general-purpose registers, with zeros being shifted in at the top. The amount to shift is specified as an immediate value in the instruction.

Syntax: LSRL<cond> RdaLo, RdaHi, #Imm

Example:

```
MOVW  R0, #0x4000
MOVT  R0, #0x4000 // R0 = 0x40004000
MOV   R1, R0
LSRL  R0, R1, #1  // R0:R1 = R0:R1 >> 1
                  // R0:R1 = 0x20002000:0x20002000
```

LSLL – Logical Shift Left Long. Logical shift left by 1 to 32 bits of a 64-bit value stored in two general-purpose registers. The amount to be shift may be specified as an immediate value, or in the bottom byte of a general-purpose register. If the shift amount is negative the shift direction is reversed.

Syntax: LSLL<cond> RdaLo, RdaHi, #Imm
               LSLL<cond> RdaLo, RdaHi, Rm

Example:

```
MOVW  R0, #0x4000
MOVT  R0, #0x4000 // R0 = 0x40004000
MOV   R1, R0
MOV   R3, #-3     // left shift value = -3 (right)
LSLL  R0, R1, R4  // R0:R1 = R0:R1 >> 3
                  // R0:R1 = 0x08000800:0x08000800
```

As a logical shift left and arithmetic shift left are the same we do not need an arithmetic shift left instruction. Furthermore, as the ASRL instruction, which has a shift amount specified in a register, can shift in either direction depending upon the sign of the shift amount, we only need an LSRL instruction with a shift specified by an immediate value.

Additionally, we have a set of signed and unsigned saturating and/or rounding shift instructions, with variants which operate on a single 32-bit register and others which operate on a register pair (like the above). In each case, we show both the signed (begins with S) and unsigned (begins with U) instruction pairs together. Some instructions allow the shift amount to be specified with an immediate value encoded in the instruction, others allow the shift amount to be specified in the lower byte of a general-purpose register. The right shift instructions are shown first, then the left shifts.

SRSHR, URSHR – Signed/Unsigned Rounding Shift Right. Signed/Unsigned rounding shift right by 1 to 32 bits of a 32-bit value stored in a general-purpose register.

Syntax:
```
SRSHR Rda, #Imm
URSHR Rda, #Imm
```

Example:
```
MOVW     R2, #0X8888
MOVT     R2, #0X0088        // R2 = 0X00888888
URSHR    R2, #4             // R2 = 0X00088889
```

In the example, a shift right of four places is performed. As this is a rounding shift, in effect, a value of 1 << 3 (a 1 left-shifted three places) is added before performing the shift and the result is rounded up to the next value.

SRSHRL, URSHRL – Signed/Unsigned Rounding Shift Right Long. Signed/unsigned rounding shift right by 1 to 32 bits of a 64-bit value stored in two general-purpose registers.

Syntax:
```
SRSHRL RdaLo, RdaHi, #Imm
URSHRL RdaLo, RdaHi, #Imm
```

SQRSHR – Signed Saturating Rounding Shift Right. Signed saturating rounding shift right by 0 to 32 bits of a 32-bit value stored in a general-purpose register. The shift amount is read in as the bottom byte of Rm. If the shift amount is negative, the shift direction is reversed. This means that there is no corresponding SQRSHL instruction.

Syntax:
```
SQRSHR Rda, Rm
```

SQRSHRL – Signed Saturating Rounding Shift Right Long. Signed saturating rounding shift right by 0 to 64 bits of a 64-bit value stored in two general-purpose registers. The shift amount is read in as the bottom byte of Rm. If the shift amount is negative, the shift direction is reversed. This means that there is no corresponding SQRSHLL instruction.

Syntax:
```
SQRSHRL RdaLo, RdaHi, Rm
```

SQSHL, UQSHL – Signed/Unsigned Saturating Shift Left. Signed/unsigned saturating shift left by 1 to 32 bits of a 32-bit value stored in a general-purpose register

Syntax:
```
SQSHL Rda, #Imm
UQSHL Rda, #Imm
```

Example:
```
            MOVW         R2, #0X4567
            MOVT         R2, #0X0123          // R2 = 0x01234567
            SQSHL        R2, #2               // R2 = SSAT32(R2 << 2)
                                              // R2 = 0x48D159C


            MOVW         R2, #0X3210
            MOVT         R2, #0X7654          // R2 = 0x76543210
            SQSHL        R2, #2               // R2 = SSAT32(R2 << 2)
                                              // R2 = 0x7FFFFFFF
                                              // (Saturated)
```

SQSHLL, UQSHLL – Signed/Unsigned Saturating Shift Left Long. Signed/unsigned saturating shift left by 1 to 32 bits of a 64-bit value stored in two general-purpose registers.

Syntax:
```
            SQSHLL RdaLo, RdaHi, #Imm
            UQSHLL RdaLo, RdaHi, #Imm
```

UQRSHL – Unsigned Saturating Rounding Shift Left. Unsigned saturating rounding shift left by 0 to 32 bits of a 32-bit value stored in a general-purpose register. The shift amount is read in as the bottom byte of Rm. If the shift amount is negative, the shift direction is reversed. This means that there is no corresponding UQRSHR instruction.

Syntax:
```
            UQRSHL Rda, Rm
```

UQRSHLL – Unsigned Saturating Rounding Shift Left Long. Signed saturating rounding shift left by 0 to 64 bits of a 64-bit value stored in two general-purpose registers. The shift amount is read in as the bottom byte of Rm. If the shift amount is negative, the shift direction is reversed. This means that there is no corresponding UQRSHRL instruction.

Syntax:
```
            UQRSHLL RdaLo, RdaHi, Rm
```

6.3 Miscellaneous Instructions

Armv8.1-M makes a few other additions and changes to the instruction set.

CLRM – Clear Multiple Registers. This new instruction allows us to set to zero the value of registers given by a list. The valid registers are the APSR, LR/R14, and R0–R12.

Syntax:
```
            CLRM<c> <Register List>
```

Example:
```
            CLRM {R0, R1, R3}
```

This will write the value 0 into registers R0, R1 and R3.

VSSCLRM – Floating-point Secure Context Clear Multiple. This writes zero values to the VPR and the specified floating-point/Helium registers and can only be executed in Secure state. The VPR is always cleared, and the floating-point registers may be specified either as 32-bit S registers, or as 64-bit D registers. In both cases, the register numbers must be continuous. (The opcode encoding simply says how many registers should be cleared and the number of the lowest register.)

Syntax: VSSCLRM<c> <Register List>

Example:
VSSCLRM {d0-d7}

VMRS, VMSR – A further change is to the operation of the VMRS (Move to general-purpose Register from floating-point Special register) and VMSR (Move to floating-point Special register from general-purpose Register) instructions. Previously, these instructions were only able to access the FPSCR. These instructions are now able to access (in Secure state only) all of the floating-point special registers, allowing saving and restoration of the Non-secure floating-point context, FPSCR and VPR registers.

Syntax: VMRS<c> <q> <Rt>, <special register>

Example:
VMRS R0, VPR   // Read the Helium Predicate Register into R0.

6.4 Questions

1. What is the difference between a WLS and a DLS instruction?

2. Why might we use the LCTP instruction?

3. Does the LSLL instruction use Helium registers?

CHAPTER 7

Helium Programming

In this chapter, we discuss practical considerations around writing code for processors which include Helium. We will look at various coding options, including vectorizing compilers, use of intrinsic functions, libraries and assembly language, and cover best practice for each of these. We will also look at low-level topics such as boot code initialization of Helium and interrupt handling.

7.1 Compilers and Tools

Arm provides a range of software development tools, including:

- **Keil MDK** (Microcontroller Development Kit) – This is the most popular toolchain for Cortex-M projects. It includes the μVision IDE.

- **Arm Development Studio** – A complete development environment for any Arm IP including Cortex-A, Cortex-R and Cortex-M processors.

- **Arm Fast Models** – These provide a modeling environment and processor models which can be used to create custom virtual platforms for early software development. This is typically used by hardware developers to create system models to be used prior to the availability of real hardware.

- **Arm Fixed Virtual Platform** (FVP) – This is a virtual development board built with Arm Fast Models for software development without a physical board.

At the time of writing, there are no off-the-shelf microcontroller implementations containing CPUs with Helium technology. This makes it difficult to give precise instructions to the reader on running the example code in later chapters. Code in this book has been tested on the Arm Fast Model of the Cortex-M55 CPU (which can be obtained from the Arm website), or on the Arm MPS3 FPGA based prototyping system, which allows chip designers to prototype their design before tape-out. A Cortex-M55 cycle model which implements Helium may be obtained from: https://ipx.arm.com/models?type=Cortex-M55.

In order to follow the examples in this book and experiment with Helium, it is suggested that readers should obtain Arm tools and install the CMSIS library on their chosen target.

The Keil MDK can be obtained from http://www2.keil.com/mdk5/.

Version 5.30 or later is required in order to have Helium support. The "Getting Started" user guide describes how to install and use the product. The installer also adds the CMSIS library, which we will look at later in this chapter. The CMSIS library contains numerous examples and detailed instructions on running these. This library is described later in the chapter. We will refer to the DSP and machine learning sections of the library frequently in later chapters. Instead of the Keil tools, you could also download Arm Development Studio, from https://developer.arm.com/.

A Fast Models evaluation package can also be downloaded from the Arm developer website. Versions are available for both Windows and Linux. Version 11.10 or later is required for a model of Cortex-M55.

This includes a FVP, for development where no board is available. The ARM_AEMv8M FVP can be configured to enable Helium (with floating-point), by setting the following parameter values:

▦ `cpu0.enable_helium_extension=1`

▦ `cpu0.vfp-present=1`

▦ `cpu0.vfp-enable_at_reset=1`

Other models may have differently named parameters to control the Helium implementation. There is an example Hello World program for the Armv8.1-M Fast Model, which can be used to demonstrate that you have Helium code running on your model. It can be found at:

https://github.com/ARM-Software/Tool-Solutions/tree/master/fast-models-examples/armv8.1-m

7.1.1 Arm Compiler 6

Arm® Compiler 6 is the most advanced C and C++ compilation toolchain from Arm and is developed alongside the Arm architecture. It can generate efficient code for the full range of Arm processors and target applications. Arm Compiler 6 is a component of Arm® Development Studio, Arm® DS-5 Development Studio, and Arm® Keil® MDK, but is also available as a stand-alone product. It combines tools and libraries from Arm with an LLVM-based compiler framework.

The Arm Compiler 6 toolchain includes comprehensive support for Helium. It supports automatic vectorization of code for Helium, which allows standard C code to take advantage of Helium and means that minimal work is required to produce optimized code. Over time, it is expected that the compiler will see performance and code size improvements, as information from real-world use-cases can be used to generate improvements in code generation.

The compiler also provides support for intrinsics, in which each Helium operation looks like a function call. There are special data types for the Helium vectors of different sizes and types. The intrinsics are common across both Arm Compiler 6 and GCC. Coding in this style requires you to map your code to Helium operations and can be a time-consuming process, requiring good knowledge of the code and architecture.

The components in Arm Compiler 6 are:

▦ **armclang** – The compiler and integrated assembler that compiles C, C++, and GNU assembly language sources. It is based on LLVM and Clang (a compiler front end for LLVM that supports C and C++). To target Cortex-M55, use `-mcpu=cortex-m55` on the armclang command line. There are options to specify various Helium capabilities. For example, Cortex-M55 without Helium would require `-mcpu=cortex-m55+nomve` and Cortex-M55 with integer-only Helium would need `-mcpu=cortex-m55+mve+nomve.fp`.

▦ **armasm** – A legacy assembler used for code with an older syntax style. The armclang integrated assembler and GNU syntax must be used for all new assembly files that include Helium instructions.

- **armlink** – The linker combines the contents of one or more object files with one or more object libraries to produce an executable. Again, the command line switch `--cpu=8-M.Main.dsp` should be used.

- **armar** – This allows sets of ELF (Executable and Linkable Format) object files to be collected together in archives or libraries.

- **fromelf** – The image conversion utility can convert Arm ELF images to binary formats. Disassembly of code with fromelf requires a `--cpu` switch (like for the linker) to recognize Helium instructions.

7.1.2 GCC Helium Capability

The GNU Compiler includes support for Helium, enabled with the `-march` switch set to `armv8.1-m. main`. You can specify:

- `+mve` – The MVE integer instructions.

- `+mve.fp` – The MVE integer and single-precision floating-point instructions.

Alternatively, if you are using a specific CPU implementation which supports Helium, you can use a command line switch like `-mcpu=cortex-m55`.

At the time of writing, GCC does not include an auto-vectorization capability for Helium.

7.1.3 Debug/Trace/Profile Options for Helium CPU Cores

Arm's debug tool offerings support Helium CPUs. These are Development Studio 2020.0 onwards (Bronze edition and upwards) and µVision from Keil MDK v5.30 onwards. As you would expect, this includes disassembly of Helium instructions and updated register views showing the vector registers in a variety of selectable formats and the VPR (vector predication status and control register) and other registers. The tools also include a FVP of a Cortex-M55 system. These are models of Arm IP, allowing software developers to write, profile, trace and debug code prior to silicon availability. This provides a great way to learn the details of the new instructions without the need for hardware development boards.

The Armv8.1-M architecture includes debug enhancements which may be useful for DSP/ML applications. It is now possible to set a breakpoint with an associated counter. This means that instead of stopping every time a pinpointed location in the code is reached, we can have the processor only halt when a certain count value is reached. This means that we could, for example, stop near the end of a loop rather than having to step through many iterations of it. This might be useful for stopping the processor when a filter has stabilized, for example. We can also now choose to mask certain bits when performing the comparison for a data watchpoint. This allows to look for a range of values rather than one specific value.

7.2 Options for Programming Helium

There are several ways that a programmer can make use of the Helium features in a CPU:

- Libraries which have been optimized for Helium provide the simplest method. CMSIS-DSP and CMSIS-NN, described below, are open-source examples of this.

- Auto-vectorization compiler techniques can automatically optimize your C/C++ code to take advantage of Helium. If the compiler is able to detect opportunities for vectorization, it can produce output which is as good as handwritten low-level code, but without the requirement to have detailed knowledge of the underlying micro-architecture. Code written in C will also be faster to create, easier to debug and be portable across systems.

- Helium intrinsics are function calls that the compiler replaces with appropriate assembly language instructions. This gives direct, low-level access to the Helium instructions and features from high-level code.

- Hand-coded Helium assembler can, in some circumstances, allow experienced programmers to achieve more optimal solutions than any of the above options.

In the rest of this chapter, we will look at each of these options in turn.

7.3 Libraries

The widespread licensing of the Arm processors means that the same Cortex-M CPU may be available from many different semiconductor companies, each with their own range of microcontrollers, which span a broad range of requirements in terms of memory, peripherals, price etc. This means that you can select the right microcontroller to meet your needs and continue to use the same knowledge and tools irrespective of which device you choose.

Modern microcontrollers may contain a variety of sophisticated peripherals, including things like an LCD interface, USB, or Ethernet. These are likely to be supplied with driver software. This means that most products today are likely to be using third-party code, possibly including operating systems, libraries, open-source communications stacks etc. This means that there is a need to make high-level code portable between different microcontrollers and tools.

7.3.1 CMSIS

CMSIS (Cortex Microcontroller Software Interface Standard) is the result of a consortium comprising Arm and a number of silicon and tools vendors, which aims toward software portability and reusability. It provides a vendor-independent hardware abstraction layer. CMSIS consists of different components that support software reuse, giving a standard way to interface to the processor and peripherals, real-time operating systems, and middleware components. It is divided into a set of different specifications.

CMSIS is compatible with Arm Compiler 6, the GNU Arm Embedded toolchain and commercial toolchains, such as IAR. Full documentation and open-source code for each of the different parts of CMSIS can be found on GitHub:

https://arm-software.github.io/CMSIS_5/General/html/index.html

There are three components which are of specific interest to Helium developers:

- **CMSIS Core** – The core component provides a minimal hardware abstraction layer (HAL) for Cortex-M devices, with standardized definitions for the various system registers, exceptions, and methods for system initialization and device-specific header files. It gives users and tools a standardized way to access the CPU and peripherals. It includes the definitions of Helium intrinsic functions (described in this chapter).

- **CMSIS DSP** – This is a library of DSP functions, with different functions for operating on 8-bit integers, 16-bit integers, 32-bit integers, and 32-bit floating-point values. It includes basic and complex math functions, filters, transforms, matrix operations, motor control, interpolation, statistical functions, and more. The library contains versions of these functions which have been optimized for Helium.

- **CMSIS NN** – This is a library of optimized software kernels that perform neural network functions on Cortex-M processors with minimal memory overhead. Again, these functions can use Helium for maximum performance. We will look at CMSIS NN in much greater detail in Chapter 12.

CMSIS is integrated into IDEs from Arm, including Keil MDK and Arm Development Studio. In Keil MDK, the ARM::CMSIS pack can be installed using the MDK pack installer. In Arm Development Studio, use Pack Manager to install the Generic->ARM.CMSIS pack. Documentation on the Arm website describes how to get started with using CMSIS. CMSIS includes a number of examples and running some of the CMSIS DSP examples with Helium enabled can be a good way to get started with Helium code.

There are three C preprocessor defines which are used to select Helium versions of CMSIS code. All of them should be defined for a CPU which supports Helium floating-point; only the first two should be used for a CPU which has Helium but no floating-point. They may be automatically defined in config files for Cortex-M55 and so may not need to be set manually.

```
#define ARM_MATH_HELIUM
#define ARM_MATH_MVEI          // Integer
#define ARM_MATH_MVEF          // Floating-Point
```

7.4 Automatic Vectorization

Compiler technology now allows us to automatically detect opportunities in high-level code to use Helium instructions to perform vector operations in parallel. This process is known as auto-vectorization. This code may be as efficient in terms of speed and size as hand-optimized assembly or C code containing intrinsics, but requires significantly less time to write and debug and does not require detailed knowledge of the target micro-architecture. The C code is also significantly more portable.

Although the C source code is portable between different architectures, it may sometimes be necessary to make compiler-specific changes in order to achieve the best code generation (in some cases, even a change in compiler options may result in significant changes to the performance of the generated code).

In most cases, the best approach for programmers is to use the compiler, along with optimized code from libraries. It will only become necessary to consider other methods, such as using intrinsics, if the code produced by the compiler does not provide the necessary performance. There are also some specific hardware features (such as enabling Helium in the first place) where assembly code will be required.

It is useful to highlight some additional features of the Arm C Compiler. For example, we can define two pointers to a buffer of 32-bit floating-point values:

```
float32_t * pSrcA
float32_t * pSrcB
```

We can then do a vector-type cast and use standard C arithmetic or logical operators. For example:

```
vecDst = *(float32x4_t *)pSrcA + *(float32x4_t *)pSrcB;
```

This will generate contiguous vector load/store and arithmetic instructions. (It should be noted that this useful feature is not defined in the ACLE specification and so may not be portable outside Arm Compiler 6/GCC.)

Furthermore, we can access elements of vectors like an array or operate directly on a whole vector. For example:

```
vecDst[2] += 0.1;
```

or

```
vecDst = vecDst << 16;   // Only makes sense for integer values
```

7.4.1 Using the Vectorizing Compiler
In order to enable Arm Compiler 6 to auto-vectorize C code for Helium, you must specify the target architecture as Armv8.1-M and use the +mve switch (and typically also specify the availability of floating-point hardware). An example command line switch might be:

```
--target=arm-arm-none-eabi -march=armv8.1-m.main +mve.fp +fp.dp
```

Auto-vectorization is enabled by default at optimization level -O2 and higher. The `-fno-vectorize` option lets you disable auto-vectorization. At optimization level -O1, auto-vectorization is disabled by default. The `-fvectorize` option lets you enable auto-vectorization. At optimization level -O0, auto-vectorization is always disabled. Note that other compilers may behave differently.

Arm Compiler 6 provides some flags which can be useful in understanding whether the compiler has been able to vectorize (or not) certain parts of the code. These flags will result in extra verbosity messages printed to the screen, or to be piped into log files. These messages are called "optimization remarks:"

- `-Rpass=loop-vectorize` – identifies loops that were successfully vectorized

- `-Rpass-missed=loop-vectorize` – identifies loops that failed vectorization and indicates whether vectorization was specified

- `-Rpass-analysis=loop-vectorize` – identifies the statements that caused vectorization to fail

For strict IEEE-754 compliance (which is required by the ISO C/C++ standards), correct handling of NaN, underflow and denormalized numbers is required. Standard DSP algorithms and other numerically robust floating-point code should not require these. The useful compiler flags `-ffp-mode=fast` or `-ffast-math` allow floating-point optimizations to be performed that provide a significant increase in performance, at the cost of compliant handling of these special cases. This means that, for floating-point code, -Ofast will outperform -O3.

In order to write optimal code, it is useful to have a simple understanding of how the compiler analyzes code to find things that can be vectorized.

The first step is loop analysis. For each loop, the compiler needs to check what pointer accesses are made within the loop and whether these are safe for vectorization. It needs to work out how many loop iterations there are (and this may or may not be a number that is known at compile time). It also needs to see which data types are being used within the loop and how they could map to Helium vector registers.

The next step is to unroll the loop to an appropriate number of iterations. For example, our original C code may perform one 32-bit operation per cycle. By unrolling the loop so that each loop performs four operations per cycle and performing a quarter of the number of loops, we create code which performs an identical set of operations, but which can more easily be mapped to Helium vector operations. The compiler may also reverse the loop order (if safe to do so), so that we count down to zero rather than counting up to a value.

If our loop looks like this:

```
for(i = 0; i < (n & ~3); i++)
  pa[i] = pb[i] * pc[i];
```

It might be unrolled to something like this (inside the compiler).

```
for (i = ((n & ~3) >> 2); i>=0; i--)
{
  pa[i] = pb[i] * pc[i];
  pa[i+1] = pb[i+1] * pc[i+1];
  pa[i+2] = pb[i+2] * pc[i+2];
  pa[i+3] = pb[i+3] * pc[i+3];
}
```

After loop unrolling, the compiler will attempt to convert array accesses to use pointers, so that we now have:

```
{
  *(pa) = *(pb) + *(pc);
  *(pa + 1) = *(pb + 1) + *(pc+1);
  *(pa + 2) = *(pb + 2) + *(pc+2);
  *(pa + 3) = *(pb + 3) + *(pc+3);
  pa += 4; pb += 4; pc +=4;
}
```

This can then be mapped to corresponding Helium instructions.

Compilers may also have techniques to spot specific programming idioms, allowing code to be recognized as vectorizable that would otherwise appear to have a data dependency. For example, this code appears to have a self-dependency, but the compiler may recognize that the values on the right-hand side of the equals sign are read and then stored on the left-hand side and therefore it is not possible for the data to change during the assignment.

```
a[i] = a[i] + a[i+1];
```

Note that some compilers have a pragma (for example, nounroll) that forces a particular loop to not be unrolled.

7.4.2 Writing C for Auto-Vectorization

As we have seen, the compiler must look at your code and attempt to detect features which can be vectorized. The more features that it can detect, the better the output code will be in terms of making use of Helium. The programmer can structure code in ways which enable the compiler to do this and can also provide hints to allow the compiler to detect features that would not otherwise be able to be vectorized. These modifications are not architecture-specific and are likely to help vectorization efforts on any target. They would not be expected to have a negative performance effect on targets which do not support vectorized execution.

It is important to understand the use of the restrict keyword in C/C++ code and use it when appropriate. The C99 restrict keyword (or the non-standard C/C++ __restrict__ keyword) tells the compiler that a specified pointer does not alias with any other pointers for the lifetime of that pointer. This allows the compiler to more aggressively vectorize loops by telling it that loop iterations are independent of each other and can be executed in parallel. If the `restrict` keyword is used wrongly then the generated code may behave incorrectly. If another pointer is used to access the same memory as the pointer that has a restrict applied to it, `restrict` must not be used.

There are a number of ways of coding loops which may help or hinder auto-vectorization:

- Try to ensure that the compiler can determine whether there is a fixed iteration count at the beginning of the loop. Use loop counters of type unsigned int where possible.

- Loop termination conditions can cause significant overheads. If possible, write count-down-to-zero loops and test for equality against zero. Where this is not possible, it is better to use < conditions, rather than <= or != conditions in constructing loops. This helps the compiler know that a loop terminates before the index variable wraps. If possible, avoid exits from loops with break instructions.

- Loop partitioning may be useful. This means that loops which perform multiple tasks may perform better when rewritten as several separate loops.

- Use pragmas to explicitly indicate that loop iterations are completely independent from each other.

- Avoid "feedback" between loop iterations. A loop that has results from one iteration feeding back into a future iteration of the same loop potentially has a data dependency conflict. This may prevent it from being fully optimized. The conflict could be array elements, or a simple scalar value such as a sum. To determine whether there is such a conflict, it is necessary to examine the pattern of accesses in each array dimension that is read or written in a loop. If there is a possible overlap the loop cannot be safely vectorized if the vector order of operations can change the results.

Example code with a data dependency conflict:

```
int p[10];
p[0]=1;p[1]=1;

void func(void)
{
  int cnt;
  for (cnt=2; cnt<10; cnt++)
  {
    p[cnt] = p[cnt-1] + p[cnt-2]; // this prevents vectorization
  }
}
```

The loop contains code which sets the value of an array element depending upon the state of other elements which were modified in a previous loop iteration. Therefore, it cannot be automatically vectorized.

A special category of scalar use within loops is where a vector of data values is "reduced" to a scalar result. This is known as a reduction operation. Reductions work across the whole of a single vector performing the same operation between elements of that vector. For example, the Helium instruction VADDV.U16 Rda, Qm is a reduction operation which takes a vector of unsigned 16-bit integer values, adds each of the eight elements together, and returns a 32-bit result containing the sum in a general-purpose register.

The compiler will attempt to recognize such cases as they are frequently used in code and therefore are worth vectorizing. This is typically done by creating a vector of partial reductions that is then reduced into the final resulting scalar. Common examples include:

■ Dot product of two vectors

■ Maximum or minimum value in a vector, or index of the minimum or maximum element within a vector

■ Product of all vector elements.

Example:

```
float a[16], b[16], x;
int i, n;
...

for (i = 0; i < n; i++)
    x += a[i] * b[i];
```

This code calculates a simple dot product where x is a reduction scalar. Although intermediate values of x are affected by the order in which the calculation is done (there is a data dependency between loops), the compiler is able to recognize that the final value at the end of the loop is unchanged by reordering the loops and this code can therefore be vectorized.

Compiling this code with Arm Compiler 6.14, with the options -mcpu=cortex-m55 -Ofast ffast-math, generates the following code for the inner loop:

```
.LBB28_5: @ =>This Inner Loop Header: Depth=1
        VLDRW.U32      Q1, [R0], #16
        VLDRW.U32      Q2, [R1], #16
        VFMA.F32       Q0, Q2, Q1
        LE             LR, .LBB28_5
```

This is followed by code to reduce the four vector product sums to one and to handle the tail.

Programmers will often wish to separate complex operations into different functions. This is generally considered to be good practice, as it aids code reuse and makes code easier to read. However, function calls within a loop may prevent vectorization. Functions which are called from within a loop that would benefit from vectorization should be marked with __attribute__((always_inline)). This tells the compiler to attempt to inline the function before attempting vectorization. Inlining means that the call to the function will be replaced by the code from the body of the function. The compiler will not do this if this would cause incorrect behavior. If functions to be inlined are used in multiple source files, they should be placed in a header file.

On some architectures or compilers, it may be the case that best performance is obtained by treating variables as 32-bits wide. For code targeting Helium, it is always better to use the smallest data type which can hold the required range of values. Helium can process four times as many 8-bit values per vector operation, or twice as many 16-bit values, when compared with 32-bit values. Double-precision floating-point should be avoided, as Helium does not support vector operations on this data type.

7.4.3 Vectorization Example

Here, we will look at modifications that can be made to the following piece of simple C code in order to make it more likely to be vectorized. Most of these changes are architecture-agnostic (i.e. they would also apply to writing code for Neon or other SIMD architectures).

```
void calculate (double *a, double *b, double *x, double *y, int n) {
        int i;
        for (i=0; i<n; i++) {
            a[i]= x[i] * y[i];
            b[i]= a[i] - x[i] + y[i];
        }
}
```

We can immediately identify some problems which would prevent this code from being vectorized:

■ The arrays are of double-precision floating-point. If it is safe to use single-precision, we should change this. (Of course, there may be instances where the algorithm requires double-precision floating-point.)

■ The compiler does not know that a, b, x and y point to independent locations (i.e. that they are non-overlapping arrays). It has to make the assumption that they are aliased and that x[3] might be the same memory location as b[2], for example. We need to use the `restrict` keyword to tell the compiler this.

■ The number of loops to be performed is not fixed. If we are able to hint to the compiler that n is a multiple of 4, by masking off the bottom two bits, it will be easier to vectorize.

This gives the following code:

```
void calculate(float *restrict a, float *restrict b, float *restrict x, float *restrict y,
int n) {
        int i;
        for (i=0; i <(n~3); i++) {
            a[i]= x[i] * y[i];
            b[i]= a[i] - x[i] + y[i];
        }
}
```

Running this modified code on a Cortex-M55 model showed a performance gain of nearly a factor of four (929 cycles compared with 258, for n = 64). This speedup is mainly because the original code used the scalar floating-point hardware whereas the modified code is able to use vector registers to perform four operations in parallel.

7.5 Helium Code Using Intrinsics

Intrinsics are a set of C/C++ functions which allow you to use Helium without having to write assembly code directly. The Helium intrinsics specification is contained in the ACLE documentation. The implementation of the functions is included in a header file, available both in Arm Compiler 6 and GCC. The functions contain short assembly language sections which are inlined into the calling code. The M-Profile Vector Extension (MVE) Intrinsics Reference documentation contains a full list of the Helium intrinsics.

Using intrinsics has several advantages:

▧ The programmer has direct access to the Helium instruction set, allowing fully optimized code to be written and all Helium features to be utilized.

▧ C/C++ can be used for most code, with the Helium intrinsics being used only when required for optimizations that the vectorizing C compiler cannot perform. It means that low-level code is used only when necessary.

▧ C and C++ code containing Helium intrinsics can be ported to a new target with fewer or no code changes compared with code written in assembly language.

▧ Using intrinsics avoids many of the difficulties associated with coding directly in assembly language (covered later in this chapter).

However, use of intrinsics requires much more knowledge of the architecture than using library code or relying on the compiler.

As we have seen, intrinsics are pseudo-function calls that the compiler replaces with an appropriate instruction or sequence of instructions.

The Helium intrinsics are defined in a special Arm Compiler header file, arm_mve.h.

This header also defines a set of vector data types of different sizes, for example:
```
int16x8_t – vector of eight 16-bit short int values (held in a Q register)
float32x4_t  – vector of four 32-bit float values (held in a Q register)
```

Example:
```
int16x8_t result, a, b;
result = vaddq_s16(a,b);
```

See the online reference documentation for a complete list of intrinsics:

https://developer.arm.com/architectures/instruction-sets/simd-isas/helium/mve-intrinsics

In the C preprocessor, the macro __ARM_FEATURE_MVE can be set. Bit 0 indicates whether Helium integer instructions are available and bit 1 indicates whether Helium floating-point instructions are available. We may therefore see code like this used, so that the header file is included only when Helium is available:

```
#if __ARM_FEATURE_MVE & 1
#include <arm_mve.h>
```

7.5.1 Coding with Intrinsics

One of the main advantages of coding using intrinsics, rather than native assembly language, is that it allows the compiler to take care of things such as array lookups and register allocation. Any variable which has been defined as a vector type will be allocated into a Helium vector register. Parameters of vector type will be passed into functions in Helium registers.

The ACLE specification defines the format for the intrinsic function prototypes. The actual definitions are contained in arm_mve.h and there are more than 4000 of them. This is because, while there are fewer than 200 Helium instructions, there is a separate function prototype for each data type. As we shall see, there are also a range of predication options for each function.

Each of the intrinsics is available with or without the __arm_ prefix. It is possible to make the __arm_ prefix mandatory (to avoid namespace pollution) by defining the macro:

```
__ARM_MVE_PRESERVE_USER_NAMESPACE
```

The naming convention for the intrinsic functions is relatively easy to follow. Each of them begins with "v" (for Vector) and the operation name (which generally maps to an assembly language instruction), then flags (the "q" flag means it operates on 128-bit vectors), then an underscore ("_"), and then the type of data.

As we have already seen, Helium operates on 128-bit vectors of the elements of the same scalar data type. This means that C/C++ code needs to be able to declare variables as vector data types. These are named as a lane type and a multiple. Lane names are based on the types defined in stdint.h. The base types are int8_t, uint8_t, int16_t, uint16_t, int32_t, uint32_t, int64_t, uint64_t, float16_t and float32_t and then the multiple is the value required to give a 128-bit vector. So, we have, for example uint8x16_t which is a vector of 16 int8_t values.

Additionally, we also have vector array data types, which are defined for multiples of two and four of all the vector types, for use in certain load and store operations. For a vector type <type>_t the corresponding array type is <type>x<length>_t. A vector array data type is a structure which contains a single array element, called val.

For example, an array of four int16x8_t types can be represented as:

```
struct int16x8x4_t { int16x8_t val[4]; };
```

The various vld4q intrinsic functions are used to load two 64-bit contiguous blocks of data from memory and deinterleave the data into four Q registers with a stride of four (discussed in Section 5.3). The output of this function is therefore of type int16x8x4_t. These functions (like the similar vld2q, vst2q and vst4q) contain multiple Helium instructions, so that vld4q will include vld40, VLD41, VLD42 and VLD43.

As intrinsics are C functions, normal C typing rules will be followed. This is more restrictive than Helium instructions, which can use any register as any type of vector, provided that the sizes match.

Therefore, an intrinsic function is provided to cast from one vector type to another. This exists only to provide information to the compiler. It does not actually change the contents of the register or cause any instruction to be generated in the binary code.

Example:
```
int16x8_t vreinterpretq_s16_u32(uint32x4_t a);
```

If we define int32x4_t x;

we cannot write: uint32x4_t y = x;

Instead, we must write: uint32x4_t y = vreinterpretq_u32_s32(x);

Similarly, the vcvtq class of intrinsic functions must be used to convert between integer and floating types. This maps to the Helium VCVT instruction.

Example:

If we again define int32x4_t x;

we cannot simply write: float32x4_t z = x;

Instead, we need to write: float32x4_t z = vcvtq_f32_s32(x);

There are a number of intrinsic functions which do map directly to assembly language instructions. The vcreateq intrinsic can be used to construct vectors from scalars. The vcreateq intrinsic uses two VMOV instructions to return a 128-bit vector formed from the concatenation of two 64-bit values. The vdupq intrinsic can also be used to construct a vector (using the VDUP instruction). Arm Compiler 6 also allows us to directly initialize a vector, as if we were initializing an array.

Example:

```
uint32x4_t x = {1, 2, 3, 4};
```

The `vgetq_lane` intrinsic is used to read the value from a specific lane within a register, while the `vsetq_lane` intrinsic is used to write a value to a specified lane. The `vuninitializedq` intrinsic is used to create a vector whose contents we don't care about.

Scalar data types are defined to match the vector types, so that `float32_t` is defined as an alias for float, `float16_t` is defined as an alias for `__fp16` and `mve_pred16_t` is defined as an alias for `uint16_t`. This latter type is used to provide lane predication through intrinsics.

7.5.2 Intrinsics Predication

Earlier in this book, we have seen how Helium permits vector predication to allow instructions to perform operations only on selected lanes. The intrinsic functions have predicated variants for those instructions which support this. Four different suffixes are used to show this predication:

- _m (merging) – indicates that false-predicated lanes are not written to and keep the same value as they originally had.

- _p (predicated) – indicates that false-predicated lanes are not used in the vector operation. For example, `vaddvq_p_s8`, where the false-predicated lanes are not added to the resulting sum.

- _z (zero) – indicates that false-predicated lanes are filled with zeros. These are only used for load instructions.

- _x (don't-care) – indicates that the false-predicated lanes have undefined values.

Some predicated intrinsics may have a dedicated first parameter of the same type as the result, used to specify the value in the result vector for the false-predicated lanes.

For example, consider the intrinsic:

```
float16x8_t vaddq_m[_f16] (float16x8_t inactive, float16x8_t a,
float16x8_t b, mve_pred16_t p);
```

This will add the value of the elements in the first source-vector register to either the respective elements in the second source-vector register or a general-purpose register. The result is then written to the destination-vector register. The function will write to each of the 16 lanes of the result vector, either the result of the add between the corresponding lanes of vectors a and b, or the corresponding lane of vector inactive, depending on whether that lane is true- or false-predicated in p. The argument "inactive" must have the same width (per vector element) as the return type of the intrinsic.

This intrinsic function potentially emits three instructions:

```
VMSR P0, Rp      // Load predicate register with the parameter p.
VPST             // The following instruction is in a predicate block
VADDT.F16 Qd,Qn,Qm // Qd is the inactive value,  Qn is a, Qm is b.
```

The predicate mask must have all bits set to the same value for each of the bits corresponding to the size of the input lane. In other words, if, for example, the input is of 32-bit size, the corresponding four bits of the predicate mask must be identical to each other. Usually, this means that the code which produces the predicate mask value must use an element size equal to (or larger than) the element size of the instruction which uses the mask. The following example illustrates this.

We create a mask by performing a comparison between two vectors a and b, which hold unsigned 8-bit integers.

```
mve_pred16_t mask8 = vcmpeqq_u8(a, b;)
```

Figure 7.1 shows an example of this instruction being executed. The 16 pairs of .U8 values in a and b are compared and the corresponding bit in VPR.P0 is set if they are equal.

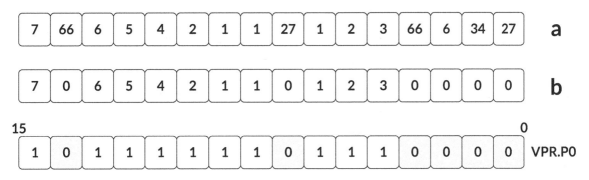

Figure 7.1: VCMPEQ.U8 example

If we now use VPR.P0 to predicate subsequent instructions, we see the following:

```
uint8x16_t r8 = vaddq_m_u8 (a, b, mask8); // This will work correctly
uint16x8_t r16 = vaddq_m_u16 (c, d, mask8);  // This will not work correctly
```

Figure 7.2 illustrates the problem.

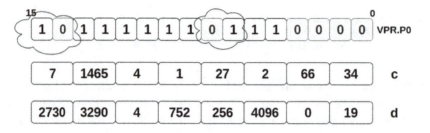

Figure 7.2: Mismatch of VPR.P0 bits and element size

When we have an instruction which is using 16-bit-wide lanes, we have two bits in VPR[15:0] for each of them. If those bits are non-identical, the behavior is unpredictable.

The same consideration applies even if we create the predicate mask manually. For example:

```
mve_pred16_t mask8 = 0xAAAA;        // 1010101010101010 binary
                                    // predicate every 2nd byte.

uint8x16_t r8 = vaddq_m_u8 (a, b, mask8); // This will work correctly

uint16x8_t r16 = vaddq_m_u16 (c, d, mask8);   // This will not work
```

It is possible to access a polymorphic implementation of most intrinsics. This is indicated by omitting the type suffix, so that instead of calling, for example, `vclzq_u8()`, we simply call `vclzq()`. The compiler can select the appropriate code through C's `_Generic` selection mechanism. This is only possible on input parameter types and it is still necessary to supply the correct number of parameters. This can be quite convenient, as it can make changes to data types used in a piece of code easier. Note that this is not possible for most load and store operations, because it is not possible to infer the element type from the input variables due to the option to widen or narrow. (For example, we would use `VLDRH` to widen 16-bit values to 32-bit values.) There are polymorphic `vld1`/`vst1` variants for contiguous loads and stores without a widening or narrowing operation.

7.5.3 Intrinsics Dot Product Example
In this section, we will look at some code that makes use of intrinsic functions.

We will start with some C code to perform a floating-point multiply accumulate on two input arrays, psrcA[] and psrcB[].

```
void arm_dot_prod( float32_t * pSrcA, float32_t * pSrcB, uint32_t blockSize)
{
result =0.0;
while (blocksize >0U) {
   result += (*psrcA++) *(*psrcB++);
   blockSize--;
   }
return(result);
}
```

The intrinsic functions we need to use are:

- `vdupq()` – sets each element of a vector register to the value of a general-purpose register. Here we use it to initialize the accumulator vector values to 0.

- `vld1q()` – loads a vector from memory, using the `VLDR` instruction.

- `vfmaq()` – performs a vector fused multiply accumulate.

The code shown here is taken from:

https://github.com/ARM-software/CMSIS_5/blob/master/CMSIS/DSP/Source/BasicMathFunctions/arm_dot_prod_f32.c

It begins by declaring variables and initializing the sum. Note the use of `f32x4_t` as a short form of `float32x4_t`.

```
void arm_dot_prod_f32(
    const float32_t * pSrcA,
    const float32_t * pSrcB,
    uint32_t    blockSize,
    float32_t * result)
{
    f32x4_t vecA, vecB;
    f32x4_t vecSum;
    uint32_t blkCnt;
    float32_t sum = 0.0f;
    vecSum = vdupq_n_f32(0.0f);
```

The main loop loads four values into one vector register, four values into a second register and multiplies four pairs of single-precision floating-point numbers per cycle and accumulates the result into a vector.

```
/* Compute 4 outputs at a time */
    blkCnt = blockSize >> 2U;
    while (blkCnt > 0U)
    {
        /*
         * C = A[0]* B[0] + A[1]* B[1] + A[2]* B[2] + .....+ A[blockSize-1]*
B[blockSize-1]
         * Calculate dot product and then store the result in a temporary buffer.
         * and advance vector source and destination pointers
         */
        vecA = vld1q(pSrcA);
        pSrcA += 4;

        vecB = vld1q(pSrcB);
        pSrcB += 4;

        vecSum = vfmaq(vecSum, vecA, vecB);
        /*
         * Decrement the blockSize loop counter
         */
        blkCnt --;
    }
```

Figure 7.3 illustrates what is happening in the loop.

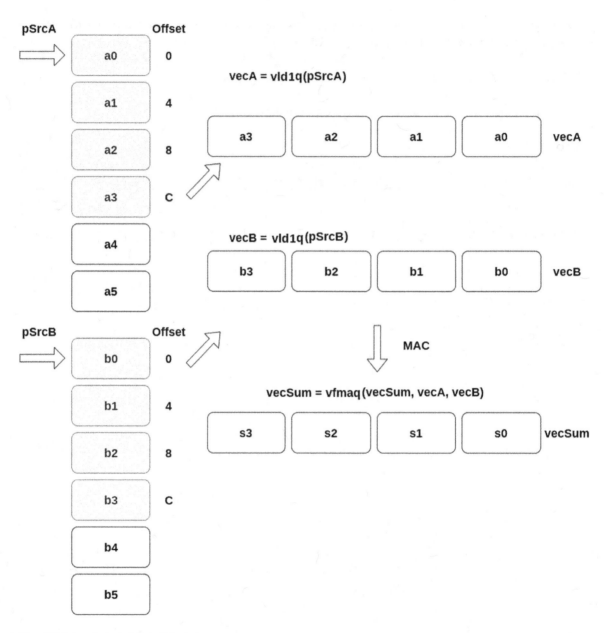

Figure 7.3: Dot-product calculation with intrinsics

Next, we need to take care of the fact that our original blockSize may not have been a multiple of four. We can use a predicated version of the vfmaq intrinsic to update only the required number (0, 1, 2 or 3) of lanes. At the end of the code, we now have a vector which contains four sum values. In order to get the final result, we need to perform a reduction and add these together. This is done by the CMSIS function `vecAddAcrossF32Mve()`. This simply does `vgetq_lane(in, 0) + vgetq_lane(in, 1) + vgetq_lane(in, 2) + vgetq_lane(in, 3)` and is defined in arm_helium_utils.h.

```
    blkCnt = blockSize & 3;
    if (blkCnt > 0U)
    {
        /* C = A[0]* B[0] + A[1]* B[1] + A[2]* B[2] + .....+ A[blockSize-1]*
B[blockSize-1] */

        mve_pred16_t p0 = vctp32q(blkCnt);
        vecA = vld1q(pSrcA);
        vecB = vld1q(pSrcB);
        vecSum = vfmaq_m(vecSum, vecA, vecB, p0);
    }

    sum = vecAddAcrossF32Mve(vecSum);

    /* Store result in destination buffer */
    *result = sum;

}
```

It is straightforward to modify this code to operate on half-precision `.F16` values instead. Here, we can perform eight operations per iteration. Code for this can be seen at:

https://github.com/ARM-software/CMSIS_5/blob/develop/CMSIS/DSP/Source/BasicMathFunctions/arm_dot_prod_f16.c

However, the final reduction process is slightly more complex. We have to sum a vector of eight `.F16` elements to produce a `.F16` result. The CMSIS function `vecAddAcrossF16Mve()` in arm_helium_utils.h does this.

One way to do this would be to use the `vgetq_lane()` intrinsic function, which allows us to extract a particular element from a vector. We can simply write code like:

```
result = vgetq_lane(vecSum,7) + vgetq_lane(vecSum,6) + vgetq_lane(vecSum,5) + vgetq_
lane(vecSum,4) + vgetq_lane(vecSum,3) + vgetq_lane(vecSum,2) + vgetq_lane(vecSum,1) +
vgetq_lane(vecSum,0)
```

However, this is quite inefficient. We can do better by using the `vrev32q`, `vrev64q` and `vaddq` intrinsics, as illustrated in Figure 7.4. Initially, the vector register contains eight values, vecSum7 … vecSum0. A pair of `vrevq` and `vaddq` intrinsics allows us to produce four intermediate sums. A further pair of these intrinsics adds these to produce two intermediate sums. Finally, we can use `vgetq_lane` and a final `vaddq` to produce the sum of all eight elements in the bottom lane of the register.

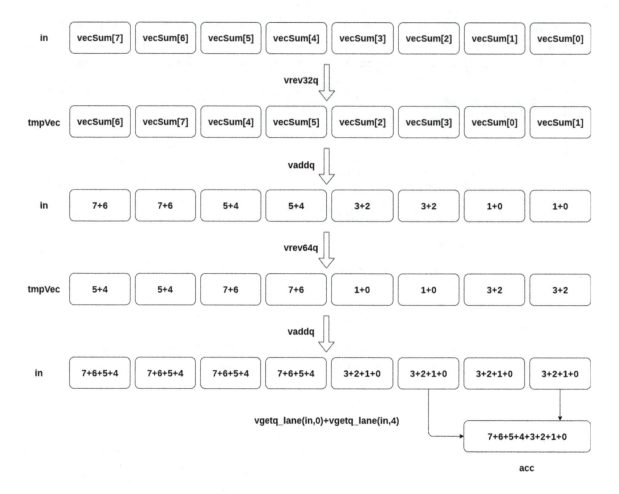

Figure 7.4: Float16 reduction

7.5.4 Intrinsics Scatter-Gather Example
We now look at an example which makes use of scatter-gather.

The complex conjugate of a complex number $z \equiv a + bi$ is defined to be $\bar{z} \equiv a + bi$. The complex conjugate of a matrix is the matrix obtained by replacing each element with its complex conjugate. This operation is often combined with transposition in matrix algebra. If we have an array of complex numbers, pointed to by pSrc, stored in memory as float32 values as real, imaginary pairs, to calculate the complex conjugate, we simply need to invert the sign bit of every odd (imaginary) value.

```
void arm_complex_conjugate_f32 (
float32_t * pSrc, uint32_t blockSize)
{
        uint32_t  blckCnt;
        float32x4_t vecDst;
        uint32_t  cnt=1;
    uint32_t vecStrides = vidupq(&cnt, 2);
    blkCnt = blockSize/4;
```

```
    while (blkCnt >0U)
    {
      vecDst=vldrwq_gather_shifted_offset_f32(pSrc, vecStrides);
      vecDst = vecDst * -1.0;
      vstrwq_scatter_shifted_offset_f32(pSrc,vecStrides, vecDst);
      vecStrides= vidupq(&cnt, 2);
      blkCnt--;
    }
}
```

There are several features to note in this code. We use `vidupq(&cnt,2)` to create the initial vector values in `vecStrides` of {1, 3, 5, 7}. This is generated by the initial value of `cnt` (1) and the increment of 2 specified in the intrinsic call. At the end of the instruction, `cnt` is automatically updated to the next value of 9.

Within the loop, we use the intrinsic `vldrwq_gather_shifted_offset_f32` to load a vector of values from `pSrc`, at the offsets given by `vecStrides`. This will generate an instruction which causes the offset values in the vector to be shifted left two places in the address calculation, so that the load is of words 1, 3, 5 and 7 rather than simply adding the offsets directly to the base address.

The intrinsic `vstrwq_scatter_shifted_offset_f32` uses the same offsets to perform a write only to the imaginary components. Finally, within the loop, we execute `vidupq` to produce the new offsets for the next loop iteration (remember that `cnt` is updated to point to the next value each time).

Note that both Arm Compiler 6 and GCC allow us to write code like `vecDst = vecDst * -1.0`. However, this alternative syntax is not defined in the Arm ACLE specification and to guarantee portability, we should write:

```
vecDst = vmulq(vecDst, -1.0f);
```

7.5.5 Intrinsics Tail Handling

When writing vector code, a common issue is how to deal with remainders if the data to be processed is not a multiple of the vector size. Normally, this would be done with some backup scalar code. As we saw in Section 3.4, Helium includes predication features for tail loops to avoid this and Arm Compiler 6 can generate code which uses this. We can also do this using intrinsics and the predication features we saw in the previous section.

The create tail predicate instruction (`VCTP`) sets up a predicate pattern in VPR.P0. This means that the following instructions will operate only on none, some, or all of the elements in the vector, depending on the number of remaining items. As we saw previously, appending _z to the `vld1q` intrinsic means that the lanes which are not to be loaded are instead filled with zeros. The _m suffix means that the unused lanes retain their previous values. The _p suffix for `vst1q` means that the false-predicated lanes are not written to memory.

Code like the following example will make the compiler produce a tail-predicated Do loop, with no requirement for a scalar epilogue.

```
void arm_mult_f32_mve_tp(const float32_t * pSrcA, const float32_t * pSrcB, float32_t *
pDst, uint32_t blockSize)
  {
    f32x4_t vecA, vecB;
    while ((int32_t)blockSize > 0)
    {
        mve_pred16_t p = vctpq_f32(blockSize);
        vecA = vld1q_z(pSrcA, p);
        vecB = vld1q_z(pSrcB, p);
        vst1q_p(pDst, vmulq_x(vecA, vecB,p), p);
        vstrwq_p(pDst, vmulq_m_f32(vuninitializedq_f32(), vecA, vecB,
p), p);
        pSrcA += 4;
        pSrcB += 4;
        pDst += 4;
        blockSize -= 4;
    }
  }
```

7.5.6 Intrinsic Functions Workflow

Writing vectorized code using intrinsic functions involves making some judgments. Does the algorithm have enough scope for vectorization to make the effort of creating the code worthwhile? How important is the portability of C code versus the speed (and complexity) of creating code using intrinsic functions? It may be that scalar code is fast enough, or the vectorizing compiler is good enough that the extra effort is not necessary.

Usually, it makes sense to begin by creating portable, scalar code. This allows you to debug the algorithm and acts as a reference for checking the correctness of your code that uses intrinsics. It also acts as a baseline for timing so that you can measure whether you've been able to make things run faster. You should profile this code and see where the bottlenecks are. They are not always in the expected locations. In some cases it may be useful to include a runtime check to see whether Helium is present and fallback to the scalar code if it is not.

Good practice is to begin with a view that you might use intrinsics in the future. For example, you might consider what would be the best layout of data structures for efficient memory access. For best performance, we need to keep the vector hardware busy. We can get the maximum throughput by using the narrowest type elements that will fit the data, allowing us to fit more into each vector. Similarly, if we exceed the maximum number of available vector registers within a loop, things will slow down because of memory spills. These considerations will help the compiler, as well as making things easier later should we need to use intrinsics.

Once you have working code, you should typically expend effort on trying to get the compiler to auto-vectorize before attempting to use intrinsics. Similarly, you should check whether it is possible to make use of library code from CMSIS (and other places).

Once you have identified that it is worthwhile refactoring parts of your code to make use of intrinsics, it can be a good idea to group that code into separate files. Keeping this code separate may help with future maintenance or porting efforts. It is usually easier, in any case, to separate vector code from scalar or control code.

It is important to test for correctness of your vector code by comparing the results against your reference code. You should also test for timing, that is, have your efforts made things faster or not?

7.6 Using Assembly Code

It is rarely necessary (or useful) to write Helium instructions directly in assembly code. It is typically only necessary in unusual cases where the programmer can do a better job of allocating registers than the compiler, for example where there are simply too many clobbered and input/output variables. (A "clobbered" variable is one which will be changed, but is not one of the outputs, in the context of inline assembly code.)

7.6.1 Inline Assembly Code

The inline assembler is part of the C compiler, and the compiler still performs register allocation and function entry/exit. It will also attempt to optimize the resulting code, so that the result may be functionally equivalent to what you write, but not necessarily identical. The inline assembler allows us to use instructions which are not available in C, or to optimize time-critical code.

In Arm Compiler 6, inline assembly code uses GNU syntax rather than the old-style armasm syntax. A brief introduction to inline assembler is given here, but the interested reader should study the full documentation.

The inline assembler is invoked using __asm, followed by a list of assembler instructions inside braces or parentheses. You can specify inline assembler code using the following formats:

- A single line, for example:

```
__asm("instruction[;instruction]");
__asm{instruction[;instruction]}
```

- Multiple lines, for example:

```
__asm
{
    ...
    instruction
    ...
}
```

C or C++ style comments can be used anywhere in an inline assembly language block. Inline assembly code uses instructions in the same way as a native assembly language function, but registers (and constants) are specified in a different way. In general, an inline assembly statement has the format:

```
asm(code : output operand list : input operand list : clobber list );
```

In the code section, operands are referenced by using a percent sign (%) followed by the symbol name enclosed in square brackets. The lists of output and input operands are optional and map symbolic names to C variables. The lists of output and input operands consist of a comma-separated list of a symbolic name enclosed in square brackets, followed by a constraint string and a C expression enclosed in parentheses.

So, we might have an instruction like:

```
asm("add %[result], %[input], #1":[result] "=r" (y):[input]"x" (i):);
```

The clobber list tells the compiler about things that will be changed as a result of the instruction (but whose final value is not important), to prevent incorrect optimizations. "Memory" is a valid keyword for the clobber list and will force the compiler to store and reload any cached variables, as memory may have been changed by the instruction. Including a register in the list ensures that the compiler will not reuse it for other purposes in the code.

All input and output operands are described by a symbolic name enclosed in square brackets, followed by a constraint string, followed by a C expression in parentheses. Every assembly language instruction has requirements for its operands. Therefore, we need to express these constraints when passing constants, pointers or variables. Constraint codes define how to pass operands between assembly code and C/C++ code.

There are three categories of constraint codes:

- **Constant operands.** These are used to provide an immediate operand to an instruction. There are specific constraints for the immediate ranges of different instructions.

- **Register operands.** The compiler allocates a register to store the value, which may be input and/or output. The compiler will generate an error if not enough registers are available.

- **Memory operands.** These are used with load and store instructions and a register is allocated to hold a pointer to the operand.

Some commonly used constraint characters are listed:

Character	Meaning
h	Register operand must be an integer or floating-point type. This can be one of R8–R12 or LR.
i	A constant integer, or the address of a global variable or function.
l	Register operand must be an integer or floating-point type. This can be one of R0–R7.
m	A memory reference. This constraint causes a general-purpose register to be allocated to hold the address of the value instead of the value itself.
n	A constant integer.
r	Register operand must be an integer or floating-point type. This can be one of R0–R12 or LR.
t	Register operand must be a 32-bit floating-point or integer type. This can be one of S0–S31.

Character	Meaning
w	Register operand must be a floating-point or vector type, or a 64-bit integer. This can be one of S0–S31, D0–D31, or Q0–Q15, depending on the size of the operand type.
I	A constant in the range 0 to 255 for 16-bit instructions or the modified immediate value for 32-bit instructions.
J	A constant in the range −1 to −255 for 16-bit instructions, or −4095 to 4095 for 32-bit instructions.
K	An 8-bit value shifted left any amount for 16-bit instructions, or the bitwise inverse of a modified immediate value for 32-bit instructions.
L	A value in the range −7 to 7 for 16-bit instructions, or the arithmetic negation of a modified immediate value for 32-bit instructions.

Optionally, a modifier may be prepended before the constraint character. All output operands require a constraint modifier and there are no modifiers for input operands.

Modifier	Meaning
=	This operand is only written to, and only after all input operands have been read for the last time. Therefore, the compiler can allocate this operand and an input to the same register or memory location.
+	This operand is both read from and written to.
=&	This operand is only written to. It might be modified before the assembly block finishes reading the input operands. Therefore, the compiler cannot use the same register to store this operand and an input operand. Operands with the =& constraint modifier are known as early clobber operands.

Further information may be found in the appropriate armclang or GCC documentation.

There are a few Helium-specific points to note. As we have the possibility of a 64-bit scalar output from certain instructions, we need to be able to specify the lower and higher parts of a 64-bit register pair and we do this with %Q and %R.

For example:

```
"vrmlaldavha.s32 %Q[sum], %R[sum], q0, q1 \n" /* sum is int64_t*/
```

Similarly, to be able to enforce even/odd scalar register pairing, we can use "+Te" and "+To". This is required for those instructions which produce a 64-bit scalar output, stored in two general-purpose registers, where there is a restriction that <RdaLo> must be an even-numbered register and <RdaHi> an odd-numbered register. For example:

```
  __asm volatile (…
" viwdup.u32 q2, %[wOfs], %[wLim], %[wInc] \n"
: [wOfs] "+Te" (wOffset), [wLim] "+To" (wLimit) :..: q2)
```

7.6.2 Inline Assembly Example
A function to read two arrays of data, multiply corresponding items together and store the result in a third array might look like this in inline assembly.

```
__asm volatile (
    ".p2align 2 \n"
    " wlstp.32 lr, %[len], 1f \n"
    " 2: \n"
    " vldrw.32 q0, [%[pA]], #16 \n"
    " vldrw.32 q1, [%[pB]], #16 \n"
    " vmul.f32 q2, q0, q1 \n"
    " vstrw.32 q2, [%[pD]], #16 \n"
    " letp lr, 2b \n"
    " 1: \n"
    :[pD] "+r"(pDst),[pA] "+r"(pSrcA), [pB] "+r"(pSrcB)
    :[len] "r"(blockSize) :"q0", "q1", "q2", "lr", "memory");
```

Low-overhead loops are more efficient when the loop start address is 32-bit aligned. Normally, the compiler will take care of this, but alignment directives should be added when using assembly code, which is why the line ".p2align 2 \n" is required.

The WLSTP and LETP instructions set up a tail-predicated While loop. The inner body of the loop simply has two vector loads, a vector multiply and a vector store.

There are a number of key points to notice about how inline assembly code is written:

■ The local labels for the loop are shown with a number and a colon, "2:" and "1:" in this case, and referred to within the WLSTP and LETP instructions as "1f" (forward) and "2b" (backward).

■ The \n linefeed characters are required at the end of each line.

■ After the final line of code, we have a colon, followed by the list of output operands. Each entry consists of a symbolic name enclosed in square brackets, a constraint string and a C expression enclosed in parentheses. So, the pDst variable in C is referred to as pD in our assembly code, the pSrcA variable is referred to as pA in our code and the same for pSrcB and pB. We refer to these pointers in our code using, for example, [%[pA]].

■ After the list of output operands, we have a colon and then a list of input operands, in a similar format. The C variable blockSize is referred to using %[len] in the code.

■ After the list of input operands, we have a colon and then the list of things that will be clobbered (potentially changed) by the code. In this case, that means the Helium registers Q0, Q1, Q2 and the integer core LR register (used as the loop counter). In general, using a hard-coded register in inline assembly may prevent best optimization results. It is better to pass a variable and let the compiler choose the register.

■ The constraint strings in this example are simple. When passing constants, variables or pointers to inline assembly code, the compiler needs to know how they should be passed. We have "r" which specifies an integer core register, and "+r" which specifies an integer core register that may be changed by the code (and so must be listed as an output).

When there are a lot of registers involved in an inline assembly block with a low-overhead loop structure, we can avoid the use of an intermediate register by telling the compiler to assign the loop counter in LR. This helps to reduce register pressure. We need to also modify the assembly instruction which sets up the loop to use LR instead of the variable name.

```
register unsigned loopCnt __asm("lr") = len

  __asm volatile (
".p2align 2 \n"
" wlstp.32            lr, lr, 1f \n"
```

In this case, LR does not need to be part of the clobbered list.

7.6.3 Native Assembly Language Functions

It is, of course, possible to write functions entirely in assembly language and to call these from C. When writing such functions, it is necessary to be aware of the rules of the Procedure Call Standard for the Arm Architecture. The full document can be accessed on the Arm website.

- Registers Q4–Q7 must be preserved across subroutine calls.

- Registers Q0–Q3 do not need to be preserved (i.e. the caller may need to push and pop them from the stack before and after the function call). These registers may be used to pass arguments or to return results (lowest numbered registers are used first).

- The VPR mask bits must be zero upon entry and exit; the VPR.P0 bits are not required to be preserved.

The C code which calls an assembly language function will need to declare that function using the `extern` keyword, within the C source. The assembly code will be stored within a separate .s file, and must use the `.globl` and `.type` directives to declare itself as a global function.

7.7 Porting DSP Code from Other Architectures

It is not possible to give detailed instructions on porting DSP code, but there are some general guidelines and advice which may be useful. It is usually very helpful if you understand how the original code works: in particular, which algorithms are implemented (and how), and what use (if any) is made of intrinsics and assembly language and DSP-specific features, such as circular buffers.

If your code to be ported is written making use of some standard set of intrinsics (for example, the OpenCV Universal intrinsics, widely used in computer vision), then it should port to Helium in a straightforward manner. Code which is targeted at Arm's Neon SIMD instruction set should also be relatively easy to port to Helium.

In general, the goal should be to end up with C code which the compiler can vectorize. If your code is written in C, any architecture-specific features will need to be removed/replaced and you will then need to look for problems which would prevent such code being vectorized.

In some cases, it may make sense to reimplement the functionality rather than attempt to simply port the code. The choice of the best algorithm for certain tasks depends on the underlying architecture. For example, performing a FFT with higher-radix algorithms, such as radix-8, requires fewer multiplications. In some architectures, it will also improve program speed because of implicit loop-unrolling. On Helium, however, the eight vector registers would require data to spill to memory and this algorithm would be slower than a radix-2 FFT. We'll see in Chapter 9 that CMSIS-DSP Helium FFT versions are based around mixed radix-2/-4 kernels, as radix-4 is well suited to Helium. Similarly, Helium produces best performance when memory operations and arithmetic operations can execute in parallel (beat overlapping) and this may also be a factor in choice of algorithm.

7.8 Helium Low-Level Code

In this section, we'll briefly look at the code required to enable Helium after reset. We'll then consider the effect of Helium on exception handling, including how the hardware deals with interrupting partly-completed instructions and how Helium can affect interrupt latency.

7.8.1 Enabling Helium

The standard Cortex-M System Control Space contains registers for system management, known as the System Control Block (SCB). In order to make use of Helium, the programmer must enable it through writes of these two registers:

- 0xE000ED88 CPACR (Coprocessor Access Control Register)

- 0xE000ED8C NSACR (Non-secure Access Control Register)

The CPACR specifies the access privileges for coprocessors and the Floating-Point Extension (FP Extension). If the CPU implements Helium, it also specifies the access privileges for that. The register can only be accessed from a privileged mode and only by word-sized accesses. There are two banked versions of the register (Secure and Non-secure).

Bits [21:20], which control CP10, are the ones which define the access rights to both the Floating-Point Extension and to Helium. The possible values of this field are:

- 0b00 All accesses to the FP Extension and Helium result in a NOCP UsageFault.

- 0b01 Unprivileged accesses to the FP Extension and Helium result in a NOCP UsageFault.

- 0b11 Full access to the FP Extension and Helium.

So, we can enable Helium by executing code like:

```
#define CPACR (*((volatile unsigned int *)0xE000ED88))
 CPACR = CPACR | (0xF << 20);
```

(The CP11 write is a convention for compatibility purposes and is not strictly required.)

CMSIS core includes definitions for each of the SCB registers. If our boot code is using CMSIS, we could simply write the following line of code to enable Helium:

```
SCB->CPACR |=     ((3U << 10U*2U)|  /* enable CP10 Full Access */
                   (3U << 11U*2U)); /* enable CP11 Full Access */
```

If our system is one which makes use of the Armv8-M Security Extension (TrustZone), we also need to think about the NSACR. This controls the Non-secure access permissions for the FP Extension/Helium and coprocessors CP0 to CP7, and can only be accessed from Secure state. The relevant bits are:

■ CP11, bit [11] CP11 access.

■ CP10, bit [10] CP10 access.

Both bits must be programmed to the same value:

■ 0 – Non-secure accesses to the FP Extension or Helium generate a NOCP UsageFault.

■ 1 – Non-secure accesses to the FP Extension or Helium are permitted.

For Cortex-M55 there is a specific micro-architectural feature which should be enabled by boot code: the low-overhead loop cache is disabled at reset and needs to be enabled to get optimal low-overhead loop performance, by writing a 1 to CCR.LOB (bit 19).

This is done in the Cortex-M55 CMSIS startup code, which can be found at:

https://github.com/ARM-software/CMSIS_5/blob/develop/Device/ARM/ARMCM55/Source/system_ARMCM55.c

7.8.2 Detecting Helium
If code is to be portable between devices, it may be necessary to check at runtime for the presence of Helium on the current hardware. The Media and VFP Feature Register 1 (MVFR1) allows us to do this. Bits [11:8] indicate the level of support, as follows:

■ 0b0000 Helium is not available

■ 0b0001 Helium is available (Integer only)

■ 0b0010 Helium is available (Integer and floating-point)

7.8.3 Exception Handling

Processors which implement the Armv8.1-M architecture support a variety of exceptions, including a set of system exceptions and a set of interrupts, commonly called IRQ. When an exception event takes place and is accepted by the processor core, the corresponding exception handler is executed. A vector table is used to determine the starting address of the exception handler. The vector table is an array of word data in memory, each word representing the starting address of the handler for an exception type.

When an exception takes place, the registers R0–R3, R12, LR, PC, and Program Status (PSR) are automatically pushed onto the stack by CPU hardware. This will either be the Process Stack Pointer (PSP) or the Main Stack Pointer (MSP), depending on the code that was running. The block of eight words of data being pushed to the stack is commonly called a stack frame. The reason these specific registers are stacked is that these are caller-saved registers, according to the Arm Architecture Procedure Call Standard. You may see this referred to as the integer caller-saved section of the stack frame. This automatic stacking reduces interrupt latency and enables extra optimizations like tail chaining. Immediately after stacking, the stack pointer indicates the lowest address in the stack frame. Armv8-M requires that the stack frame is double-word aligned, and the processor will automatically decrement the stack pointer, if necessary, to enforce this.

When using floating-point or Helium code, or if an exception causes a change of security state, the processor might automatically stack additional registers to form an extended stack frame. Recall that the FPU registers are shared with the Helium vector unit. Exactly what is done depends upon the state of a bit in a control register. If CONTROL.FPCA is 1 when the exception is taken, then there are the following possible modes for the floating-point context:

■ Stack the floating-point context.

■ Reserve space on the stack for the floating-point context. This is called "lazy" floating-point context preservation.

When lazy context preservation is selected, the floating-point registers will be pushed onto the stack only when a floating-point (or Helium) instruction is executed by the exception handler. This means that unnecessary memory accesses can be avoided when an exception handler does not require floating-point or Helium code to be executed. The standard Armv8-M exception stack frame format is modified, so that the VPR register is stored in the previously reserved location above FPSCR, as shown in Figure 7.5.

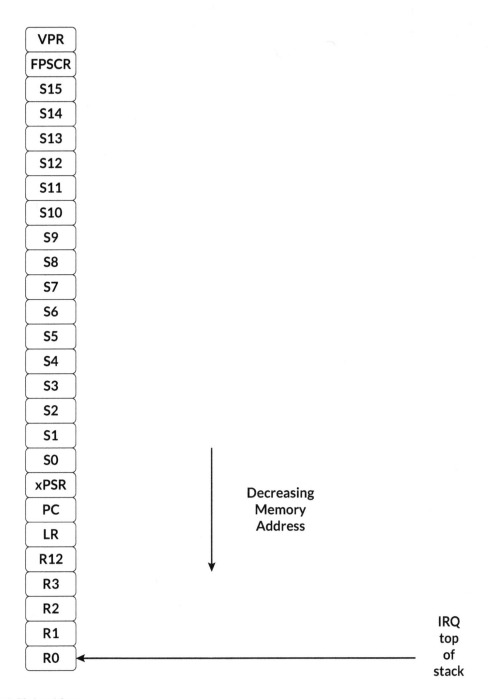

Figure 7.5: Modified stack frame

One complication that Helium creates is that we now have the possibility of exceptions occurring in the middle of the execution of a beat-wise vector instruction. That is, we potentially have multiple partially executed instructions at the point when the exception occurs. The exception return address always points to the oldest incomplete instruction.

The value RETPSR.ECI, stored in the exception stack frame, gives information about how many beats of the instruction at the return address, and how many beats of the subsequent instruction, have already been executed. The field ECI[7:0] is equivalent to EPSR[26:25,11:10,15:12].

The possible values of this field ECI[7:0] are:

0b00000000	No completed beats.
0b00000001	Completed beats: A0.
0b00000010	Completed beats: A0 A1.
0b00000011	Reserved.
0b00000100	Completed beats: A0 A1 A2.
0b00000101	Completed beats: A0 A1 A2 B0.
0b0000011X	Reserved.
0b00001XXX	Reserved.

In the list above, the letters correspond to the instruction at the return address (A) and the instruction after it (B). The numbers show which beats of those instructions have been completed. For example, A0 A1 A2 B0 denotes that the first three beats of the instruction at the return address and the first beat of the instruction which follows it have been completed.

Interrupt Latency

A DSP system must have some ability to respond to external devices. For example, an ADC or other peripheral may use an interrupt signal to indicate to the DSP that action is required. The worst-case time taken for the DSP to respond to that interrupt is called the *interrupt latency* and needs to be considered when calculating the processing power required for a specific sample rate.

Interrupt latency depends upon several factors, which may vary between architectures and may include some or all of the following:

- Time to complete pending memory transactions.

- The length of the instruction pipeline which must be flushed and refilled by the interrupt handler code.

- In systems which use reentrant interrupts (where a higher-priority interrupt is allowed to interrupt a lower-priority handler), the length of time for which further interrupts are disabled.

The Armv8-M architecture includes numerous features (such as automatic stacking, tail chaining, hardware prioritization of interrupts, and preemption) which reduce interrupt latency. Helium provides the ability to implement features such as tight loops without requiring interrupts to be disabled, which can be a significant advantage over stand-alone DSP cores. The ability to interrupt multi-beat instructions and continue them after the exception has been handled means that use of the SIMD/vector capability does not compromise interrupt latency.

7.9 Questions

1. What is CMSIS?

2. What optimization level do we need to specify to the compiler to enable auto-vectorization?

3. What is an intrinsic function?

CHAPTER

Performance and
Optimization

8

In most cases it is useful to have some understanding of the performance of the system. This may be, for example, to improve the user experience, to prove that some real-time constraint is always met, or to reduce power consumption by increasing efficiency. Performance analysis can reveal opportunities to do things better and to prevent problems. It should not be reserved only for when things have gone wrong.

It is important to focus on measuring the performance of the whole system. Although a problem may be seen during the execution of a specific application, it is often the case that the bottleneck causing the problem is located within hardware or software components outside that code. Similarly, performance and optimization work best when carried out as close to the real system as possible.

Most systems spend most of their time executing a relatively small proportion of the total codebase. (Pareto's principle is often quoted in this context, i.e. 20% of code takes 80% of CPU time). Tools therefore need to be used to identify the best places to apply optimization efforts. Profiling tools allow you to identify which pieces of code are executed most frequently and which take the most clock cycles to execute. They may also allow you to identify bottlenecks, where performance is constrained by a particular function. Performance data may be collected through software instrumentation, execution tracing, or time-based sampling. Note that, in some cases, when a slow piece of code has been identified it may be better to consider whether to change the algorithm rather than try to speed up the existing code.

In this chapter, we will look at the hardware and tools available to profile and measure performance of Helium code. We will also cover the effect of the CPU memory system on performance and look at the effects of instruction overlapping on execution cycle counts.

8.1 Profiling Code/Measuring Performance

In order to understand the performance of our code, we need some ability to measure it. This can be as simple as a stopwatch, or `printf()` statements within code, or can be as complex as OS-provided profiling tools or external cycle trace hardware. Arm CPUs which implement Helium include built-in hardware specifically to allow developers to measure performance of code.

There are two main approaches to collecting data. One is to sample the state of the system at a periodic time interval. We can simply record which function is being executed at that moment and build a profile over time. A smaller sampling interval will produce more detailed data but (if the sampling is software-based) may increase execution time. Another approach is to sample based on the occurrence of events. In complex systems, it may be necessary to control profiling information capture to focus on the areas of interest and avoid capture of large amounts of non-useful data. Profiling tools will typically provide information such as a call graph (showing how many times each function was called) and a flat profile (which shows how much runtime was spent in particular functions).

Some Arm Cortex-M CPUs (including Cortex-M3, Cortex-M4 and Cortex-M7) have a DWT (Data Watchpoint and Trace) unit implemented. This provides functionality which includes the ability to count clock cycles and events, such as instruction execution, exceptions etc. This functionality is provided by the PMU (Performance Monitor Unit) on Arm's Cortex-A CPUs. In Cortex-M CPUs, the Power Management Unit is also called the PMU, and so care is needed not to confuse the two. Exactly what features are present in the DWT unit is determined by the CPU implementer.

System timers provide a simple way to benchmark code, particularly in bare-metal systems or where the operating system does not provide any profiling utilities. The programmer can enable the timer with an appropriate instruction, run the code that is to be inspected, and then stop the timer and look at the cycle count information. This simply shows how long the code took to be executed and does not directly show where any performance bottleneck is located.

The trace features provided by the optional Embedded Trace Macrocell (ETM) hardware provide a much greater level of information suitable for benchmarking. They allow high-level profiling of code, for example, providing counts showing how many cycles were spent in each function of the program and finer-grained profiling within those functions. The ETM provides accurate cycle trace data, showing the execution of each instruction. The volume of data it can produce means it requires software tools to be used to control which data is collected and to provide visualization of the results in a form that the programmer can use.

Arm's software solution for performance analysis, which supports the ETM and other hardware, is the Streamline Performance Analyzer. This is primarily aimed at bare-metal and real-time operating system (RTOS) performance analysis. It can be used to locate performance hotspots in the system and to understand what changes can be made to critical code sections and observe the resulting performance effects. It allows power-management frameworks to be improved and supports multi-core systems.

8.1.1 Helium Performance Counters and Ratios
A new feature added to the Arm v8.1-M architecture provides support for PMU features, similar to those found in Cortex-A processors. This is done by extending the profiling counters in the DWT unit. Although the profiling counters are physically the same (and so debug tools cannot use the PMU and legacy DWT features at the same time), they are accessed using different memory addresses. The PMU allows profiling code to perform measurements such as cache hit/miss rates and pipeline stalls.

The PMU provides a noninvasive way to collect CPU execution information, as enabling it does not change execution timing of subsequent code in any way.

The PMU provides a cycle counter which counts the number of execution cycles (there is an optional 1/64 divider). It also provides a set of counters which count occurrences of events. The number of events and the events which can be counted vary between different cores and so it is necessary to consult the Technical Reference Manual for the specific CPU in use, and the Arm Architecture Reference Manual for exact details. Events which can normally be counted include things such as the number of instructions executed, cache hits or misses etc. The PMU can be configured to generate an interrupt on a counter overflow. For example, this can happen if the count is too large for the 32-bit register.

Normally, it is necessary to combine information from multiple counters to generate parameters to be optimized: for example, counting the total number of clock cycles and the total number of instructions executed to generate a clocks per instruction figure, or the total number of memory accesses and number of cache hits to generate a cache hit percentage figure.

The table shows the PMU registers and their associated address and description. CMSIS-Core includes definitions of all of the PMU registers, so that they can be accessed without reference to their fixed memory addresses. There may be up to 30 such registers in the table whose names finish with n (i.e. one register per implemented counter). The addresses of these registers are four bytes apart (i.e. PMU_EVCNTR0 is at 0xE0003000, PMU_EVCNTR1 is at 0xE0003004 and so on).

Address	Name	Type	Description
0xE0003000	PMU_EVCNTRn	RW	PMU Event Counter Register
0xE000307C	PMU_CCNTR	RW	PMU Cycle Counter Register
0xE0003400	PMU_EVTYPERn	RW	PMU Event Type and Filter Register
0xE000347C	PMU_CCFILTR	RW	Reserved, RES0
0xE0003C00	PMU_CNTENSET	RW	PMU Count Enable Set Register
0xE0003C20	PMU_CNTENCLR	RW	PMU Count Enable Clear Register
0xE0003C40	PMU_INTENSET	RW	PMU Interrupt Enable Set Register
0xE0003C60	PMU_INTENCLR	RW	PMU Interrupt Enable Clear Register
0xE0003C80	PMU_OVSCLR	RW	PMU Overflow Flag Status Clear Register
0xE0003CA0	PMU_SWINC	WO	PMU Software Increment Register
0xE0003CC0	PMU_OVSSET	RW	PMU Overflow Flag Status Set Register
0xE0003E00	PMU_TYPE	RO	PMU Type Register
0xE0003E04	PMU_CTRL	RW	PMU Control Register

The PMU_TYPE register is read by software to check what PMU features are available on the current hardware; for example, how many counters there are.

PMU_TYPE (RO, 0xE0003E00)

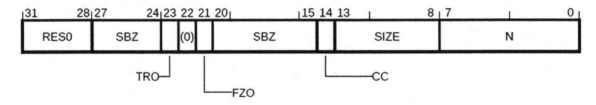

- TRO, bit[23] – Trace-on-overflow support. This bit reads as one.

- FZO, bit[21] – Freeze-on-overflow support. This bit reads as one.

- CC, bit[14] – TCycle counter present. This bit reads as one.

- SIZE, bits[13:8] – Size of counters. This field reads as 0b011111, which indicates PMU_CCNTR and 31 event counters implemented.

- N, bits[7:0] – Number of counters implemented in addition to the cycle counter, PMU_CCNTR. This reads as an IMPLEMENTATION DEFINED value.

The PMU_CTRL register is used by software to reset and enable counters, and to control trace features.

PMU_CTRL (RW, 0xE0003E04)

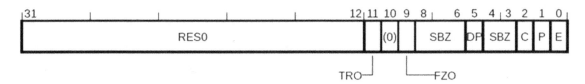

- TRO, bit[11] – Enables Trace-on-overflow. When it is 1, trace is enabled whenever any of the first eight counters overflows an 8-bit value.

- FZO, bit[9] – Enables Freeze-on-overflow. When it is 1 it stops events being counted once PMU_OVSCLR or PMU_OVSSET are non-zero.

- DP, bit[5] – Disable cycle counter when event counting is prohibited. This bit is an alias of the DWT_CTRL.CYCDISS bit.

- C, bit[2] – Cycle counter reset. Reset the PMU_CCNTR counter; does not clear the PMU_CCNTR overflow bit to 0. This bit is write-only, reads as 0.

- P, bit[1] – Reset all event counters, not including PMU_CCNTR, to zero; does not clear any overflow bits to 0. This bit is write-only, reads as 0.

- E, bit[0] – When this bit is 0, all counters, including PMU_CCNTR, are disabled; when 1, all counters are enabled by PMU_CNTENSET.

The PMU_EVCNTR registers are used to access the actual count values.

PMU_EVCNTR

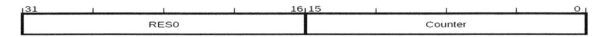

- Counter, bits[15:0] –

  - Event counter n, counts whenever the selected event occurs.

  - Value of event counter n, where n is the number of this register; n is a number in the range 0–30. The size of this counter is 16 bits.

The PMU_EVTYPER registers are used to select which type of event should be counted by each timer. The list of events which can be counted is specific to a particular CPU implementation, but there are certain architecturally mandated events.

PMU_EVTYPER

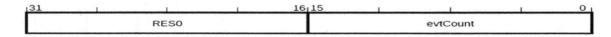

- evtCount, bits[15:0] –

  - Event to Count; the event number of the event that is counted by event counter PMU_EVCNTR<n>.

  - If the associated counter does not support the event number that is written to this register, the value read back is UNKNOWN.

There is a set of PMU Count control registers, which are used to enable or disable individual counters and to control interrupt and overflow behavior. They all have a similar format, with one bit per event counter and bit 31 used to access the cycle counter.

PMU_CNTENSET/PMU_CNTENCLR: Count Enable Set/Clear Registers

- Used to set and clear the enable bit for each counter.

PMU_OVSSET/PMU_OVSCLR: Overflow Flag Status Set/Clear Registers

- The bit representing a counter gets set automatically on overflow.

- To reset you need to write 1 to the bit in order to clear the flag.

PMU_INTENSET/PMU_INTENCLR: Interrupt Enable Set/Clear Registers

- Used to set and clear the overflow interrupt enable bit for each counter.

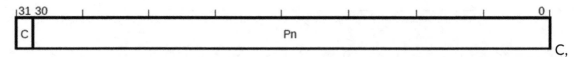

- C, bit[31] – PMU_CCNTR bit.

- Pn, bits[30:0] –

    - Event counter PMU_EVCNTR<n> bit.

    - Bits [30:N] are RAZ/WI, where N is the number of counters and the value of PMU_TYPE.N.

Section B.14.7 of the Armv8.1-M Architecture Reference Manual lists the supported events which can be counted. That list is not reproduced here. Architecture Reference Manual sections B.14.8 and B.14.9 provide more detail on what is being counted by specific events.

There are two sets of distinctions to be aware of. One is that some events are considered "Architectural", which means that they are the same across all implementations. For example, when a particular segment of code is executed the number of instructions executed will be the same, as would the number of branches, number of loads etc. Other events are considered to be "Micro-architectural", which means that they expose implementation-specific details such as the numbers of cache misses or number of clock cycles taken to execute a piece of code.

A further distinction is made between events that a processor is required to implement and events that are optional. For example, a processor that allows speculative execution of vector loads may choose to implement counters for this, but an architecturally compliant implementation is not required to do so. Within the list of required PMU events, there are also certain provisos (e.g. a processor which does not implement a L1 unified or data cache is not required to count how many cache linefills occurred). Individual CPU implementations may also provide their own additional, implementation-specific events.

CMSIS-Core provides support for the PMU. The CMSIS/Core/Include directory has the header files pmu_armv8.h and core_armv811ml.h or core_cm55.h which include the relevant definitions. The user needs to define __PMU_PRESENT and __PMU_NUM_EVENTCNT, which will typically be done in the CMSIS device header file. For example:

```
#define __PMU_PRESENT 1U               /* PMU present */
#define __PMU_NUM_EVENTCNT 31U         /* Number of PMU event counters */
```

The Linux operating system provides kernel tools, such as Perf, which can generate useful data using the PMU counters in more complex systems. In an embedded system we may need to access the counters directly, using the debugger, or by including code in the application which enables the counters and generates results for us. In this example we'll count clock cycles, number of instructions executed, L1 data cache misses and also use the Software increment counter (SW_INCR), using the CMSIS Core PMU functions.

```
   // Initialise counter variables
   unsigned int cycle_count = 0;
   unsigned int l1_dcache_miss_count = 0;
   unsigned int instructions_retired_count = 0;
   unsigned int sw_increment = 0;

   /* Enable the PMU */
   ARM_PMU_Enable();

   /*
    *  Configure Event Counter Reg 0 to count instructions retired
    *  Configure Event Counter Reg 1 to count L1 D-Cache misses
    */

   ARM_PMU_Set_EVTYPER(0, ARM_PMU_INST_RETIRED);
   ARM_PMU_Set_EVTYPER(1, ARM_PMU_L1D_CACHE_MISS_RD);
```

The constants `ARM_PMU_INST_RETIRED` and `ARM_PMU_L1D_CACHE_MISS_RD` specify the numbers corresponding to the event that we wish to count. Their values (0x8 and 0x39 respectively) are defined in CMSIS Core. Now that we have the counters set up, we can proceed to use them. Before running the code that we wish to benchmark, we reset the counters to zero and tell them to start counting.

```
   // Reset Event Counters and Cycle Counter
   ARM_PMU_EVCNTR_ALL_Reset();
   ARM_PMU_CYCCNT_Reset();

   // Start incrementing Cycle Count Register
   // and Event Counter Registers 0, 1, & 2

ARM_PMU_CNTR_Enable(PMU_CNTENSET_CCNTR_ENABLE_Msk|PMU_CNTENSET_CNT0_ENABLE_Msk|PMU_
CNTENSET_CNT1_ENABLE_Msk|PMU_CNTENSET_CNT2_ENABLE_Msk);
```

We can now execute the code to be profiled or benchmarked. After this is done, we need to stop the counters from incrementing and read the results from the PMU.

```
   /*
       Run whatever code here you want to profile/measure/benchmark
   */

   // Stop incrementing Cycle Count Register and
   // Event Counter Registers 0 & 1

ARM_PMU_CNTR_Disable(PMU_CNTENCLR_CCNTR_ENABLE_Msk|PMU_CNTENSET_CNT0_ENABLE_Msk|PMU_
CNTENSET_CNT1_ENABLE_Msk);

   // Increment Event Counter Register 2

   ARM_PMU_CNTR_Increment(PMU_SWINC_CNT2_Msk);

   // Get cycle count, number of instructions retired,
   // number of L1 D-Cache misses (on read), and how many times
   // software has manually incremented event counter 2

   cycle_count = cycle_count + ARM_PMU_Get_CCNTR();

   instructions_retired_count = instructions_retired_count + ARM_PMU_Get_EVCNTR(0);
```

```
l1_dcache_miss_count = l1_dcache_miss_count + ARM_PMU_Get_EVCNTR(1);

sw_increment = sw_increment + ARM_PMU_Get_EVCNTR(2);
```

Section B.4.10 of the Architecture Reference Manual lists the counters which the PMU is required to support. These generic event types provide a great deal of useful information and we can rely on their presence, so we will look at them in closer detail.

The cycle counter is, perhaps, the most common starting point for measurements. Normally, we want to know how many cycles were required to execute a particular piece of code. Looking at cycle counts lets us identify where our program is spending most of its time and where optimization effort is most likely to be productive. By itself, however, it may not provide very much information about *why* something is happening.

Event type 0x000 is called SW_INCR. This is a software-controlled counter (and so unlike most of the other counters, it is not strictly noninvasive, as it requires some code changes to be used). Software running on the processor can increment the counter by writing to the PMU_SWINC register. It is up to the programmer to decide how to use it. It might be used to count frames of data processed, or a specific error condition occurring, for example.

The event types 0x023 (STALL_FRONTEND) and 0x024 (STALL_BACKEND) can be useful to count occasions where no operation was issued. This can indicate code locations where the instructions per clock figure is lower than expected and where there may be scope for optimization.

We will briefly look at cache-related performance issues in Section 8.3.1. Events 0x003 (L1D_CACHE_REFILL) and 0x004 (L1D_CACHE) provide a powerful mechanism for optimizing cache performance of code. By combining these measures (numbers of cache accesses and cache linefills), we can focus on cache hit/miss rates associated with code and data structures in memory.

There are two mandatory events which relate specifically to Helium code. Event 0x200 (MVE_INST_RETIRED) allows us to count the number of Helium instructions executed. Event 0x201 (MVE_LDST_RETIRED) lets us count Helium loads and stores.

There are many optionally implemented events which (if present) can be used to give much finer detail about the causes of performance issues in Helium code. For example, event 0x2CC (MVE_STALL) counts stall cycles caused by a Helium instruction. There are further events which give more detail to point toward the possible problem, for example, event 0x2D4 (MVE_STALL_DEPENDENCY) counts stalls caused by a Helium register dependency, where one instruction is stalled waiting for a register used in a previous instruction to become available.

Ratios of counter values can also be useful. We might, for example, want to look at the ratio of loads and stores (by counting MVE_LDST_RETIRED, which gives the total number of Helium loads and stores, along with MVE_LD_RETIRED, which counts just Helium loads). Similarly, we could look at MVE_LD_CONTIG_RETIRED/MVE_LD_RETIRED to measure the number of contiguous loads relative to the total number of loads.

8.1.2 Embedded Trace Macrocell

Cortex-M microcontrollers include a wide range of debug features. An external debugger can be connected to the chip using a JTAG or single wire interface. Often, this is done through a debug adapter device (such as the Keil ULINK2), which plugs into a USB port on the computer running the debugger. This allows us to download code to the device, start and stop program execution, step through code line by line and set breakpoints so that execution stops at a chosen line of code. We can also examine and change memory and processor registers and create watchpoints (causing the processor to stop when a certain memory location or peripheral is accessed). Many Cortex-M microcontrollers also provide trace, allowing real-time collection of information from the code, which can include execution history of the entire program, tracing of certain data values etc. This can be an important feature when trying to debug problems which are related to the interactions of real-time events, or where stopping code execution for debug purposes may not be feasible (for example, motor control applications). The exact features included in a device are configured by the hardware designer.

In order to debug code containing Helium instructions it will be necessary to use debug tools which are aware of the new instructions, special registers etc. It is likely that a debugger used for previous Cortex-M devices would need to be upgraded to a newer software version.

8.2 Performance Considerations

There are some general considerations which apply when analyzing benchmark results or profiling code on Arm CPUs. As Helium is likely to be deployed in performance-sensitive areas, it is more likely that such code will be profiled and so it makes sense to start with simple things to consider, which include:

- **System Configuration** – Many Arm CPUs include hardware which is disabled by default after reset, but which can significantly affect performance. For example, it may be necessary for boot code to enable Caches, the Memory Prediction Unit or features such as branch prediction. If these are turned off, then cycle counts may be significantly higher. If the system is profiled in a different configuration to that of the final target, misleading results may be obtained.

- **Bare metal versus operating system (OS)** – Benchmarking or profiling small code segments stand-alone may produce misleading results when compared with running the same code under an OS. For example, interrupt handling may cause changes to the contents of caches that can significantly affect cycle timing compared to profiling the same code with exceptions disabled.

- **Use of semi-hosting library function calls** – During the initial development phase, the programmer may use standard C functions (for example, `printf()` or file i/o) which may not be used in the final design, or which have not yet been ported to the target. These are handled by the debugger and may take many thousands of extra cycles to execute. Benchmarking code with these in place may give very misleading results.

It is also important to consider the status of the system being used for benchmarking/profiling. Obviously, the final production hardware will give the best, most accurate results. However, it is likely to be available late in the development period and, in most cases, it would be desirable to have measured code performance before this point. In some cases, there may be a development board available which is based on the microcontroller design that will be used in the final product. This may be lacking some features or peripherals or may not have an identical memory map, but may well be sufficiently close to the final device to provide useful results. Using such a board can be a good way to perform benchmarking before the production device is available.

8.3 Performance and the Cortex-M Memory System

Programmers creating optimized Helium code for their system need to be aware of the effect the memory system can have on performance. The numbers of cycles taken to read data from memory (or write data to memory) can have a very significant impact. In some systems, external memories may add significant numbers of "wait states", meaning that access will be slow. Therefore, placement of data and code within the system becomes important.

Many Cortex-M based microcontroller devices support the use of caches and/or internal Tightly-Coupled Memory (TCM) (areas of memory-mapped, dedicated RAM local to the processor), which can give significantly faster access times than external memory, and so understanding of the correct usage of these can be important. Processors which implement the Armv8.1-M architecture have a range of options for memory system implementation. There may be no cache, a unified cache, or separate (Harvard) instruction and/or data caches. Similarly, there may be one or more areas of TCM. There may also be an MPU which handles both the instructions responsible for checking address access permissions and memory attributes for all accesses.

8.3.1 Cache

A cache is a small, fast memory typically located between the CPU and main memory. It holds copies of instructions and data that are stored in external memory. Its advantage is that cache accesses happen faster (take fewer clock cycles) than accesses to main memory. A cache holds only a portion of the contents of main memory, and so it stores both the address of the item in main memory and the associated data. When the CPU needs to access a specific address, it will first look for it in the cache. If it finds the address in the cache, it will use the cached data instead of attempting an external memory access. This technique can significantly improve the overall system performance by providing much faster access to code and data. It can also reduce the overall system energy requirement by reducing the number of external memory accesses.

Only certain Cortex-M CPUs have the option of implementing caches. Although the cache size is small relative to the amount of memory in some systems, it may be orders of magnitude larger in comparison with the CPU itself. Therefore, adding a cache can be relatively expensive on small microcontroller devices. In addition, a cache will only improve performance when the memory system is relatively slow in comparison to the CPU. For many Cortex-M systems, it is possible to operate memory at similar clock speeds to the processor and a cache may have little benefit. A further drawback of caches is that program execution time can be non-deterministic. As the cache holds only a subset of the contents of main memory, it is not typically possible for an application to be sure that the instruction or data from a specific address is to be found in the cache. This means that the execution time of a piece of code can vary significantly from one time to the next.

The cache architecture is usually Harvard, that is, only instructions can be fetched from the instruction cache, and only data can be read from and written to the data cache. However, it is also possible to implement unified caches (which hold both instructions and data).

Caches only benefit execution times when a program reuses the same addresses over time (temporal locality) and when it uses instructions or data that are close together in memory. Both of these things will generally be true for DSP and ML functions using Helium. As we will see, such code tends to rely heavily on loops, meaning that the same code is executed repeatedly. Furthermore, access to data is often repeated and/or sequential. For these reasons, we typically see that such algorithms do run faster when able to make use of caches. Even when caches are not in use, close attention to the layout of data in memory can significantly improve performance.

One consequence of cache usage is that an application cannot normally rely on a particular code segment or a piece of data being resident in the cache. (Even if the program itself uses the cache deterministically, the behavior of interrupt handlers may modify the cache contents.) Therefore, execution times of code may vary significantly, and in seemingly non-deterministic ways. Modifying code may move it in memory and may change cache behavior. Similarly, changing the location of data buffers may change the cache behavior and the timing of code. It is important to be aware of these effects when tuning for performance. For example, the cycle timing of code run on "bare metal" may differ from that under an OS, because of cache effects. Similarly, enabling or disabling interrupts while profiling code may change the cache behavior.

In general, best performance is obtained by enabling cache and using cache wherever possible. Ensuring that critical code segments and their data fit within the cache will produce best performance. This might mean placing frequently accessed data close together in memory. As fetching a data value from memory means reading a whole line of data, best performance is obtained by accessing data in a sequential manner. For example, code which accesses rows of data in an array may execute faster than code which accesses columns. Sparse arrays may use cache less efficiently than packed arrays.

The Performance Monitors are able to generate cache hit rates, the number of cache hits divided by the number of memory requests during execution of a particular piece of code. Miss rates can be measured similarly, and one may also be able to calculate hit or miss rates on code, data reads, and data writes separately.

When dealing with arrays which are large in comparison to the cache size, it may be useful to consider rewriting code to use loop tiling. For example, if calculating a large matrix by vector multiplication, where we have to multiply each element in each array with each element in the other array, a simple implementation would proceed in a way in which one array is accessed row-wise (resulting in good cache performance) but the other is accessed column-wise, ensuring that there will usually be a cache miss on each multiply. By refactoring the code to use more loops and more sequential accesses, better performance will be achieved.

8.3.2 Tightly-Coupled Memory

Tightly-Coupled Memory (TCM) is an area of memory connected directly to the processor via a dedicated interface. It typically provides single-cycle access, avoiding arbitration delays and latency that may exist for other memories. Unlike a cache, it is memory mapped, and it is the responsibility of the system designer to statically map and place specific code segments and/or important data into the TCM. It might be used, for example, to hold exception vectors, or interrupt service routines, or time-critical control loops which require deterministic execution times. Unlike cache, the TCM provides fast memory access without a loss of determinism.

Only certain Cortex-M processors have the option of including TCM. This is typically available as an instruction TCM (which also supports data access to literal data embedded within code) and/or a data TCM (which can only hold data). On those processors which support TCM, their size (and whether the TCM is present) is determined by the implementer of the microcontroller and so this will differ between devices. In some cases, there may be more than one "bank" of TCM, or the interface may be wider than 32-bits, allowing multiple instructions or data items to be accessed per cycle. Some processors include support for direct access to the TCM through a dedicated interface. This allows a direct memory access (DMA) to move data into the TCM for use by the processor. For performance reasons, it is common to place frequently used data in the TCM, using a linker script.

8.4 Performance Considerations for Dual-Beat Micro-Architectures

All modern processor implementations make use of hardware pipelining, so that the processor can achieve greater instruction throughput. It means that on the same hardware clock cycle, a processor with a simple three-stage pipeline might be fetching one instruction from memory, decoding another instruction and executing another. Normally, this is completely transparent to the programmer.

In a Cortex-M processor which implements Helium, the Helium instructions are fetched normally with other non-Helium instructions, and there will be a common pipeline stage which decodes all instructions. However, each processor implementation may have a different pipeline to execute Helium instructions. It may be that some processors are able to dual-issue Helium instructions, some may have a dedicated load/store path to memory for Helium, and so on.

As we saw earlier in the book, the architecture permits instructions to proceed beat-wise. This means that 128-bit wide Helium operations can be carried out over multiple cycles. The implementation is permitted to overlap these instructions, so that, for example, vector loads and ALU operations may be performed in parallel. The CPU micro-architecture will typically have multiple parallel execution units for Helium. The precise detail of this will differ between implementations but, for example, we might have separate execution pipelines for floating-point/multiply operations, vector integer operations and load/store instructions. A consequence of this is that interleaved instructions from different groups will execute faster than repeated instructions using the same pipeline. By reordering instructions within inner loops, it may be possible to achieve better performance. Normally, we would expect the C compiler to be aware of such effects and to schedule instructions accordingly, but it can be useful to understand this behavior when using intrinsics, or when looking at compiler output.

For example, the sequence:

```
VLDRW
VLDRW
VMLA
VMLA
```

will typically be slower than when the same instructions are interleaved, for example:

```
VLDRW
VMLA
VLDRW
VMLA
```

Best performance is likely to be obtained by avoiding consecutive load/stores or consecutive ALU (or multiplier) operations. It is usually better to alternate between these.

In general, it is usually better to avoid mixing vector and scalar instructions, but we may be able to improve performance by inserting scalar instructions which do not have a dependency on preceding vector instructions between two vector operations of the same type (for example, between two VLDRs).

Instruction latencies can differ between CPU implementations (and may not always be given in documentation). Cycle delays may occur because of register dependencies between successive instructions stalling the processor or preventing the overlap of vector instructions. This can happen where values are moved between scalar and vector registers (for example, loading a value from memory into a scalar register and then using that scalar register as an input to a following vector instruction).

Generating a scatter/gather offset using VIDUP or VDDUP has some latency in Cortex-M55 and so better performance is achieved if this is done two or more instructions earlier than the actual load or store.

8.5 Performance Example

We will look at some code which takes two arrays of complex numbers, multiplies each complex vector by another complex vector and generates an array containing the complex number results. The data in the complex arrays is stored in an interleaved fashion (real, imaginary, real, imaginary etc.). The parameter numSamples represents the number of complex samples processed.

The basic algorithm is easy to understand. For each pair of complex numbers $(a + bi)$ and $(x + yi)$, we will calculate $(ax - by) + (ay + bx)i$. The simple, unvectorized C code looks like this:

```
for (n = 0; n < numSamples; n++) {

    pDst[(2*n)+0] = pSrcA[(2*n)+0] * pSrcB[(2*n)+0] - pSrcA[(2*n)+1] * pSrcB[(2*n)+1];

    pDst[(2*n)+1] = pSrcA[(2*n)+0] * pSrcB[(2*n)+1] + pSrcA[(2*n)+1] * pSrcB[(2*n)+0];
}
```

where pSrcA points to the first input array, pSrcB points to the second input array, pDst gives the location to write the outputs, and numSamples gives the number of samples in each array.

The C compiler is able to vectorize this code. It produces an inner loop which commences with four VLDRW.32 instructions, loading four vector registers, each containing four floating-point values. In total, 16 floating-point values are in the vector registers, representing eight complex numbers. Each loop iteration performs four VMUL instructions, a VSUB and a VADD (representing the *ax – by* and *ay + bx* calculations). We then have two VSTR instructions to write out the results.

However, the total size of the inner loop is 41 instructions and the total sequence takes 51 cycles to execute on Cortex-M55. This is because the second line of the function requires us to multiply elements which are not in the same lanes within the vectors (we need to multiply the real components, in even-numbered array locations, by imaginary components, in odd-numbered array locations). This requires 29 VMOV instructions to reorder data (some can be of 64-bit size, others are 32-bit).

Let us assume that profiling shows that this function is a bottleneck in our system and that it is worth optimizing its speed. We can optimize this code by reimplementing it using Helium intrinsic functions.

We can read 128-bits of data using the vldrwq_f32 intrinsic. We do that twice per iteration, to read data from pSrcA and data from pSrcB. The data that is held in the two Helium registers is interleaved.

By using the vcmulq intrinsic, with no rotation, we multiply the odd lanes of the first input by the corresponding even component from the second vector. We then write the results to the odd lanes of the output register. Next we multiply the even lanes of the first vector by the corresponding even lanes of the second vector and write those results to the even lanes of the output register.

We then use the vcmlaq_rot90 intrinsic. This performs a complex multiply and accumulate. We will accumulate onto the values calculated in the previous step, in vecDst. For the imaginary values, we must add the result of the multiplication onto the previous value, as the imaginary component of $(a + bi) \times (x + yi)$ is $ay + bx$. For the real component, the instruction will flip the sign bit when performing the second multiply, so that the result is $ax - by$.

Finally, we can use the intrinsic vstrwq_f32 to write the output vector to memory.

The resulting code looks like this:

```
void arm_cmplx_mult_f32 (float32_t * pSrcA, float32_t * pSrcB, float32_t * pDst, uint32_t
blockSize)
    {
    uint32_t blkCnt;
    float32x4_t vecA, vecB, vecDst;
    blkCnt = blockSize >>2;
    while (blkCnt > 0U)
        {
        vecA = vldrwq_f32(pSrcA);
        vecB = vldrwq_f32(pSrcB);
        vecDst = vcmulq(vecA, vecB);
        vecDst = vcmlaq_rot90(vecDst, vecA, vecB);
        vstrwq_f32(pDst, vecDst);
        blkCnt--;
        pSrcA +=4;
        pSrcB +=4;
        pDst +=4;
        }
    }
```

Now, our inner loop has nine instructions. The disassembly is as follows:

```
VLDRW.U32      Q0, [R0]
VLDRW.U32      Q1, [R1]
VCMUL.F32      Q2, Q1,Q0,#0
VCMLA.F32      Q2, Q1,Q0,#0x5a
VSTRW.32       Q2, [R2]
ADDS           R2, R2,#0x10
ADDS           R1, R1,#0x10
ADDS           R0, R0,#0x10
LE             LR, #-0x1e
```

We can remove three instructions (and four clock cycles per loop) by removing the ADD instructions and making use of the post-incrementing VLDR instruction variant. This means that we would need to write VLDRW.U32 Q0, [R0],16 and so on. It is highly likely that a future compiler update will be able to automatically perform this optimization itself.

We can do this by creating an assembly language function. The function now looks like this:

```
    PUSH        {LR}
    WLSTP.32    LR, R3, loop_end
start:
    VLDRW.32    Q0, [R1],#16
    VLDRW.32    Q1, [R0],#16
    VCMUL.F32   Q2, Q1, Q0, #0
    VCMLA.F32   Q2, Q1, Q0, #90
    VSTRW.32    Q2, [R2]
loop_end:
    LE          LR, start
    POP         {pc}
```

Using the cycle counters (and the Cortex-M55 counters for pipeline stalls), we can see that there is still scope for improvement. The loop takes eight cycles to execute and calculates four complex multiplies. There are two vector loads followed by two complex multiplies. The two loads will use the same pipeline (and so cause a stall), and the two multiplies will use the same pipeline (and so cause a stall). The code performance could be improved if we could interleave these instructions, as we saw in the previous section. We can therefore optimize this still further, if required.

As the complex multiply needs both inputs in order to operate, we cannot simply swap the order of the instructions. Instead, we need to schedule the loads earlier. We can do this by using a generic technique called load scheduling by preloading and unrolling. This is not Helium-specific but is worth understanding as it is often useful.

Simple code may contain a loop for which the pseudocode looks like this:

```
[loop with counter i]
{
[load data for iteration i]
[do work for iteration i]
}
```

We modify this code into a functionally equivalent form which looks like this:

```
[load data for iteration 0]
[loop with counter i]
{
    [load data for iteration i+1 to temp]
    [do work for iteration i
    [set data for next iteration = temp]
}
```

We can hide memory latency by unrolling the loop and overlapping the work for iteration i with the loading for iteration i + 1.

To apply this to our case, we need to use an extra vector register and to unroll the loop so that we have two pairs of vector loads and two pairs of vector complex multiplies within each iteration.

```
        VLDRW.32    Q0, [R1],16        // these initial loads needed
        VLDRW.32    Q1, [R0],16        // for first loop iteration
        WLS         LR, R3, loop_end   // R3 is already shifted to
                                       // give correct number of loops
    start:
        VCMUL.F32   Q2, Q0, Q1, #0
        VLDRW.32    Q3, [R1],16
        VCMLA.F32   Q2, Q0, Q1, #90
        VLDRW.32    Q1, [R0],16
        VSTRW.32    Q2, [R2],16
        VCMUL.F32   Q2, Q3, Q1, #0
        VLDRW.32    Q0, [R1],16
        VCMLA.F32   Q2, Q3, Q1, #90
```

```
        VLDRW.32    Q1, [R0],16
        VSTRW.32    Q2, [R2],16
          LE        LR, start
    loop_end:
```

The inner loop now takes 12 cycles to execute 10 instructions (on Cortex-M55). Each loop is performing twice as many operations as the previous code, so this is an improvement. We are performing four 128-bit loads and four 128-bit multiplies in the loop, giving eight complex floating-point multiplies per iteration. On Cortex-M55, there is still a stall of two cycles because of the two instances of VLDRW followed by VSTRW, but this cannot be avoided. Other Armv8.1-M CPU implementations might not show this behavior. The cycle counter shows that this code performs around seven times faster than our original auto-vectorized C code.

8.6 Questions

1. What is the function of the PMU?

2. Why might we get different results from profiling code on bare-metal compared with running the same code with an OS?

3. Is it always the case that interleaving vector load and vector arithmetic instructions will improve performance?

CHAPTER
DSP Fundamentals

9

In this chapter, we will look at two common DSP operations, matrix multiplication and transposition, and FFT. This is not a DSP textbook, and we will assume that readers are familiar with the basic concepts of these methods. We will, however, have a brief reminder of the basics of each operation before looking at how Helium features can be used to obtain fast, efficient implementations. Throughout this and the following chapter, we will use the code in the CMSIS-DSP library as a reference. In most cases, the programmer should be able to use this library code without the need to look too closely at the low-level operation.

9.1 Matrix Operations

Many signal and image processing algorithms rely on the efficient implementation of a set of basic matrix primitives, including matrix and vector multiplication, matrix transposition and matrix inversion. Here, we'll see how Helium features allow significant speedup of these operations.

9.1.1 Matrix Multiplication

In earlier chapters we have shown several code segments which calculate dot products of two input arrays. These are, in effect, multiplying together two input vectors, with each value in one vector being multiplied by the corresponding data from the other input vector and the result being added to the accumulator.

Often, we are dealing with data in a two-dimensional matrix. For example, in machine learning algorithms, a common requirement is to calculate the dot product of a matrix and a vector, or of two matrices. As we shall see in Chapter 12, ML algorithms might only need to use 8-bit accuracy. Our example will therefore use data in Q7 format. For simplicity, we'll look at the matrix–vector product, although the principles are the same for multiplying two matrices.

Before we look at some code, let's consider how a matrix–vector product is calculated.

Let's assume we have a matrix A and a vector V. The number of columns in A must equal the number of rows in V. In other words, if A is an m × n matrix, the product A.V is defined only when V is an n × 1 column vector. The product will itself be an m × 1 column vector (i.e. the number of rows in the input matrix is equal to the number of rows in the output).

The calculation is of the following general form:

$$A.V = \begin{bmatrix} a_{11} & a_{12} & \cdots & a_{1n} \\ a_{21} & a_{22} & \cdots & a_{2n} \\ \cdots & \cdots & \cdots & \cdots \\ a_{m1} & a_{m2} & \cdots & a_{mn} \end{bmatrix} \begin{bmatrix} v_1 \\ v_2 \\ \cdots \\ v_n \end{bmatrix} = \begin{bmatrix} a_{11} \cdot v_1 + a_{12} \cdot v_2 + \cdots + a_{1n} \cdot v_n \\ a_{21} \cdot v_1 + a_{22} \cdot v_2 + \cdots + a_{2n} \cdot v_n \\ \cdots \\ a_{m1} \cdot v_1 + a_{m2} \cdot v_2 + \cdots + a_{mn} \cdot v_n \end{bmatrix}$$

It can be seen that to calculate each row of the product vector simply involves a set of multiply accumulate operations. We proceed along each row of the matrix, load the data into a Q register, load the corresponding columns from the vector into another Q register and then use one of the vector multiply accumulate instructions to perform the calculation. When dealing with Q7 data we can fit 16 values into a register, so a significant amount of parallelization is possible. Furthermore, rather than calculating one row at a time we can load several rows at once. Each will use the same vector columns for the multiply. Here, we will show only the parts of the function which are relevant to Helium, so function and variable declarations are omitted.

The first part of the code will initialize pointers to the first four rows of the input matrix and the column vector, and zero four accumulators.

```
pMat0 = pMatSrc; pMat1 = pMat0 + numCols;
pMat2 = pMat1 + numCols; pMat3 = pMat2 + numCols;
pVec = pVecSrc;

acc0 = 0L; acc1 = 0L; acc2 = 0L; acc3 = 0L;
```

Our inner loop will then load 16 bytes from matrix rows 0, 1, 2 and 3 into four vector registers, and 16 bytes from the column vector into a further register, using the vldrbq_s8 intrinsic function. We can then use the vmladavaq intrinsic (Multiply Add Dual Accumulate Across Vector) to perform 16 multiplies of Q7 fixed-point matrix values with their corresponding element from the column vector and accumulate the products. Note that we don't need to specify the size of the vmladavaq intrinsic, as the compiler knows that we are dealing with .s8 data. We do this for each of the four rows. We then update the pointers for the next items in the current rows of the matrix and do the same for the pointer into the column vector.

```
blkCnt = numCol >> 4;
while (blkCnt > 0U) {
      vecMatA0 = vldrbq_s8(pMat0);
      vecMatA1 = vldrbq_s8(pMat1);
      vecMatA2 = vldrbq_s8(pMat2);
      vecMatA3 = vldrbq_s8(pMat3);
      vecIn = vldrbq_s8(pVec, 0);
      acc0 = vmladavaq(acc0, vecIn, vecMatA0);
      acc1 = vmladavaq(acc1, vecIn, vecMatA1);
      acc2 = vmladavaq(acc2, vecIn, vecMatA2);
      acc3 = vmladavaq(acc3, vecIn, vecMatA3);

      pMat0 += 16; pMat1 += 16;
      pMat2 += 16; pMat3 += 16;
      pVec += 16;
      blkCnt--;
}
```

It can be seen that the code has been unrolled to perform four accumulations per iteration. This is done to mitigate the cost of the back-to-back loads of the matrix rows and vector. If we have only one accumulator, there are two vldrbq and a vmladava, requiring four cycles. If we unroll the loop for two accumulators, we need one vldrbq for the vector and two for the matrix rows and then two vmladava intrinsics, requiring six cycles (and so three cycles for each accumulator). If we unroll the lovslcop for four accumulators, we need one vldrbq for the vector and four for the matrix rows and four vmladava intrinsics, requiring ten cycles in total (and so 2.5 cycles for each accumulator).

Once the calculation has been performed for all of the columns in the input matrix, we can shift and saturate the results back to Q7 values and write the output to the destination vector. We then update the pointer for the next four rows in the input matrix and go around again. The __SSAT() function used here is an inline function defined in CMSIS which does a signed saturation to the specified number of bits – eight here.

```
*pDst++ =  __SSAT(acc0 >> 7, 8);
*pDst++ =  __SSAT(acc1 >> 7, 8);
*pDst++ =  __SSAT(acc2 >> 7, 8);
*pDst++ =  __SSAT(acc3 >> 7, 8);
pMatSrc += numCols * 4;
```

Our inner loop is able to perform 64 multiply accumulates per iteration, representing a very significant speedup over scalar code. This is one of several key features of Helium technology that opens up a new set of possibilities for implementing machine learning neural network algorithms on small microcontrollers.

The CMSIS-DSP library contains a number of matrix functions. For example, multiplication of matrices of Q15 fixed-point data by the function `arm_mat_mult_q15()` is done on Helium in a similar fashion to the above example, with special optimized versions for multiplication of 2×2, 3×3 and 4×4 square matrices. The code can be seen here:

https://github.com/ARM-software/CMSIS_5/blob/master/CMSIS/DSP/Source/MatrixFunctions/arm_mat_mult_q15.c

9.1.2 Matrix Transposition

In the above code, we saw how the VMLADAVA instruction allows us to parallelize the multiplications in matrix operations. In addition to this, Helium load/store features allows us to perform efficient transposition of matrices.

Consider a 4×4 square matrix:

$$\begin{bmatrix} a_{11} & a_{12} & a_{13} & a_{14} \\ a_{21} & a_{22} & a_{23} & a_{24} \\ a_{31} & a_{32} & a_{33} & a_{34} \\ a_{41} & a_{42} & a_{43} & a_{44} \end{bmatrix}$$

The transposition of this requires us to rearrange the rows and columns of the matrix, as follows:

$$\begin{bmatrix} a_{11} & a_{21} & a_{31} & a_{41} \\ a_{12} & a_{22} & a_{32} & a_{42} \\ a_{13} & a_{23} & a_{33} & a_{43} \\ a_{14} & a_{24} & a_{34} & a_{44} \end{bmatrix}$$

Our original matrix is stored as 16 sequential items in memory. If, for example, we have 32-bit data (integer, Q31 fixed-point, or single-precision floating-point), we can use the deinterleaving operations to load these 16 items into four Helium registers (using VLD4) and then four VSTR operations to write out the transposed results. A code fragment to do this might look like this:

```
uint32x4x4_t vecIn;
vecIn = vld4q((uint32_t const *) pSrc);
vstrwq(pDst, vecIn.val[0]);
pDst += 4;
vstrwq(pDst, vecIn.val[1]);
pDst += 4;
vstrwq(pDst, vecIn.val[2]);
pDst += 4;
vstrwq(pDst, vecIn.val[3]);
```

This works because we have an instruction for deinterleaving by 4. For a 3×3 matrix transposition, we have to tackle things differently. A 3×3 matrix like this:

$$\begin{bmatrix} a_{11} & a_{12} & a_{13} \\ a_{21} & a_{22} & a_{23} \\ a_{31} & a_{32} & a_{33} \end{bmatrix}$$

will produce the following when transposed:

$$\begin{bmatrix} a_{11} & a_{21} & a_{31} \\ a_{12} & a_{22} & a_{32} \\ a_{13} & a_{23} & a_{33} \end{bmatrix}$$

If we consider the layout of the array in memory, our original array has $a_{11}, a_{12}, a_{13}, a_{21}, a_{22}, a_{23}, a_{31}, a_{32}$ and finally a_{33}. We need to copy those nine items to produce a transposed array in the order $a_{11}, a_{21}, a_{31}, a_{12}, a_{22}, a_{32}, a_{13}, a_{23}$ and finally a_{33}. We can do this (again, assuming 32-bit array elements) by simply loading the first eight elements with a pair of VLDR instructions and then using a scatter-store with hard-coded offsets to produce a very efficient transpose operation. The final (ninth) element can simply be copied across at the end. An example code fragment looks like this:

```
const uint32x4_t vecOffset1 = {0, 3, 6, 1};
const uint32x4_t vecOffset2 = {4, 7, 2, 5};

uint32x4_t vecIn1 = vldrwq_u32((uint32_t const *) pSrc);
uint32x4_t vecIn2 = vldrwq_u32((uint32_t const *) &pSrc[4]);

vstrwq_scatter_shifted_offset_u32(pDst, vecOffset1, vecIn1);
vstrwq_scatter_shifted_offset_u32(pDst, vecOffset2, vecIn2);

pDst[8] = pSrc[8];
```

9.2 Fourier Transform

The FFT is a widely used DSP operation. In this section, we briefly review the fundamentals of Fourier transforms and their implementation in software using the FFT algorithm. We then look at the FFT example provided in the open source CMSIS-DSP library and see how Helium features, including bit-reversal instructions and scatter-gather loads and stores, are used.

9.2.1 Introduction to Fourier Transforms

The discrete Fourier transform (DFT) transforms a finite, discrete, time-domain sequence into a finite, discrete, frequency-domain representation. The DFT transforms N complex time-domain samples into N complex frequency-domain values.

The N-point complex DFT of a discrete-time signal $x(n)$ is described by:

$$X(k) = \sum_{n=0}^{N-1} x(n) W_N^{kn}$$

evaluated for $0 \le k < N$,

where the constants W are called twiddle factors $W_N = e^{(-j2\pi n/N)}$

The inverse DFT is described by:

$$x(n) = \frac{1}{N} \sum_{k=0}^{N-1} X(k) W_N^{-nk}$$

As calculating all N values means producing N-squared product terms, each of which is a multiplication of complex numbers, DFT can be computationally intensive for large values of N.

9.2.2 The Fast Fourier Transform

The FFT is a computationally efficient algorithm for computing a DFT. It is widely used in DSP and the terms DFT and FFT can be considered as near synonyms. It works by decomposing a large DFT into a number of smaller DFTs. At each stage of processing, the results of the previous stage are combined. This part of the computation that combines the results of smaller DFTs into a larger DFT (or vice versa) is called a butterfly. This process continues until we have a DFT of size 2, which is a simple calculation. The one-point DFT of a single sample is equal to that sample itself.

The size used by an FFT decomposition is called a radix. For example, if we have a DFT of size N and use a radix-2 approach, we can take the DFT of the first $N/2$ points and a DFT of the second $N/2$ points and combine them to produce the result. Each of the $N/2$ point DFTs can themselves be performed by calculation using smaller DFTs, in the same way. So, the algorithm proceeds by calculating $N/2$ 2-point DFTs, combining these to form $N/4$ 4-point DFTs, then $N/8$ 8-point DFTs etc., until the desired single N-point DFT is produced.

Other radices may be used, with radix-4 and radix-8 being common. Sometimes mixed-radix FFTs are used – for example, a 1000-point FFT might be performed using stages of radix-2 and radix-5.

It is not normally necessary to implement the FFT yourself. There are many standard implementations available in C or other high-level languages and an optimized set of FFT functions is provided in CMSIS-DSP.

When deciding how to decompose our N points into two sets of N/2, there is a choice to be made. The decomposition can be of even and odd points, which is called a decimation-in-time (DIT) FFT, or it can simply be done by taking the first N/2 points and the second N/2 points, which is called a decimation-in-frequency (DIF) FFT. Decimation in time means that we multiply by the twiddle factors before the addition and subtraction, while decimation in frequency means that we perform the addition and subtraction first and then multiply.

One consideration when performing an FFT is whether an additional memory buffer is required. An FFT implementation which can operate by performing calculations using only the original sample memory is called an "in place" FFT. For a radix-2 FFT, all of the butterfly operations can be performed in place, if the input array is stored (or accessed) in bit-reversed order.

Bit reversing means that the bits in a binary word are reversed from left to right. (So that, for example, 10110100 becomes 00101101.) This reversal can be done in software but takes time and is much faster in hardware. Helium includes an instruction (VBRSR) for this specific purpose. Note that what is required is the ability to index the data using bit-reversed addressing. We do not actually bit-reverse the data itself, and we are in fact only reversing some of the bits within the address.

Figure 9.1 shows an example of the use of VBRSR within an FFT. Suppose that we generate a vector of incrementing values using the VIDUP instruction. This is shown in decimal and binary at the top of the figure. We then use the VBRSR instruction to perform bit reversal. For a 128-point FFT, we would need to do this on the least-significant seven bits. The result is shown in binary and decimal at the bottom of the figure. We can then use the resulting vector of offsets to perform a gather-load of the data.

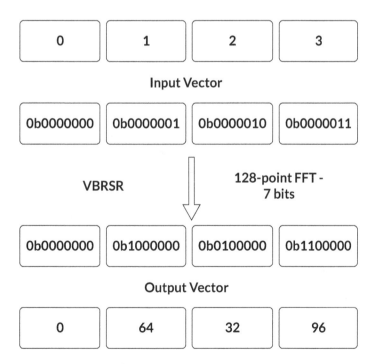

Figure 9.1: VBRSR for 128-point FFT

Figure 9.2 shows the effect of performing bit reversal of six bits (for example, for a 64-point FFT), with the same input vector.

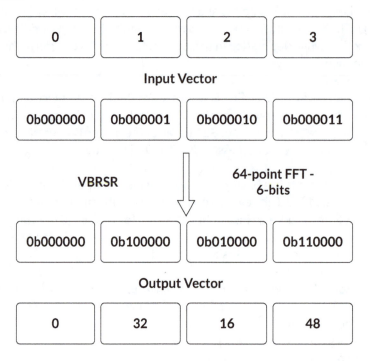

Figure 9.2: VBRSR *for 64-point FFT*

However, CMSIS-DSP often is not able to use the VBRSR instruction. When dealing with mixed-radix FFTs, the reversal formula is not straightforward. For an in-place implementation, we must take care to avoid corrupting samples which have not been read yet. Instead, pre-computed bit-reversal tables are used to provide the offsets. In both cases, for a Helium FFT implementation, we can then use scatter-gather operations to perform the operation.

9.2.3 FFT Example

Helium contains special instructions which can help us implement FFT efficiently. We've seen how the ISA includes instructions for multiplication or multiply/accumulate of complex numbers (VQDML{A, S}SDH{X}, VCMUL, VCMLA), and for addition of complex numbers with VHCADD (halving addition) and VCADD (normal addition) with both integer/fixed-point and floating-point variants. There is also the VBRSR instruction which allows us to generate bit-reversed addresses.

If we look at the FFT code in the CMSIS-DSP library, we can see how this is put into practice.

The CMSIS-DSP library contains several examples to help the user become familiar with using it. The CMSIS documentation describes how to compile and run these examples. The code can be found at:

https://github.com/ARM-software/CMSIS_5/tree/master/CMSIS/DSP/Examples/ARM

One of these examples is `arm_fft_bin_example`, which can be used with a Helium-capable processor, such as the Cortex-M55. The example takes an input test signal of 10 kHz with uniformly distributed white noise added. An FFT of this signal is calculated, which converts this time-domain signal to the frequency domain. We then calculate the magnitude of each frequency bin (an interval into which the frequency domain is divided) and calculate the one with the maximum energy (which will be 10 kHz, of course).

The code uses the CMSIS-DSP functions for complex FFT `arm_cfft_f32()`, complex magnitude `arm_cmplx_mag_f32()`, and maximum `arm_max_f32()`. The function `arm_cfft_init_f32()` is used to initialize the FFT structure. The C source for the example is contained within `arm_fft_bin_example_f32.c`. The input signal used by the example is defined in `arm_fft_bin_data.c`.

When we compile and run this code for Helium, we can see extensive use of vectorization and special features of Helium. The floating-point complex FFT uses multiple radix-4 operations and a single radix-2 stage, as required. The inner loop of the radix-4 butterfly calculation makes use of vector operations `VLDR`, `VADD`, `VSUB` and `VSTR`. So that we see code like:

```
vecSum0 = vecA + vecC;
vecDiff0 = vecA - vecC;
```

These lines are "syntactic sugar" for the `vaddq` and `vsubq` intrinsics.

It also makes use of the complex multiply instructions described in Section 4.2.3. The instructions used are `VCADD` (with rotations of 90 and 270 degrees) to perform the required addition and subtraction, and `VCMLA` and `VCMUL` to perform complex multiplication and conjugation. These are accessed through #defines.

```
#define MVE_CMPLX_ADD_A_ixB(A, B)         vcaddq_rot90(A,B)
#define MVE_CMPLX_SUB_A_ixB(A, B)         vcaddq_rot270(A,B)
#define MVE_CMPLX_MULT_FLT_Conj_AxB(A,B)  vcmlaq_rot270(vcmulq(A, B), A, B)
```

As the 128-bit vector contains four single-precision floating-point values, we operate on two complex numbers in each vector.

Once the transform is completed, the example calculates the complex magnitude values, by squaring the real and imaginary components, adding the two results and then taking the square root. The code is able to load four complex values into a vector register using `VLDR` and obtain the sum of the squares using `VMUL` and `VFMA`. Helium does not have an instruction to calculate square roots, so this is implemented using a vectorized version of the Newton–Raphson method.

Finally, the function which finds the maximum bin value, `arm_max_f32()`, is also vectorized. It iterates through the data, loading four floating-point values at a time. By performing a `VCMPGE`, we can compare the values loaded with the current maxima and use `VPSEL` (the predicated select instruction) to select the result if there is a new maximum for that lane of the vector, and the corresponding index value. When we have compared all of the values, we can use `VMAXNMV` to find the maximum within the vector.

CHAPTER

DSP Filtering

10

In this chapter, we will look at fundamental DSP operations, convolution and filtering. Again, we will assume that readers are already familiar with these.

10.1 Convolution

Convolution is of fundamental importance to DSP. It is the basis of FIR filters. It is also a fundamental operation in neural network implementation and we will revisit this in Chapter 12.

10.1.1 Introduction

The algebraic expression for convolution is represented by:

$$f(n) * g(n) = \sum_{k = -\infty}^{\infty} f(k)\, g(n - k)$$

If we have two arrays a[ ], with alen items, and b[ ], with blen items, we can see that a simple piece of code to perform a convolution of the two might look like this:

```
for (i = 0; i < alen + blen - 1; i++)
    {
    c[i] = 0;

    jmin = (i >= blen - 1) ? i - (blen - 1) : 0;
    // these steps are simply to stop us
    jmax = (i < alen - 1) ? i : alen - 1;
    // going beyond the edge of the array

        for (j = jmin; j <= jmax; j++)
            {
            c[i] += a[j] * b[i - j];
    //* here is a multiply, not the mathematical convolution symbol
            }
        }
```

where c[ ] is an output array, of length alen + blen - 1.

This algorithm is simple to understand, consisting of two nested loops multiplying and summing elements from both input arrays. However, it is difficult to vectorize as the code varies the start and end bounds of the inner loop on each iteration of the outer loop. Notice also that we access the first array with an incrementing index, but the second array with a decrementing index (i.e. we have to access this array in the reverse direction).

10.2 Filters

Filtering is a fundamental part of digital signal processing. After sampling a continuous signal in the time-domain to produce a series of samples, we process those samples to alter their frequency-domain characteristics. Usually, this means filtering out, or attenuating, specific frequency components.

There are two basic approaches to filter design:

- **Finite impulse response (FIR)** – The FIR filter's time response to an impulse is the straightforward weighted sum of the present and a finite number of previous input samples. There is no feedback component and so the effect of a specific sample is limited to a time window after it is input. A FIR filter's frequency response has no poles, just zeros. Example uses of FIR filters include audio equalization and motor control.

- **Infinite impulse response (IIR)** – The IIR filter is a recursive function. This means that its output is a weighted sum of inputs and outputs. As it is recursive, its response can potentially continue indefinitely. An IIR filter frequency response has both poles and zeros. An example use of an IIR filter might be to implement an equivalent to analog filters, such as Butterworth, Chebyshev or Bessel.

The CMSIS-DSP library contains numerous functions which perform filtering, including both FIR and IIR filters. In this section, we will take a closer look at implementing the FIR filter on Helium.

10.2.1 Introduction to the Finite Impulse Response (FIR) Filter

In this section, we will look at the FIR filter and see how Helium features can be used to efficiently perform the filter.

Figure 10.2 shows a block diagram of a FIR filter. It has four parts:

- A buffer (also called a delay line) stores a fixed number of previous input samples. Mathematically, we label the newest input sample $x(n)$ and the previous input samples as $x(n - k)$. At each new sampling event, the samples are shifted one position to the right in the diagram and the new sample is stored at the start.

- A set of filter coefficients denoted as $h(k)$.

- A block which multiplies each sample in the buffer by the corresponding filter coefficient.

- A block which sums the multiplier outputs to produce the filter output sample $y(n)$.

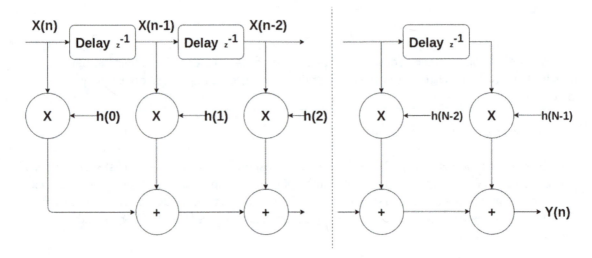

Figure 10.1: FIR filter

We can represent this mathematically as:

$$y = \sum_{k=0}^{N-1} h(k) \cdot x(n-k)$$

where $x(n)$ is the series of data values to be filtered and $h(n)$ are the filter coefficients.

10.2.2 FIR Example

Often, a FIR filter will be sufficiently long that we cannot hold all of the coefficients in registers at once. For such a filter, each output result depends upon N data values and N filter coefficients being loaded from memory. For this reason, it can be useful to calculate multiple output results at the same time, from a single load of data and coefficients. This is called a block filter implementation. Instead of moving a new sample into the delay line on each iteration, we use a delay line which is a multiple of the number of taps (coefficients) and perform the calculation when we have a full "block" of data. We therefore do not use a circular buffer, but instead move the delay line data once per block. The overhead of doing this is small for a large block size.

Let's look at the full FIR implementation contained within CMSIS-DSP. CMSIS-DSP contains an example which performs a low-pass filter. It can be found here:

https://github.com/ARM-software/CMSIS_5/tree/master/CMSIS/DSP/Examples/ARM/arm_fir_example

The example shows how to use a block FIR filter. An input signal is defined (in arm_fir_data.c) which contains two sine waves, at 1 kHz and 15 kHz, with 320 sample values. A low-pass filter with a cutoff-frequency at 6 kHz is used, leaving only the 1 kHz sine wave as the output. The filter has 29 coefficients (taps). The example shows how the FIR filter is configured and how blocks of data are passed to it. The example uses the CMSIS-DSP library function `arm_fir_f32.c()` to perform the filter.

The source code for this function can be found here:

https://github.com/ARM-software/CMSIS_5/blob/master/CMSIS/DSP/Source/FilteringFunctions/arm_fir_f32.c

The function operates on blocks of data, as previously described. The pointer pSrc points to an array of input data, pDst points to an array of output data and blockSize gives the number of values to be processed by the function. pCoeffs points to an array of coefficients, stored in time-reversed order. This means the coefficient for the oldest data value is stored first. The number of coefficients (taps) is given by numTaps.

To avoid the use of circular addressing, a state array of size numTaps + blockSize − 1 holds sample values and is pointed to by pState. For example, if we have 16 coefficients in our filter and want to process 32 samples, we need to hold both the 32 samples and the 16 sample values that preceded them. The coefficients and state variables for a filter are stored together in an instance data structure. Although coefficient arrays can be shared between different instances of the filter, the state arrays cannot be shared and a separate instance structure has to be defined for each filter.

The instance needs to be initialized by setting all values of pState to zero and setting the numTaps and required pointers pCoeffs and pState. This can be done manually or by calling the provided initialization function.

The Helium version of the function first checks whether the blockSize is greater than 8. If it is not, then vectorization is not attempted and the filter is calculated by standard C code. If the amount of data to be processed is large enough that vectorization is worthwhile, then the number of coefficients is checked. If it is below eight, then optimized functions arm_fir_f32_1_4_mve (for one to four taps) or arm_fir_f32_5_8_mve (for five to eight taps) are used. Note that the array of coefficients must be a zero padded to be a multiple of 16 even if fewer than 16 coefficients are used by the filter.

The code consists of a set of loops. We begin with a loop which uses VLDR to read 128-bits of data from the input sample and VSTR to copy it to the state array. The basic filter calculation loop reads eight coefficient values.

The code then uses a series of eight VLDRW instructions. Each VLDRW reads four sample values, with the address incrementing by one sample each time. There is then a VMUL or multiply accumulate (VFMA) which multiplies the vector by one of the coefficient values. This is repeated for all coefficient values and all samples.

We then have some code to handle any remaining calculations. If the number of samples is not a multiple of eight, the final set is handled through tail predication, with the vctp32q() intrinsic used to create a tail predicate so that the multiply accumulates only produce a result for the correct number of samples. Finally, if the number of taps is not a multiple of eight, a simple loop of VLDR and VFMA instructions is used to handle those remaining taps, four samples at a time.

CHAPTER

Application Examples

In this chapter, we will look at an easily understood example of application code for image processing and see how Helium features can be used to give a significant speedup. We will then look at Helium features for cryptography.

11.1 Image Processing

Computer graphics and video systems represent images using an array of pixels. There are some common formats used to represent the color of those pixels, typically using three or four values or color components. RGB format uses additive color mixing. It stores individual values for red, green and blue and these describe what kind of light needs to be emitted to produce a given color. There are several common RGB formats in use. For example, if we have 24 bits per pixel, this typically means that there is an 8-bit value for each color. Sometimes we might have only 16 bits per pixel, allocated as 5 bits for red, 6 bits for green and 5 bits for blue (RGB565). ARGB is RGB with the addition of an extra channel called alpha which indicates transparency.

11.1.1 Example Code

Most cameras provide a set of options to apply effects to images. Here, we look at a simple example which will take an image in 32-bit ARGB format and convert to 8-bit grayscale. To do this, we read the input RGB values and average them, so that the red, green and blue values are the same. As the human eye responds differently to different colors, we must weight them accordingly and there is a standard formula to do this.

The formula we will use is as follows:

$$Y_{out} = (R_{in} \times 0.3) + (G_{in} \times 0.59) + (B_{in} \times 0.11)$$

We are dealing with 8-bit integer input RGB values and 8-bit integer output RGB values. We can fit more data into a vector by using integer arithmetic rather than floating-point numbers. Multiplying each of the input weights by 256 and then dividing by 256 (shift by eight bits) gives us:

$$Y_{out} = ((R_{in} \times 77) + (G_{in} \times 151) + (B_{in} \times 28)) \gg 8$$

Note that there is no possibility of overflow (the max RGB value of 255, 255, 255 will produce $Y = 255$).

Simple C code to perform the translation of a single frame could look like this:

```
void grayscale(unsigned char * out, unsigned char * rgb, int pixelCnt)
{
    int Index=0;
    int outPtr=0;
    int aIn, rIn, gIn, bIn, yOut;
    while (Index < pixelCnt)
        {
            // aIn = rgb[ Index + 3];
            rIn = rgb[ Index + 2];
            gIn = rgb[ Index + 1];
```

```
            bIn = rgb[ Index];
            Index+=4;

            yOut = ((77 * rIn) + (151 * gIn) + (28 * bIn)) >> 8;

            out[outPtr++] = yOut;
        }
    }
```

When this code is compiled, it does not auto-vectorize and will perform one pixel per loop iteration. We can try to modify the C code so that it will vectorize, for example, by using the restrict keyword to indicate that the input array rgb[ ] and the output array out[ ] are non-overlapping. We would also need to reformat the loop so that the compiler knows that a multiple of 16 iterations will occur.

We can try to create a faster, vectorized version using Helium intrinsic functions.

We can use the VLD4 instructions to extract the A, R, G and B values, as we saw in Section 5.3. This intrinsic will generate four vector load instructions. The result is that we have a register with eight alpha values, a register with eight red values and so on. This means that we have now used four of the available eight registers. As the A values are not required, we can reuse that register if necessary.

```
uint8x16x4_t pixels = vld4q_u8(rgb);
rgb +=64;
```

Figure 11.1 shows the effect of this. It can be seen that a total of 64 bytes of pixel data is loaded and deinterleaved.

When we multiply two eight-bit values, we will obtain a sixteen-bit result. As we want to multiply a vector by a scalar value in a general-purpose register, we need to use VMOVL to widen the input pixel values from eight to sixteen bits:

```
uint16x8_t tmp1, tmp2, sum1, sum2;

tmp1 = vmovltq_u8(pixels.val[2]);
tmp2 = vmovlbq_u8(pixels.val[2]);
```

Recall that when discussing vector array data types in Section 7.5.1, for a vector type <type>_t the corresponding array type is <type>x<length>_t. The vector array data type is a structure which contains a single array element, called val. So, having executed the VLD4 intrinsic to deinterleave into four Helium registers, we can access the individual registers by specifying val[2] etc. Figure 11.2 shows the effect of the pair of VMOVL instructions.

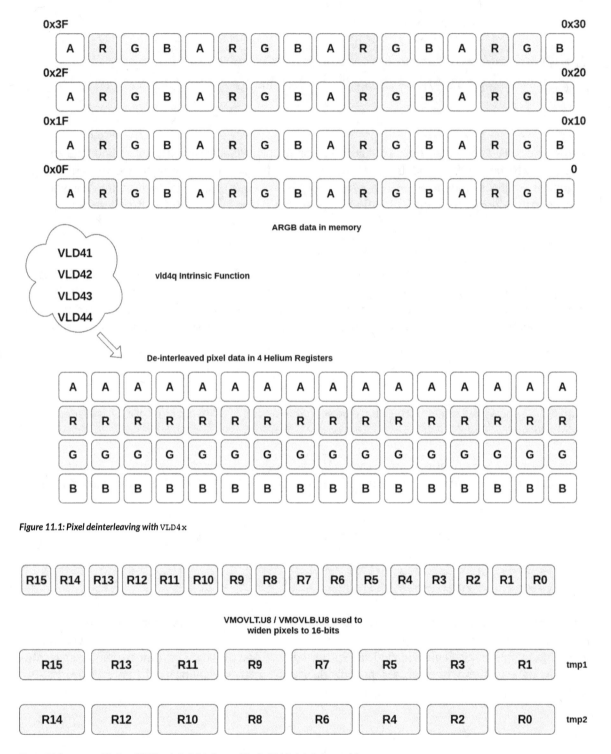

Figure 11.1: *Pixel deinterleaving with* VLD4x

Figure 11.2: VMOVL *widening of 8-bit red pixel data in a register to 16-bit data in two registers*

We now have two Helium registers, each of which contains eight sets of red pixel data, expanded to 16-bits. We can then do the vector multiply for these red values:

```
sum1 = vmulq_n_u16(tmp1, 77);
sum2 = vmulq_n_u16(tmp2, 77);
```

Then we do the same widen and multiply for the green and blue values but using VMLA to accumulate onto the already calculated values:

```
tmp1 = vmovltq_u8(pixels.val[1]);
tmp2 = vmovlbq_u8(pixels.val[1]);

sum1 = vmlaq_n_u16(sum1, tmp1, 151);
sum2 = vmlaq_n_u16(sum2, tmp2, 151);

tmp1 = vmovltq_u8(pixels.val[0]);
tmp2 = vmovlbq_u8(pixels.val[0]);

sum1 = vmlaq_n_u16(sum1, tmp1, 28);
sum2 = vmlaq_n_u16(sum2, tmp2, 28);
```

Next, we need to use two VSHRN instructions to shift and narrow back to a vector of 16 eight-bit values, in one register:

```
uint8x16_t result;

result = vshrntq(result, sum1, 8);
result = vshrnbq(result, sum2, 8);
```

Finally, we can use a VSTR instruction (through the vst1q intrinsic function) to write out the processed data:

```
vst1q_u8 (out, result);
out+=16;
```

This vectorized solution operates on sixteen pixels per iteration. If our original image does not contain a multiple of sixteen pixels, a simple solution is to handle the remaining small number of pixels using the C code already shown.

```
void grayscale_mve(unsigned char * out, unsigned char * rgb, int PixelCnt)
{
    uint16x8_t tmp1, tmp2, sum1, sum2;
    uint8x16_t result;
    uint8x16x4_t pixels;
    PixelCnt = PixelCnt>>4;

    while (PixelCnt > 0)
      {
        pixels=vld4q_u8(rgb);
        argb+=64;

        tmp1=vmovltq_u8(pixels.val[2]);
        tmp2=vmovlbq_u8(pixels.val[2]);
        sum1=vmulq_n_u16(tmp1,77);
        sum2=vmulq_n_u16(tmp2,77);

        tmp1=vmovltq_u8(pixels.val[1]);
        tmp2=vmovlbq_u8(pixels.val[1]);
        sum1=vmlaq_n_u16(sum1, tmp1,151);
        sum2=vmlaq_n_u16(sum2, tmp2,151);

        tmp1=vmovltq_u8(pixels.val[0]);
        tmp2=vmovlbq_u8(pixels.val[0]);
        sum1=vmlaq_n_u16(sum1, tmp1,28);
        sum2=vmlaq_n_u16(sum2, tmp2,28);

        result=vshrntq(result, sum1,8);
        result=vshrnbq(result, sum2,8);

        vst1q_u8(out, result);
        out+=16;
        PixelCnt--;
      }
}
```

11.2 Cryptography

As we briefly mentioned in Chapter 4, Helium contains two features which are useful for implementation of standard cryptographic algorithms: support for big-number arithmetic and polynomial multiplication. In this section, we'll review why cryptography needs these things and how Helium can be used in an efficient implementation.

11.2.1 Big Number Arithmetic

An integer in C is generally 32 bits, which gives a range of +/- 2 billion (2×10^9) approximately. Nearly all modern compilers also support a "long long" 64-bit integer type, which allows us to represent integers up to about 9×10^{18}. However, sometimes even this number is not large enough, particularly where intermediate steps in the calculation may produce very large results. Most processor hardware is able to perform arithmetic of some fixed length(s) of between 8 and 64 bits of precision. If we need larger numbers, or greater precision, a library (or programming language) which supports arbitrary-precision (sometimes called infinite-precision or bignum) arithmetic must be used.

Cryptography can involve multiplications of numbers with 300 decimal digits (995 bits). The RSA encryption algorithm, like many other cryptographic algorithms, is based on the fact that it is easy for a computer to take two very large prime numbers and multiply them, but it is extremely hard to do the opposite, that is, to take a very large number, given that it has only two prime factors, and find them. Furthermore, there are many other mathematical applications which may require use of arbitrary-precision numbers.

Helium has some instructions which help us with synthesis of arithmetic operations for large numbers. These instructions are VADC, VSBC and VSHLC, which do whole vector add, subtract and left shift operations respectively, in each case with carry in and out.

Addition (or subtraction) of big numbers is straightforward. The digits are simply added (or subtracted) in sequence, with appropriate carries, until all of the digits have been added. In our example, we'll add together two arbitrarily long binary numbers.

We can define bignum as an array of 32-bit integers:

```
typedef uint32_t * bignum;
```

We can use inline assembly code like this:

```
void bignum_add (intBlkCnt, bignum pA, bignum pB, bign pDst, uint32_t *carry)
{
      uint32_t cout;
   __asm volatile (
      "    mov        r0, #0                        \n"
      "    lsls       r0, #1                        \n" // clear carry flag
      "    wls        lr, %0, .adc_scalar_end%=     \n"
      ".adc_scalar_loop1_%=:                        \n"
      "    ldr        r0, [%1], #4                  \n" //load pA[n]
      "    ldr        r1, [%2], #4                  \n" //load pB[n]
      "    adcs       r0, r0, r1                    \n" // tmp <- a[n] + b[n]
      "    str        r0, [%3], #4                  \n" // Dst[n] <- tmp
      "    le         lr, .adc_scalar_loop1_%=      \n"
      ".adc_scalar_end%=:                           \n"
      "    mrs        %4, APSR_nzcvq                 \n" // get output carry bit
      "    ubfx       %4, %4, #29, #1               \n" // extract the C bit and move to
                                                       bit 0
      : "+r" (BlkCnt), "+r" (pA), "+r" (pB), "+r" (pDst), "+r" (carry)
      :: "lr", "r0", "r1", "memory", "cc"
   );
   *carry = cout;
}
```

The code is quite simple. It clears the processor carry flag initially. We then loop through reading four words at a time from each of the inputs (least significant word first) and use the ADCS instruction to perform the 128-bit addition. Any carry out from this addition is automatically applied to the next add. Once we have iterated through the full length of our big number, we extract the carry bit from the APSR. Similar code using the SBCS instruction can be used for subtraction.

This code is making use of the Helium While loop, but only performs 32-bits of addition per cycle, as it is not using Helium vectors. We can use the `vldrwq` intrinsic to load 128-bits at a time, and the `vadcq` intrinsic to perform a whole register 128-bit addition.

This means that we can have the body of a function which looks like this:

```
unsigned int carry = 0;
uint32x4_t      vecA
uint32x4_t      vecB ;
uint32x4_t      vecDst;

while (blkCnt > 0U)
  {
        mve_pred16_t    p0 = vctp32q(blkCnt);
        vecA = vldrwq_z_u32(pA, p0);
        vecB = vldrwq_z_u32(pB, p0);
        vecDst = vadcq(vecA, vecB, &carry);
        vstrwq_p(pDst, vecDst, p0);
        pA += 4;
        pB += 4;
        pDst += 4;
        blkCnt -= 4;
  }
```

The use of a tail-predicated loop means that our inputs may be of any length number of words and do not need to be a multiple of four.

11.2.2 Polynomial Multiplication

Finite field arithmetic is a branch of mathematics dealing with arithmetic in a field containing a finite number of elements. This in contrast to "normal" arithmetic where we have an infinite number of elements, the set of rational numbers. There are infinitely many such different finite fields.

A finite field is also called a Galois field, denoted GF(q), where q is a prime power. The simplest example is the case of a prime p, in which case GF(p) is the ring of integers modulo a prime p. The arithmetic operations addition, subtraction and multiplication are performed using the usual operation on integers, followed by reduction modulo p. For example, in GF(7), 4 + 5 = 9 becomes 2 modulo 7. GF(2) is of particular interest to us. Here, addition or subtraction is exclusive OR and multiplication is AND. Elements of a general Galois field may be represented as suitable polynomials over GF(p). For example, in the case of GF(2^n), such as GF(256) used in AES, elements are polynomials over GF(2), with each term in the polynomial represented by one bit. This representation is used in a variety of applications, including calculation of cyclic redundancy checks, Reed–Solomon error correction, and in algorithms such as AES and elliptic curve cryptography. A detailed look at this is outside the scope of this book and this introduction is simply to give some brief background on polynomial (sometimes called carryless) multiplication.

Helium implements the VMULL instruction with supported types .P8 and .P16. This allows us to perform eight parallel 8-bit polynomial multiplications (or four 16-bit polynomial multiplications).

Here, we'll look at an implementation of a 64-bit × 64-bit polynomial multiply routine, using VMULL.P16.

We can represent the two inputs as containing four 16-bit elements, like this:

A = (a3, a2, a1, a0)

B = (b3, b2, b1, b0)

The product is then:

(a3.b3) <<96 + (a2.b3) <<80 + (a1.b3) <<64 + (a0.b3) <<48 + (a3.b2) <<80 + (a2.b2) <<64 + (a1.b2) <<48 + (a0.b2) <<32 + (a3.b1) << 64 + (a2.b1) <<48 + (a1.b1) <<32 + (a0.b1) <<16 + (a3.b0) <<48 + (a2.b0) <<32 + (a1.b0) <<16 + (a0.b0)

It can be seen that in order to calculate A * B, we need to calculate the product of every Ai, Bj combination. We can do this efficiently by using VMULL.P16 four times. Each execution of the instruction produces four products.

We can do this by generating the following terms:

- A16 = A rotated right 16 bits = (a0, a3, a2, a1)

- B16 = B rotated right 16 bits = (b0, b3, b2, b1)

- B32 = B rotated right 32 bits = (b1, b0, b3, b2)

We can then use the VMULL.P16 instruction to calculate the products:

- P0 = (a3.b3, a2.b2, a1.b1, a0.b0) by using VMULL.P16(A, B)

- P1 = (a3.b0, a2.b3, a1.b2, a0.b1) by using VMULL.P16(A, B16)

- P2 = (a0.b3, a3.b2, a2.b1, a1.b0) by using VMULL.P16(A16, B)

- P3 = (a3.b1, a3.b0, a1.b3, a0.b2) by using VMULL.P16(A, B32)

Some algebraic manipulation of these terms then allows us to produce the correct result, without the need to extract, shift and add each individual 32-bit product term.

We produce a sum, S, from P1 and P2 (using XOR as this is polynomial arithmetic, as we do throughout):

$S = P1 + P2$

Writing P3.3 as the third element of P3 etc., we must calculate two intermediate results, R0 and R1:

$R0 = (0, S.2, S.3 + S.1, S.0) << 16$

$R1 = (0, P3.3 + P3.1, P3.2 + P3.0, 0)$

The final result is then:

$Result = P0 + R0 + R1$

The resulting Helium assembly code to do this is shown here:

```
// R0 points to a 64-bit polynomial in memory (input A)
// R1 points to a 64-bit polynomial in memory (input B)
// R2 points to a location to store the result (output)
//
// result is returned in Q0

PUSH {R4, R5, R6, R7}
VPUSH {Q4, Q5, Q6, Q7}
MOV R4, #0

// Widening loads - convert 4x16 bit values a3, a2, a1, a0
// into 0, a3, 0, a2, 0, a1, 0, a0
// and the same for b

VLDRH.U32 Q1, [R0] // Q1 is A
VLDRH.U32 Q2, [R1] // Q2 is B

VMULLB.P16 Q0, Q1, Q2 // Q0 will hold result (=a.b)

//Create a16 from a (= a0, a3, a2, a1)
//Effectively a rotate right 32 bits

VMOV R7, R3, Q1[3], Q1[1]
VMOV R5, R6, Q1[2], Q1[0]
VMOV Q4[3], Q4[1], R6, R5
VMOV Q4[2], Q4[0], R7, R3

//Create b16 from b (= b0, b3, b2, b1)

VMOV R7, R3, Q2[3], Q2[1]
VMOV R5, R6, Q2[2], Q2[0]
VMOV Q5[3], Q5[1], R6, R5
VMOV Q5[2], Q5[0], R7, R3
```

```
// We only need VMULLB and not VMULLT because of widening

VMULLB.P16 Q6, Q1, Q5 // Q6 is a.b16
VMULLB.P16 Q7, Q4, Q2 // Q7 is a16.b

// s = Q6 + Q7 (EOR is polynomial add) = a.b16 + a16.b

VEOR Q3, Q6, Q7 // Q3 is s

// Now manipulate S so we have (0, s2, s3 +s1, s0) << 16

VMOV.32 R7, Q3[3] // Read s3 into gpr
VMOV.I32 Q4, #0
VMOV.32 Q4[1], R7 // Move old s3 value into position 1
VMOV.32 Q3[3], R4 // Zero s3 position
VEOR Q3, Q3, Q4 // Eor value from s3 into s1
VSHLC Q3, R4, #16 // Shift left 16 R4 is just to ensure zero carry in

// And add onto result in Q0
VEOR Q0, Q0, Q3 // Eor into result

// Now create b32
// b32 = b1, b0, b3, b2
// effectively a rotate of 64 bits

VMOV R7, R3, Q2[3], Q2[1]
VMOV R5, R6, Q2[2], Q2[0]
VMOV Q5[3], Q5[1], R3, R7
VMOV Q5[2], Q5[0], R6, R5

// Last of the 4 multiplies
VMULLB.P16 Q3, Q1, Q5 // Q3 is p3 = a.b32

// now manipulate p3
// so that we have 0, p3.3 + p3.1, p3.2 + p3.0, 0

VMOV.32 R7, Q3[3] // Read p3.3 into gpr
VMOV.32 R3, Q3[2] // read p3.2
VMOV.I32 Q4, #0
VMOV.32 Q4[1], R7
VMOV.32 Q4[0], R3
VMOV.32 Q3[3], R4 //Zero p3.3
VMOV.32 Q3[2], R4 //Zero p3.2
VEOR Q3, Q3, Q4 //we now have 0,0, p3+p1, p2+p0
VSHLC Q3, R4, #32 // we now have 0, p3+p1, p2+p0, 0

VEOR Q0, Q0, Q3 // Add into result
VSTRW.32 Q0, [R2] // Write the final result
VPOP {Q4, Q5, Q6, Q7}
POP {R4, R5, R6, R7}
BX LR
```

There are a few interesting features of this code.

Multiplying two 16-bit values gives a 32-bit result, so that the result is double the input width. For a 128-bit vector register to hold the result, this means that we can only use half of the values in each input register. The VMULL instruction lets us select either the top or bottom half of each pair of input lanes. Figure 11.3 shows this.

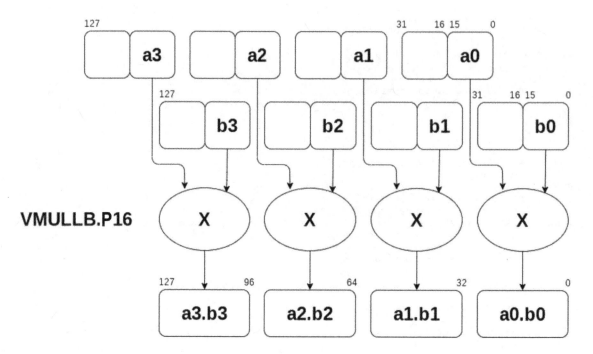

Figure 11.3: VMULLB.P16 *operation*

A widening load (VLDRH.U32) efficiently converts our 64-bit input into the desired format. The instruction reads four 16-bit values (our 64-bit input polynomial) and converts them to four 32-bit values, of which the top 16-bits are zero. Figure 11.4 shows this. We then use only the bottom half of each.

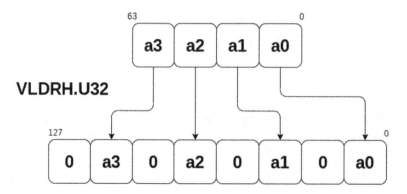

Figure 11.4: Widening load

The algorithm requires us to move data between vector lanes and to XOR together values in different lanes of the same vector. Helium does not provide instructions to do this directly, but we can do this by transferring values to and from scalar registers.

Helium has eight vector registers. If we implement the algorithm in the order described earlier, where we begin by performing all of the rotations and then perform all of the multiplies, we would need to spill intermediate results to memory. We can avoid this by reordering operations so that we have no more than eight 128-bit values in use at any time. However, if we have a block of Helium arithmetic instructions which cannot be overlapped, we can (on a dual-beat implementation, such as Cortex-M55) insert interleaved memory access instructions without any additional cycle penalty. This means that for some code, spilling values to memory can be a good approach.

When we call Helium code in a function, we must preserve Q4–Q7, which means that using those registers requires us to store and restore them on the stack. Although we can change R0-R3, we must preserve other general-purpose registers. We can optimize this code with some changes to avoid using R7 and Q7, so that these registers don't need to be saved and restored on the stack.

We can apply further optimization to this code. It can be seen that producing the vectors a16 and b16 requires four VMOV instructions for each:

```
//Create a16 from a (= a0, a3, a2, a1)
//Effectively a rotate right 32 bits

VMOV R7, R3, Q1[3], Q1[1]
VMOV R5, R6, Q1[2], Q1[0]
VMOV Q4[3], Q4[1], R6, R5
VMOV Q4[2], Q4[0], R7, R3

//Create b16 from b (= b0, b3, b2, b1)

VMOV R7, R3, Q2[3], Q2[1]
VMOV R5, R6, Q2[2], Q2[0]
VMOV Q5[3], Q5[1], R6, R5
VMOV Q5[2], Q5[0], R7, R3
```

This could be avoided by the use of scatter-load instructions (described in Section 5.2), either by using the VIWDUP instruction to generate the required offsets (0, 3, 2, 1), or by using a pre-computed set of offsets stored with the code and loaded into a vector register. This technique of using scatter-loads can be useful in the Helium implementation of many algorithms, to perform intra-vector manipulation. The code using VIWDUP is both smaller and faster and is as follows:

```
// Build offset table to load a16 and b16
MOV R4, #1 // Start value 1
MOV R5, #4 // Wraparound at 4
VIWDUP.U32 Q6, R4, R5, #1 // Results in Q6 = (0,3,2,1)
// Widening loads - convert 4x16 bit values a3, a2, a1, a0
// into 0, a3, 0, a2, 0, a1, 0, a0
// and the same for b
VLDRH.U32 Q1, [R0]     // Q1 is A
VLDRH.U32 Q2, [R1]     // Q2 is B
```

Inspection of the code shows that the calculation of b32, p3 and then adding of (0, p3.3 + p3.1, p3.2 + p3.0, 0) into the result requires quite a lot of manipulation and takes 11 instructions to perform.

Inspection of the algorithm and some algebra shows that we can instead use left shifts of 16 bits to produce two terms a'16 and b'16. It is quicker to calculate the shifted products a'16*b16 and a16*b'16 and to take two terms from one and two terms from the other. We then add both to the result, separately, using lane predication on the inner two lanes. This kind of lane predication can be a powerful way to perform operations on a per-lane basis. The resulting code looks like this:

```
// Build a'16 = (a2, a1, a0, 0) - don't need to restore a3 because
// we'll only be interested in the middle two fields.
VSHLC Q1, R4, #32

// Compute a'16 * b16 = (?, a1b3, a0b2, ?)
VMULLB.P16 Q5, Q1, Q4
// Build b'16 = (b2, b1, b0, 0) - don't need to restore a3 because
// we'll only be interested in the middle two fields.
VSHLC Q2, R4, #32
// Compute a16 * b'16 = (?, a3b1, a2b0, ?)
VMULLB.P16 Q3, Q2, Q3
// Successively add (?, a3b1, a2b0, ?)
// and (?, a1b3, a0b2, ?) via predication
VPSTT
VEORT Q0, Q0, Q5
VEORT Q0, Q0, Q3
```

This code is two instructions shorter and several cycles faster.

Finally, we can look for interlocks between successive instructions (described in Section 8.4) and reorder our code to avoid these. For example, in the code sequence above, the load of the immediate value into R4 and its write to the predication bits in P0 can be moved away from the VPSTT instruction to avoid interlock cycles. Similarly, instead of loading a16 and b16 using the generated offsets and then performing the two multiplies, we can interleave the load and multiply instructions to save two cycles (on dual-beat implementations, such as Cortex-M55).

The following sequence:

```
VLDRH.U32 Q4, [R0, Q7, UXTW #1] // Q4 = a16
VLDRH.U32 Q5, [R1, Q7, UXTW #1] // Q5 = b16
VMULLB.P16 Q6, Q1, Q5           // Q6 is a.b16
VMULLB.P16 Q7, Q4, Q2           // Q7 is a16.b
```

then becomes:

```
VLDRH.U32 Q4, [R1, Q6, UXTW #1] // Q4 = b16
VMULLB.P16 Q5, Q1, Q4           // Q5 is a.b16
VLDRH.U32 Q3, [R0, Q6, UXTW #1] // Q3 = a16
VMULLB.P16 Q6, Q3, Q2           // Q6 is a16.b
```

(Note also that the register numbers have changed, to avoid having to use Q7, saving a 128-bit stack write and read.)

Our final, optimized code then looks like this:

```
pmul64:
        // R0 points to a 64-bit polynomial in memory (input A)
        // R1 points to a 64-bit polynomial in memory (input B)
        // R2 points to a location to store the result (output)
        // R3, R4, R5, R6 and Q0-Q6 used as temporaries
        // R4-R6, Q4-Q6 preserved.

        PUSH {R4, R5, R6}
        VPUSH {Q4, Q5, Q6}
        MOV R3, #0

        // Build offset table to load a16 and b16
        MOV R4, #1 // Start value 1
        MOV R5, #4 // Wraparound at 4
        VIWDUP.U32 Q6, R4, R5, #1  // Results in Q6 = (0,3,2,1)
        // Widening loads - convert 4x16 bit values a3, a2, a1, a0
        // into 0, a3, 0, a2, 0, a1, 0, a0
        // and the same for b
        VLDRH.U32 Q1, [R0]     // Q1 is A
        VLDRH.U32 Q2, [R1]     // Q2 is B
        VMULLB.P16 Q0, Q1, Q2 // Q0 will hold result (=a.b)
        VLDRH.U32 Q4, [R1, Q6, UXTW #1] // Q4 = b16
        VMULLB.P16 Q5, Q1, Q4         // Q5 is a.b16
        VLDRH.U32 Q3, [R0, Q6, UXTW #1] // Q3 = a16
        VMULLB.P16 Q6, Q3, Q2         // Q6 is a16.b
        // Build a'16 = (a2, a1, a0, 0) - don't need to restore a3 because
        // we'll only be interested in the middle two fields.
        VSHLC Q1, R4, #32

        // s = Q5 + Q6 (EOR is polynomial add) = a.b16 + a16.b
        VEOR Q5, Q5, Q6 // Q5 is s
        // Now manipulate S so we have (0, s2, s3 + s1, s0) << 16
        VMOV R5, R4, Q5[3], Q5[1]
        EOR R5, R5, R4
        MOV R4, 0x0FF0
        VMSR P0, R4
        VMOV Q5[3], Q5[1], R5, R3
        VSHLC Q5, R3, #16 // just to ensure zero carry in
        // And add onto result in Q0
        VEOR Q0, Q0, Q5 // Eor into result

        // Compute a'16 * b16 = (?, a1b3, a0b2, ?)
        VMULLB.P16 Q5, Q1, Q4
        // Build b'16 = (b2, b1, b0, 0) - don't need to restore a3 because
        // we'll only be interested in the middle two fields.
        VSHLC Q2, R4, #32
        // Compute a16 * b'16 = (?, a3b1, a2b0, ?)
        VMULLB.P16 Q3, Q2, Q3
        // Successively add (?, a3b1, a2b0, ?)
        // and (?, a1b3, a0b2, ?) via predication
        VPSTT
        VEORT Q0, Q0, Q5
        VEORT Q0, Q0, Q3

        VSTRW.32 Q0, [R2] // Write the final result
        VPOP {Q4, Q5, Q6}
        POP {R4, R5, R6}
        BX LR
```

Note that this code could be further optimized, if being used inside a loop for calculation of larger polynomials. For example, the requirement to push and pop vector registers can be avoided, and the predicate and offset register values could be computed just once, outside of the loop.

Synthesizing larger polynomial multiplication operations

Many algorithms require much larger polynomials, 128- or 256-bit lengths being common. We can synthesize larger multiplications by the normal long multiplication process of performing smaller multiplies and shifting and adding (for polynomials, carryless addition is performed using XOR, as we have seen). To perform a 128-bit multiply, we would need to use the above 64-bit multiply code four times.

An alternative approach is to construct an n-bit polynomial multiplier using the Karatsuba algorithm. This essentially is a divide-and-conquer approach. We can calculate the product of two numbers using three multiplications (each half of the original size) plus some additions and shifting. The algorithm is not specific to polynomial multiplication, but can also be used to speed up long multiplications in conventional arithmetic.

Let us consider two polynomials with their digits split into two halves {a,b} and {c,d}.

The product of the two is then calculated by the following steps:

1. `ac = a * c // multiply the top halves of each input`

2. `bd = b * d // multiply the bottom halves of each input`

3. `ab_mul_cd = (a XOR b) * (c XOR d) // remember that XOR is add for`
   `polynomial, so this is ac+ad+bc+bd`

Now that we have performed the three multiplications, we simply have to shift and add to produce the result. First, we calculate an intermediate term:

4. `ad_plus_bc = ab_mul_cd XOR ac XOR bd // leaves us with just ad + bc`

Finally, we produce our result. Using the previously seen notation to denote the four parts of the result and the top and bottom halves of the intermediate values, we have:

- `Result.3 = ac.1`

- `Result.2 = ac.0 XOR ad_plus_bc.1`

- `Result.1 = bd.1 XOR ad_plus_bc.0`

- `Result.0 = bd.0`

This means that we can, for example, calculate a 256-bit polynomial multiplication by performing three 128-bit polynomial multiplications. Although this approach uses fewer multiplies, it needs more addition and vector manipulation, so it is typically faster only for sufficiently large polynomials.

CHAPTER 12

Neural Networks and Machine Learning

In the rapidly growing IoT area, many systems involve sensors gathering data, which might include audio, video, GPS location, or environmental data, such as temperature, humidity etc. This data is typically processed in the cloud, meaning that the edge device requires a network connection. As more data is collected, a significant amount of computing power is required to generate useful results. This normally means uploading data to a server on the network and the server sending back processed data which the edge device can then act upon. Increasingly, such systems use machine learning (ML) techniques.

Machine learning is an exciting new area in the field of artificial intelligence, where machines adapt the algorithm based on experience. A model is used to perform computational operations on a set of input data to produce some useful output. Instead of this being achieved by a program implementing some fixed algorithm, the model is "trained" using a data set and this trained model is then used to make "inferences" from new data supplied to it. ML algorithms were initially rolled out on powerful computers, either on data farms in the cloud, or on the desktop, often using Graphics Processors (GPUs) or specialized accelerators for performance. Neural-network (NN)-based solutions have demonstrated high levels of accuracy for applications such as speech recognition, natural language processing and image classification.

It is now possible to deploy neural network algorithms on Cortex-M microcontroller-based edge devices. This has some clear advantages, including the following:

- **Cost** – A microcontroller and sensor node may cost only a few cents in volume production. In some systems there may be additional savings from not requiring the edge device to have networking or wireless capability.

- **Latency and bandwidth** – Deploying the algorithm at the edge removes the delays and bandwidth costs associated with networked communication to a central server. It also makes the system easier to deploy, and more reliable, in locations with limited network connectivity.

- **Power consumption** – A Cortex-M device will consume orders of magnitude less power than a more sophisticated system with powerful CPUs and a GPU. It may also require less energy to perform classification of data at the node compared to the cost of network communications to a server.

- **Privacy and security** – Potentially sensitive image or audio data is processed locally, rather than being uploaded to the cloud.

Helium further extends this capability by offering a large increase in NN performance.

It is important to recognize that there are some important constraints which apply to such devices. In particular, the processor performance will be significantly lower than on a server. Many applications have a real-time requirement and are always-on. This means that there is a fixed budget for the total number of operations that can be carried out within a NN inference. Furthermore, microcontrollers have very limited memory availability and it will typically be necessary to fit the entire NN model within the available kilobytes. These issues can be handled both by careful optimization of the NN itself and by optimizing the low-level code for performance and memory footprint.

Google's MobileNet v1 image classification model (introduced in 2017), which runs on smartphones, has a memory requirement of more than 15MB, and needs more than 400 million multiply accumulate operations. Clearly, to make such models useful on edge devices, they need to be smaller (to fit in limited memory), and to be computationally cheaper to execute. We can do this by reducing their capabilities (perhaps recognizing only a few words, or image types), by reducing accuracy, or by reducing the data size (for example, by using smaller input image dimensions). As we shall see, we can also convert models to use integer arithmetic and make use of built-in hardware features of Helium.

In this chapter, we will review neural networks, before looking at CMSIS-NN, an open-source library of optimized software kernels that maximize the NN performance on Cortex-M cores. We will look at the process of converting a model from a standard neural network framework (e.g. Caffe or PyTorch) to CMSIS-NN. We will look at TensorFlow Lite and give an example of training a model and deploying it to a CPU with Helium. Finally, we will briefly introduce the CMSIS-DSP library functions which can be used to implement "classical" ML techniques, which do not use neural networks.

12.1 Introduction to Neural Networks

Neural networks are a class of ML algorithms. They are widely used in a range of applications, including image classification, object detection, natural language processing and speech recognition.

This book will only look at how Helium technology can be used to efficiently implement neural networks and the reader should refer to other sources if further information on ML algorithms is required. However, we will provide a simple overview, in order to illustrate how key Helium features are employed.

Technology in this area is advancing rapidly, but common types of NN include multi-layer perceptron (MLP), convolutional neural networks (CNNs) and recurrent neural networks (RNNs).

The basis for neural networks is a computational model of a neuron. This has a set of inputs with associated weights and produces an output using an activation (or transfer) function. Each neuron also has a bias, effectively a static input (e.g. of 1.0) to which a weight must also be applied. The weighted inputs are summed and then the activation function maps the input value to the output signal. Examples might include a hyperbolic tangent (tanh), or a sigmoid function which outputs a value between 0 and 1 with an s-shaped distribution. A rectifier function (which outputs 0 for a negative input, and a ramp where the output equals the input for positive inputs) is most commonly used today. These neurons are connected together to form neural networks.

The MLP is modeled on the human brain and is structured so that there is a set of neurons, each of which is stimulated by connected nodes. Figure 12.1 shows a very simple network of three layers.

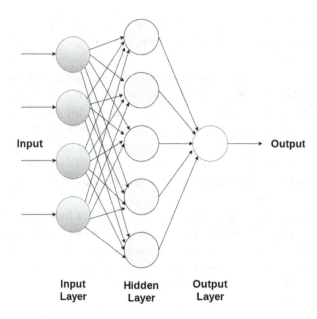

Input   Input   Hidden   Output
               Layer   Layer   Layer

Figure 12.1: Neural network layers

The input (or visible) layer is typically shown with one neuron per input value in the dataset (e.g. one per pixel if we are processing images) and may not actually be a neuron, but simply pass inputs through to the next layer. Hidden layers are not externally visible. There may be many hidden layers and the word "deep" is applied to such networks. The output layer is responsible for outputting a value (or vector) in the required format. Once a model of a neural network has been created, it needs to be trained. This means that we apply a set of training data to the network and automatically tune the weight values of each neuron, by an iterative process, to attempt to produce a neural network with the desired characteristics.

12.1.1 Convolutional Neural Networks

CNNs are most commonly used for image recognition, but have many other applications (e.g. AlphaGo, which famously beat the world's best human Go player, used CNNs to evaluate positions and to suggest moves to try).

In simple terms, image recognition means that we will supply an input image, which will be a 3-D array of pixel values. For example, a 640 × 480 image might be represented by a 640 × 480 × 3 array of byte values showing the RGB intensity at each pixel. The output from the algorithm is a set of numbers which describe the probability of the image being a member of a particular class (for example, a 0.95 chance that this is a cat).

The first layer of a CNN is a conv (convolutional) layer. This takes a filter (also called a kernel or neuron) which is moved across the whole image. It is a small array of numbers (weights, also just called parameters) with the same depth as the input. The area to which the filter is applied is called the receptive field.

The filter is convolved across the input image, so that for each unique location that the filter can fit we produce a number, which is calculated by multiplying the pixel values of the image with the corresponding filter value and summing the multiplications. The resulting two-dimensional array is called an activation map, or feature map. Typically, we will use more than one filter, to retain more spatial information. Filters typically act as feature identifiers. This means that they are able to detect simple characteristics such as colors, curves, straight lines etc.

CNNs typically contain multiple conv layers. This means that the output activation map of one conv layer provides the input to another conv layer. When we apply further filters, we are able to detect higher-level features, such as combinations of a curve and a straight line. As more layers are added to the network, activation maps representing increasingly complex features are produced. Furthermore, the filters have a larger receptive field and are influenced by a larger area of the original image.

Between conv layers, we will typically have Rectified Linear Units (ReLU) and/or Pooling layers. A ReLU is used to introduce nonlinearity to the system, by applying the function $f(x) = \max(0, x)$ to all inputs. In other words, all negative activations are set to 0. This is simple to perform in hardware and increases the non-linear properties of the network. Pooling layers essentially down-sample the input, to reduce the number of parameters/weights and hence memory footprint and cycle count. Additionally, it reduces the possibility of overfitting a model.

The final layer, at the end of the network, is the fully-connected layer. This takes an input volume (the output of the preceding layer) and computes an N-dimensional vector, where N is the number of possible classifications that the model produces. So, if our network is able to classify images as a flower, a cat or a person, it might produce four outputs – an 80% chance of being a flower, 5% chance of being a cat, 5% chance of being a person and 10% chance of being something else. A Softmax function, an activation function which converts numbers into probabilities that sum to one, is often used. It outputs a vector which represents the probability distributions of a list of potential outcomes.

CNNs are created by a training process. This requires a set of images, each of which is labeled with what it represents, which are applied to the model to cause the filter weights to be adjusted through a process called backpropagation. The process is repeated for each batch of training images, usually for a fixed number of iterations.

Backpropagation can be thought of as four separate processes per iteration. During the forward pass, we apply a training image to the network and look at the output. As we started with a random set of weights, the output is unable to perform any classification. This output goes to the loss function, which calculates a value based on the output of the network compared with the expected output from the training data (e.g. if the label says the image is a cat, the expected output is 100% cat and 0% for everything else). In order to produce a network which correctly predicts, we need to minimize the loss. To do this, we must perform a backward pass, which determines which weights have the largest effect on the loss and how to adjust them to reduce the loss. The final step is the weight update, where the weights are updated. The rate at which these changes are made is called the learning rate. A higher learning rate (bigger changes to weights per iteration) may mean that we produce an optimal set of weights more quickly, but may result in the optimum point not being reached.

12.1.2 Recurrent Neural Networks

Recurrent neural networks are a class of neural network that are used in situations where we have a series of data. An example might be natural language processing, where we have a series of words to handle. Unlike a CNN, where we might have a single image as the input, an RNN works where the order of inputs in a sequence can affect the output. RNNs are made from a set of modules in which we produce a hidden state vector by multiplying a matrix of weights with the input, and adding the result of a set of recurrent weights multiplied with the "hidden state" vector from the previous time step. These recurrent weight matrices are the same for all time steps.

A gated recurrent unit (GRU) gives us a more complex way of calculating the hidden state vector, which allows the model to better handle long-distance dependencies. It is broken into three parts, an update gate, a reset gate, and a memory container. In simple terms, if the update gate value is close to 1 the current input is ignored, and the previous hidden state is retained. Conversely, if it is close to zero the hidden state value is ignored, and the output depends only on the current input. In other words, it controls how much the previous hidden state influences the current hidden state. The reset gate allows the model to drop information that is not relevant to the future output. If its value is close to 1, the memory container keeps the previous hidden state, if it is close to 0, it ignores the previous hidden state.

A LSTM (long short-term memory) unit works in a similar way to a GRU. An LSTM cell contains three "gates." Each gate has a (sigmoid) neural net layer and a multiply operation. The sigmoid layer outputs a value between 0 and 1 which describes how much of each component should be allowed through to the next stage, where 0 means nothing gets through and 1 means everything gets through. The "forget" gate controls what information from the current cell state will be thrown away. The "input" gate decides which values will be updated and creates a vector of new candidates and the "output" gate filters exactly how much of the cell value is output.

12.2 CMSIS-NN

It is not practical to run the full ML framework on a Cortex-M device. Instead, we typically want to run the code bare-metal, or with a minimal OS, to make efficient use of the available memory and clock cycles. Arm NN translates a trained model to code that runs on Cortex-M cores using CMSIS-NN functions.

CMSIS-NN is a library of efficient neural network kernels for Arm Cortex-M processor cores. It aims to maximize the performance and minimize the memory requirements, in order to be able to operate successfully on such devices. The functions are used by an application to implement the NN inference application and can easily be targeted for common machine learning frameworks such as TensorFlow etc. CMSIS-NN APIs may be used directly in application code. CMSIS-NN is publicly available, free and comes with an Apache 2.0 Open Source license. The utility functions provided (and the DSP functions in CMSIS-DSP) allow construction of more complex NN modules such as LSTM. The code is divided into two parts:

- **NN Functions** – This includes functions implementing standard neural network layer types, including convolution, depthwise separable convolution, fully connected (i.e. inner product), pooling, and activation. In some cases, multiple versions are provided – one a standard version that works in all situations, others which are optimized for particular use cases, but which may have parameter limitations or require input in a specific form.

- **NN Support Functions** – This includes support functions used in NN functions, such as data conversion and activation tables. The provided functions can also be used within an application for more complex NN modules not provided within the library. An example – an implementation of a GRU layer (discussed in Section 12.1) – showing how to create these can be found here:

https://github.com/ARM-software/CMSIS_5/tree/develop/CMSIS/NN/Examples/ARM/arm_nn_examples/gru

One key feature of CMSIS-NN is that the library functions operate on fixed-point (8- or 16-bit) data. From the hardware point of view, this reduces the energy cost of computation and reduces the memory required to store network weights and activations. This conversion to low-precision fixed-point does require some developer effort to perform the necessary quantization but does not appear to degrade the accuracy of the NNs.

CMSIS originally used a fixed-point quantization which uses a power-of-two scaling, which allows bitwise shift operations to be used for scaling. This legacy quantization format is being replaced by one which is compatible with TensorFlow Lite for Microcontrollers.

12.2.1 CMSIS-NN Optimizations

CMSIS-NN includes a number of important optimizations for efficient NN implementation. The most important low-level operation in a neural network is matrix multiplication and so optimization of this code is vital. For large matrices, it is particularly important to reduce the total number of memory loads.

A convolution layer computes the dot product between filter weights and a small receptive field in the input feature map. A neural network performing image recognition may spend more than 90% of cycles performing convolution and require billions of floating- point operations to complete. It proceeds by reordering and expanding the input through an `im2col` image-to-column function, and then performing a matrix multiply, which is implemented using a GEMM algorithm. GEMM stands for GEneral Matrix-matrix Multiplication.

As we saw earlier, an image can be regarded as a 3-D array (with the third dimension being the red, green and blue pixel values). We convert this into a 2-D array which can be treated as a matrix. Each convolution kernel is applied to a small 3-D cube within the image, so we take all of the values from that cube and write them as a column within a matrix (this is `im2col`, image-to-column). We do the same for the convolution kernel weight values, creating rows in the second matrix. The image-to-column process requires us to copy input values into multiple column locations. This can represent a significant amount of memory usage, which may be a problem in a microcontroller system. The library code therefore expands only two columns at a time. This allows us to get the best performance from the matrix multiplication code while keeping the memory overhead low. By interleaving data movement and compute, we can minimize memory footprint and achieve better performance.

There are two common image data formats for 3-D convolution layers, channel-height-width (CHW) and height-width-channel (HWC). The data layout has no impact on matrix multiplication, but HWC format gives more efficient data loading, as data for each (x, y) location is stored contiguously. This format is therefore preferred by the CMSIS-NN library.

Implementation of pooling layers is improved by splitting pooling into separate x and y directions (i.e. along the width and then the height). This allows the results of finding max and average values in the x direction to be reused in the y direction. Pooling is done in place, to avoid the need for extra memory. This does, of course, mean that the input data is destroyed. Activation functions such as sigmoid/ tanh are implemented using table lookups, rather than computation. ReLU is comparatively easy to accelerate by SIMD code which converts any negative value to a zero.

12.2.2 CMSIS-NN Helium Optimization

For C code, when a Helium-capable target is specified and the appropriate optimization levels are selected, the compiler will auto-vectorize where it is able to do so. Additionally, the CMSIS-NN library contains many Helium-specific optimizations. These are enabled by using `#define ARM_MATH_MVEI`. These two factors provide a significant performance increase for running machine learning algorithms. This happens without any need for the programmer to do anything apart from select appropriate configuration options.

We have already seen how Helium can enable vectorization of calculations, such as matrix multiplication and convolution, for DSP. These operations are also fundamental to neural networks. In CMSIS-NN, there are Helium-optimized versions of these. For example, there is a NN support function, `arm_nn_mat_mul_core_4x_s8()`, which does a matrix multiplication of four rows and one column, using a loop of `VLDRB` and `VMLADAVA` instructions. The loop is unrolled, so that we use four `LDRB` instructions to load values from four rows. The load and multiply instructions are interleaved, so that instruction overlapping can take place, and tail predication is used.

If we look in the CMSIS-NN Convolution functions folder, the function `arm_convolve_s8()` has its own Helium-specific `im2col` function, to allow efficient computation of the convolution. It then calls the NN-supporting matrix multiply code just described. Other parts of the operation can also be vectorized. For example, the depthwise convolution function in `arm_depthwise_conv_s8.c` performs requantization on its output. It makes use of a Helium-specific quantization inline function `arm_requantize_mve` which performs the operation on a vector of four 32-bit values, making it much faster than the standard Cortex-M equivalent.

Additionally, there are Helium-specific versions of many neural network elements, including pooling, Softmax and fully connected layers. Let's look at one of these in more detail. In CMSIS-NN Softmax Functions, we have `arm_softmax_s8.c`. The standard implementation of Softmax involves the calculation:

$$y_i = \frac{e^{x_i}}{\sum_j e^{x_j}}$$

However, calculations using the natural logarithm e are expensive on a microcontroller, and so is division. The function begins by iterating over the input, looking for the maximum value. This is straightforward to vectorize, using a loop of `VCTP`, `VLDRB` and `VMAX` instructions to read the data and find the maximum. To calculate e^x we use an inline function called `arm_nn_exp_on_negative_values()` which is defined in arm_nnsupportfunctions.h. This uses a Taylor expansion to perform a fixed-point calculation, which is valid only for a small range of negative input values.

The same file contains two other inline functions, `arm_divide_by_power_of_two()` and `arm_sat_doubling_high_mult()`, which are used heavily by the Softmax code. Each of these has a Helium-optimized version, denoted by the _mve suffix.

The standard `arm_sat_doubling_high_mult()` function uses the C multiply operator followed by a shift and a comparison to do the saturation. The `arm_sat_doubling_high_mult_mve()` version simply uses one `VQRDMULHQ` instruction to handle four multiply/saturate operations in parallel and is an order of magnitude faster.

Similarly, the `arm_nn_divide_by_power_of_two()` function uses a right shift to calculate the result, an `AND` operation to calculate the remainder, and then a pair of "if" and increment operations to perform rounding. The Helium version is able to use just four vector instructions, `VDUP`, `VSHR`, `VAND` and `VQADD`, to handle four divisions.

12.3 TensorFlow Lite for Microcontrollers

In developing a machine learning solution for a Helium-based Cortex-M device, we must choose a neural network model type and generate a trained model, bearing in mind the hardware constraints of the device. We then need to turn this into a deployable model and use optimized CMSIS-NN functions to produce code for our hardware.

TensorFlow is a free, open-source software library for machine learning. It was originally developed at Google. Its website, https://www.tensorflow.org/, provides a wide range of tutorials and introductory material which make it easy to create and deploy machine learning models.

TensorFlow Lite is a set of tools which make it easier to run TensorFlow models on smaller devices, such as phones, IoT edge nodes and microcontrollers, where a small binary size is required and less computing power is available. There are two main parts. The TensorFlow Lite interpreter runs specially optimized models on these smaller devices. The TensorFlow Lite converter converts TensorFlow models into an efficient form (i.e. with improved performance and smaller binary size) for use by the interpreter. Various platforms are supported, including Android, IoS and embedded Linux, and APIs are provided for C++, Java, Python and other languages. There are also a set of pre-trained models for common machine learning tasks which can easily be customized. TensorFlow Lite is already used on billions of mobile devices, in applications such as Google Photos and Gmail.

TensorFlow Lite for Microcontrollers (TFLM) is a port of TensorFlow Lite. It allows us to run models on very small microcontroller devices. It does not require standard C/C++ libraries, or operating system support. The core runtime and a useful machine learning model can fit within an Arm Cortex-M device in less than 32kB.

There are many widely available resources to learn about TensorFlow and many freely available examples covering image classification, keyword detection etc. This section of this book does not aim to duplicate existing tutorials, but will instead discuss the process of training and deploying a model onto a Helium-based microcontroller device.

In order to do this, we will need to train a TensorFlow model (or download an example). Training is not performed on the target microcontroller. We will then need to convert this model to the standard TensorFlow Lite format, perform quantization and convert to a C byte array.

After that, we need to write code to collect data (e.g. from a microphone, camera or other sensors), run the model using the TensorFlow Lite for Microcontrollers C++ library, including handling of low-level memory management for the library. We then need to include code to use the output from the model in our system. Finally, we need to deploy this code on our target.

There are some constraints that we need to be aware of. The memory available on your device to store the model will act as a limit, as may the available processing power for real-time execution. Using a quantized model will help as these are smaller and execute more efficiently. The TensorFlow Lite for Microcontrollers library supports only a subset of the functions available in TensorFlow. Further functionality is being added over time, so it will be necessary to consult documentation for details of this. Currently, for example, certain types of RNN models cannot be supported.

12.3.1 TensorFlow Lite for Microcontrollers and CMSIS-NN
In the TensorFlow repository, the directory micro/kernels/cmsis-nn contains optimized kernels that make use of CMSIS-NN. These are selected by adding `TAGS=cmsis-nn` to the make command line.

CMSIS-NN supports a "legacy" API and one that supports TFLM's symmetric quantization scheme. The TFLM-compliant API includes support for input and/or filter offset, per-channel rather than per-layer quantization, fused activation, a per-layer output offset, and more complex requantization. As further development of CMSIS-NN will focus on the new API, it follows that Helium optimizations are primarily also to be found in the functions which support this TFLM API. The majority of these functions have the _s8 suffix. We'll look at the legacy API in Section 12.4.

12.3.2 Model Conversion
Once we have a model, it needs to be optimized to allow it to be run within the constraints of a microcontroller device. As we have already seen, one key step is quantization for both size and speed.

Full quantization of both weights and activations to integers normally requires measurement of the dynamic range of inputs and activations, so that the conversion is correctly calibrated. Weights and activations are represented by two's-complement 8-bit values, in the range -128 to $+127$, although activations do not necessarily have the zero point at zero.

Best results can be achieved by performing quantization-aware training, but this may not be possible when using pre-trained models. Pre-trained fully quantized models are available from the TensorFlow Lite model repository.

A trained TensorFlow model needs to be converted to a FlatBuffer and modified to use TensorFlow Lite operations. This is done use the TensorFlow Lite converter Python API, which produces a .tflite file. The Unix command xxd is used to convert this into a C source file which contains the model as a char array.

12.3.3 Deploying the Model on a Cortex-M CPU with Helium

Executing a TensorFlow Lite model on a target device, based on some input data, is known as an inference. We must use the TensorFlow Lite interpreter in order to perform an inference. This involves:

- Loading the model into memory. In the microcontroller environment, this is typically done by encoding the model as an array in C code.

- Transforming the input data into the format required by the model.

- Using the TensorFlow Lite API to execute the model. This may involve building the interpreter and allocating tensors.

- Use the output.

The TensorFlow repository on github contains (in the root directory micro) the TensorFlowLite for Microcontrollers C++ library. As the repository is large, a number of scripts and example project files are included to extract the relevant source files for ease of deployment onto the target.

When deploying code in our target, we must include the library headers, include the model, set up logging and reporting of errors (this will be target-dependent), load the model, and load the operations resolver (as a model will only use a subset of the available operations this will be model-specific). (In a microcontroller environment, it does not make sense to load unused code.) We need to allocate memory for input, output and temporary storage for intermediate calculations, create an instance of the interpreter, and allocate tensors.

12.3.4 Keyword Spotting Example

Keyword spotting (KWS) is becoming an extremely important part of the user interface of smart devices, allowing the user to interact through normal speech. Detection of the keyword may wake up the device and activate the full-scale speech recognition either locally, or in the cloud. In some simpler applications, the keyword may be a voice command to a smart device (for example, turning something on or off). Providing a good user experience needs high accuracy and real-time response. As the keyword spotting code typically has to be always-on, there will often be tight constraints on the power budget. One way to handle this has been to transmit continuous audio data to the cloud. This adds significant latency, has privacy issues for the end user, and can represent a significant load on the network. These factors mean that it is desirable for the KWS code to run at the edge. Neural networks are widely used to implement keyword spotting and so Helium's ability to significantly accelerate this kind of code makes it likely to be widely used.

Running neural network code on a microcontroller with limited computing power and memory availability means that we must make good choices about which type of NN to use. A microcontroller system may have anything from a few tens to a few hundred kB of memory available. This means that the input/output layers, weights and activations of the neural network must fit within this small memory budget. Additionally, the total number of operations per neural network inference may be constrained by the clock speed of the microcontroller, which will be much lower than found in a server or even a mobile phone processor.

These constraints mean that choosing the best model for the task is an important step. There is a trade-off between model size and accuracy. Generally, we need to use small models. The model needs to be small enough to fit into the target. Models can be made smaller by using fewer (and smaller) layers in the network architecture. However, this is likely to lead to underfitting problems. So, it is usually best to use the largest model that will fit in the system, allowing 16kB for the runtime.

A KWS system usually consists of a source of input audio data, a feature extractor and a neural network classifier.

The input audio signal is divided into equal-sized, overlapping frames. Each frame is passed to the feature extractor. This is an engineered algorithm, taken from non-NN-based speech processing research, which translates the time-domain speech signal into a set of frequency-domain spectral coefficients, which enables dimensionality compression of the input signal.

A large amount of research has been carried out in recent years into the most efficient techniques for extracting keywords from audio speech data. There are several standard neural network architectures which can be used. We have already looked at different types of NNs, including CNNs and RNNs. For keyword spotting, deep networks have the smallest number of operations per inference and are well suited to systems with very limited processor power, although their memory requirements are relatively high. CNNs are more accurate but need more processing power. For a small microcontroller, a model type called a Depthwise Separable Convolutional Neural Network (DS-CNN) typically achieves the best accuracy and furthermore is less compute-/memory-intensive.

The DS-CNN performs a convolution on each channel in the input feature map with a separate 2-D filter and then a further 1×1 convolution to combine the outputs in the depth dimension. Decomposing a 3-D convolution into 2-D convolutions followed by 1-D convolutions is more efficient in the number of parameters and operations. This makes a deeper and wider NN architecture possible in a microcontroller.

Running the Example

There is an example included in TFLM called micro_speech. Instructions for deploying this example to a range of platforms are provided with the example. There is also a detailed description for Cortex-M mbed platforms, entitled "Build Arm Cortex-M voice assistant with Google TensorFlow Lite," available from developer.arm.com. It is difficult to give exact instructions here, as this will depend upon the board being used.

You will need a PC on which you have installed Arm tools, the CMSIS library, Python3 and its associated package installer `pip`, plus other standard Unix tools such as `make` (4.2.2 or higher) and `git`. You may also need to install some Python libraries.

You can download the TensorFlow repository with the command:

```
git clone https://github.com/tensorflow/tensorflow.git
```

It should then be possible to build the binary using:

```
make -f tensorflow/lite/micro/tools/make/Makefile micro_speech_bin
```

To use the CMSIS library, you need to add `TAGS="cmsis-nn"` and/or potentially you may need to specify an option for TARGET.

If your target is not one of those that is supported, you may need to modify the code for your environment.

The file command_responder.cc contains a method `RespondToCommand`, which may use a serial port or turn on a different LED, depending upon whether "yes", "no" or an unknown word was detected. You may need to modify this to produce suitable output in your environment. The file audio_provider. cc captures audio from the microphone. You need to provide a suitable equivalent for your own board or provide pre-recorded samples. The main code checks for new audio by looking at the timestamp on the ring buffer which holds the data.

When you have built the binary, it should be possible to demonstrate your device responding to the words "yes" and "no."

12.4 Converting a Neural Network for Helium

In addition to the TensorFlow Lite example just described, it is possible to take a working model from some other framework (e.g. Caffe, PyTorch etc.) and manually convert it to CMSIS-NN to run on a Helium-capable device.

There is a very detailed description of this conversion process here:

https://developer.arm.com/solutions/machine-learning-on-arm/developer-material/how-to-guides/converting-a-neural-network-for-arm-cortex-m-with-cmsis-nn/

Note that there is almost nothing which is Helium-specific in what follows. As we saw earlier, simply enabling the use of Helium within the library and C compiler is sufficient to obtain better performance. It is therefore possible to follow one of the examples on the Arm website and elsewhere which give step-by-step instructions for using specific models and applications such as image recognition etc.

For example, this page describes how to use a standard image recognition ML model on a Cortex-M processor:

https://developer.arm.com/solutions/machine-learning-on-arm/developer-material/how-to-guides/image-recognition-on-arm-cortex-m-with-cmsis-nn/single-page

The flow for porting a model to CMSIS-NN involves the following stages:

1. **Layer Mapping** – Map layers to those supported with CMSIS-NN. If the model uses layers which are not implemented within the library, it will be necessary to implement these yourself, using CMSIS-NN support functions and CMSIS-DSP.

2. **Data Layout** – Ensure that the data layout of the model matches that required by CMSIS-NN and reorder weights if necessary.

3. **Quantization** – Select an appropriate quantization scheme and fixed-point format. Select the input and output Q-format for each layer depending upon the constraints for the layer type and quantization scheme.

4. **Implementation** – Create the CMSIS-NN implementation, including allocation of buffers, function calls, correctly ordered and quantized weights and biases.

5. **Testing** – Test the implementation and reiterate if necessary.

6. **Optimization** – Optimize the code.

Layer Mapping
As we have seen, CMSIS-NN supports many common types of layers. You must identify the mapping between each layer in your model and its CMSIS-NN equivalent. If the layer type is not directly supported, you must implement it yourself. Two common layer types which are not currently implemented are GRU and LSTM. A GRU implementation is provided in CMSIS/NN/arm_nn_examples/gru and this example may be used as a starting point for understanding how to implement other layers. An LSTM layer could be implemented using sigmoid and tanh activation functions and fully connected layers from CMSIS-NN with vector product functions from CMSIS-DSP.

Data Layout
The ML framework may order data in memory differently compared to CMSIS-NN. For example, the elements in a matrix can be arranged in row or column order, and we have even more possibilities

with inputs with more dimensions. This typically applies to fully connected and convolution layers. We need to ensure that weights are reordered such that we get the same output from CMSIS-NN and the original ML layer. Note that there is a separate weight reordering which can be used for optimization purposes.

Quantization

Neural networks are generally trained with floating-point weights and activations. It has been shown that running an NN with reduced-precision floating-point or integer/fixed-point weights causes minimal loss in accuracy. This process of quantization can be done either by performing "quantization-aware" training, or post-training. We can quantize only the model weights, or both weights and activations.

Quantization reduces the precision of the model parameters from their default of 32-bit floating-point numbers. By using 8- or 16-bit representations, we can make the model 50% or 75% smaller. Helium can perform more 8- or 16-bit calculations per instruction and so we can also reduce latency or perform more operations per cycle. In systems which uses caches, the model parameters may better fit within the cache. In general, quantization to float16 gives insignificant levels of accuracy loss, while quantization to integers may produce a higher level of accuracy loss (although still usually acceptable). We also have the potential to quantize weights and activations differently.

The comments which follow apply to the legacy quantization scheme of CMSIS-NN. As we saw in Section 12.3, a different quantization scheme is used with TensorFlow Lite.

Switching a model from floating-point to fixed-point arithmetic has the potential to introduce errors and reduce accuracy. Training a quantized network should produce better results but is more complicated and precludes the use of pre-trained models. Some frameworks provide tools which allow networks to be trained with quantization effects, but these are typically not completely identical to the fixed-point CMSIS kernels.

Instead, we may choose to quantize a network which is already trained. This is simpler and the process is the same regardless of the framework originally used. We select a word size of 8- or 16-bits and can then simply generate the weights and biases. Most CMSIS-NN functions have an 8-bit version and a 16-bit version. Usually, the same size is used throughout, otherwise conversions between 8-bit and 16-bit would be required between layers.

For the activation values, quantization requires us to know the range of values. This requires applying a range of inputs to the network (ideally the full training pattern) and recording statistics about the values at the input and output of each layer. This needs to be at least the minimum and maximum values, but potentially also information about the distribution of values, to allow experimentation with several quantization schemes later. A simple approach is to use the full range of values from the minimum to the maximum, but better results may be achieved by concentrating on the most common values, or by quantization schemes which discard outliers. As the network performance may depend on the quantization scheme chosen, it may be necessary to repeat this step for some layers to improve performance.

When a quantization scheme has been selected, the Q-format for the layer inputs and outputs can be chosen. Some layers impose constraints on the output format. For example, the max pool CMSIS-NN implementation requires that the same Q-format is used for input and output. Fully connected layers and convolutional layers allow the output format and input format to differ by shifting the biases and the output values.

The Q-format for each layer is selected by iterating through, starting at the input. The input Q-format is derived on the statistics of the training patterns. If the input layer is fully connected or convolutional, the output Q-format is selected based upon the output statistics. Otherwise, the output Q-format is governed by the layer type and the input format.

Once you know the Q-format of the input and output of the fully connected and convolutional layers, then you can compute the bias shift and out shift. During the computation of the model, the fixed-point representation for different types of data (inputs, weights, biases, and outputs) might not be identical. The scaling factors for biases and outputs are passed as parameters to the functions. As the scaling is based on powers of two, bitwise shifts can be used for scaling. We use the input parameters, `bias_shift` and `out_shift` to do the scaling, so that we have:

```
bias_shift = Ninput + Nweight - Nbias
out_shift = Ninput + Nweight - Noutput
```

where `Ninput`, `Nweight`, `Nbias` and `Noutput` are the number of fractional bits in the inputs, weights, biases, and outputs.

Implementation

The process to generate a CMSIS-NN implementation is to go through each layer in turn, starting with the first layer. If it is a fully connected or convolutional layer, the reordered weights and biases must be quantized, and the coefficients placed into C arrays. You then generate a function call to the appropriate code, with the bias, out shift and Q-format already calculated. For other layers, a function call with the appropriate parameters is required. Each layer may need memory buffers to be allocated, including input and output buffers (may be the same, e.g. for pooling layer) and in some cases a temporary buffer for working data.

Once the network has been implemented, its input and output must be considered. It will normally be necessary to create code which converts input from sensors in your system to the Q-format expected by the input layer of the network. The constraints of this format conversion may be a factor when implementing the model. The output may also need some post-processing to be in a format usable by subsequent code in your system.

Testing

It is necessary to test the implementation. Obviously the first step is to ensure that the model has been implemented correctly. However, because the quantization and use of a fixed-point implementation can significantly affect performance, it is important to also measure and compare the performance on a full set of test patterns, with the original model.

Optimization

CMSIS-NN has several versions of some functions. For some layers, there are specific _opt versions which require weights to be reordered. There are also versions which are optimized for particular layer dimensions. Using the most efficient version of each layer increases performance and may reduce memory footprint. Memory usage may also be reduced by reusing those buffers within the network which are not used simultaneously.

12.5 Classical Machine Learning

So far in this chapter, we have looked at neural networks. However, the field of machine learning is broader than this. CMSIS-DSP includes functions to implement other statistical machine learning techniques including Support Vector Machine (SVM), Gaussian naïve Bayes classifier, and Clustering Analysis. Such methods can be significantly faster to execute than neural networks and, unlike neural networks, it is generally possible to explain how they reach an inference. However, their implementation requires greater expertise than simply using a pre-trained neural network. Typical applications include image recognition, classification of audio, natural language processing and anomaly detection.

As this book is focused on Helium, the interested reader should refer elsewhere for an introduction to these. CMSIS-DSP contains examples and documentation, which will work unmodified on a CPU which supports Helium and running these examples is a recommended starting point.

Here, we will briefly summarize what is available in CMSIS-DSP and point out some of the Helium-specific optimizations. The classical ML functions only support single-precision floating-point.

The new functions are contained in the following CMSIS-DSP directories:

- **SVM Functions** – This provides functions for implementing an SVM. An SVM is a machine-learning model that uses classification algorithms for two-group classification problems. After training an SVM model with sets of labeled training data for each category, it can categorize new sets of input. Four kinds of classifier are supported: linear, polynomial, radial basis function, and sigmoid.

- **Bayesian Estimators** – This provides support for implementing Bayes classifiers, which are simple probabilistic classifiers, predicting the most likely class of some input.

- **Distance Functions** – Clustering algorithms partition a set of points into different clusters of similar points. They use methods to measure how close or similar the points are and often rely on a distance function for that purpose. CMSIS-DSP provides many commonly used distance functions.

- **Support Functions** – This directory mainly contains type conversion and sort and copy operations for general DSP support, but has two functions to compute weighted sums for classical ML algorithms.

- **Statistics Functions** – Again, this directory primarily contains functions for general DSP use, such as mean, standard deviation etc. However, it has two ML-related functions, `arm_entropy_f32()`, which calculates the entropy of a probability distribution, and `arm_kullback_leibler_f32()`, which calculates the Kullback–Leibler divergence between two probability distributions.

Many of these CMSIS functions have vectorized Helium versions which are selected by the preprocessor define `ARM_MATH_MVEF`. For example, the function `arm_gaussian_naive_bayes_predict()` is able to make use of the `VLDR`, `VMUL`, `VADD`, `VFMA` and `VSUB` instructions, along with tail predication, to perform four calculations in parallel. For those parts of the algorithm which are not handled directly by Helium instructions, vectorized inline functions can be used. For example, the function `vrecip_medprec_f32()` defined in arm_vec_math.h uses Newton's method to calculate the reciprocal on a vector of four single-precision floating-point values and the inline function `vlogq_f32()` uses vector operations with a look-up table.

Similarly, vectorized Helium code can be found in the library for SVM (e.g. arm_svm_linear_predict_f32.c), distance functions (for example, arm_chebyshev_distance_f32.c), support functions (for example, arm_barycenter_f32.c) and statistics (e.g. arm_kullback_leibler_f32.c).

Answers

Chapter 1
1. 128. There are eight 128-bit wide registers, each of which can store sixteen 8-bit values.

2. Arm Architecture Armv8.1-M

3. No. The FPU provides optional support for double-precision floating-point, but Helium provides vector operations only for single-precision and half-precision numbers.

Chapter 2
1. Single instruction, multiple data

2. +127

3. Half-precision floating-point potentially allows us to perform double the number of calculations per instruction compared with single-precision, which can give a significant performance boost. The memory footprint of storing half-precision values is half that of single-precision, which may be a factor where we have large arrays and limited memory.

Chapter 3
1. S4–S7

2. Four

3. Tail predication

4. Unsigned 32-bit integer

Chapter 4
1. `VADD`

2. `VFMA` multiplies two vector registers. `VMLA` multiplies a vector register by a scalar value.

3. IT (If-Then) causes entire instructions to be executed or not. `VPT` allows individual lanes within a vector register to be predicated.

Chapter 5
1. Narrows – it takes 32-bit vector values and writes out bytes to memory.

2. `0x1040`

3. A scatter-gather load reads from a set of non-contiguous addresses, whose offsets from the base are given by a vector register. A normal load reads from a set of sequential, contiguous memory addresses.

Chapter 6

1. `DLS` ensures that there will always be at least one iteration of the loop. `WLS` will cause a branch to the end of the loop (specified by the label) if the iteration count is zero.

2. The `LCTP` instruction is used to break (early terminate) out of a tail-predicated loop.

3. No. The `LSLL` instruction operates on a 64-bit value held in two general-purpose registers.

Chapter 7

1. CMSIS is a hardware abstraction layer for Arm-based microcontrollers, which provides a standard software interface. It includes Helium-enabled libraries for DSP and machine learning.

2. We need to use –O2 or higher.

3. An intrinsic function is a built-in function which is replaced during compilation by a specific sequence of low-level instructions.

Chapter 8

1. The PMU allows software to non-invasively gather information about software execution, including cycle times, numbers of instructions and many other event types.

2. Code running under an OS might be affected by many factors. For example, interrupt handling may cause code or data to be lost from the cache, or the code may be contending with some other application for use of a shared resource.

3. Interleaving different types of instruction can improve performance on CPUs (such as Cortex-M55) with dual-beat implementations of Helium. However, it is not architecturally guaranteed that all CPU implementations will show this behavior; a CPU implementation with a different pipeline structure might not.

Abbreviations/Acronyms

The following abbreviations and acronyms are used in this book.

ADC	Analog-to-digital converter
ALU	Arithmetic logic unit
API	Application programming interface
APSR	Application program status register
Arm ARM	Arm Architecture Reference Manual
CMSIS	Cortex Microcontroller Software Interface Standard
CNN	Convolutional neural network
CPU	Central processing unit
DFT	Discrete Fourier transform
DS-5	Development Studio 5
DSP	Digital signal processing (or digital signal processor)
DWT	Data watchpoint and trace unit
ETM	Embedded trace macrocell
FFT	Fast Fourier transform
FIR	Finite impulse response
FPSCR	Floating-point status and control register
FPU	Floating-point unit
GCC	GNU C compiler
GRU	Gated recurrent unit
HAL	Hardware abstraction layer

HPC	High-performance computing
IoT	Internet of Things
ISA	Instruction set architecture
JTAG	Joint Test Action Group (the IEEE1149 standard for boundary scan test and debug)
LR	Link register
LSB	Least significant byte
LSTM	Long short-term memory
MAC	Multiply-accumulate
MDK	ARM Keil Microcontroller Development Kit
MISRA	Motor Industry Software Reliability Association
ML	Machine learning
MLP	Multi-layer perceptron
MPU	Memory protection unit
MSP	Main stack pointer
MVE	M-Profile Vector Extension
NN	Neural network
NPU	Neural processing unit
OEM	Original equipment manufacturer
PC	Program counter
PMU	Performance monitor unit (can also be power management unit in Cortex-M CPUs)
PSP	Process stack pointer
PSR	Program status register

RAS	Reliability, availability and servicability
RNN	Recurrent neural network
RTOS	Real-time operating system
SCB	System control block
SIMD	Single instruction, multiple data
SoC	System-on-a-chip
SP	Stack pointer
SRAM	Static RAM
SVM	Support vector machine
TCM	Tightly-coupled memory
TFLM	TensorFlow Lite for Microcontrollers
VPR	Vector predication status and control register

References

The following documents are referenced in this book:

Specification	URL
Armv8.1-M Architecture Reference Manual ARM DDI 0553	https://developer.arm.com/docs/ddi0553/bi
Cortex-M55 Technical Reference Manual	https://developer.arm.com/-/media/Arm%20Developer%20Community/PDF/Processor%20Datasheets/Arm%20Cortex-M55%20Processor%20Datasheet.pdf
CMSIS Documentation	https://arm-software.github.io/CMSIS_5/General/html/index.html
Helium Intrinsics Reference	https://developer.arm.com/architectures/instruction-sets/simd-isas/helium/helium-intrinsics
Keil MDK Documentation	https://www2.keil.com/mdk5/docs

Index

The Arm Education Media Story

Did you know that Arm processor design is at the heart of technology that touches 70% of the world's population - from sensors to smartphones to super computers.

Given the vast reach of Arm's computer chip and software designs, our aim at Arm Education Media is to play a leading role in addressing the electronics and computing skills gap; i.e., the disconnect between what engineering students are taught and the skills they need in today's job market.

Launched in October 2016, Arm Education Media is the culmination of several years of collaboration with thousands of educational institutions, industrial partners, students, recruiters and managers worldwide. We complement other initiatives and programs at Arm, including the Arm University Program, which provides university academics worldwide with free teaching materials and technologies.

Via our subscription-based digital content hub, we offer interactive online courses and textbooks that enable academics and students to keep up with the latest Arm technologies.

We strive to serve academia and the developer community at large with low-cost, engaging educational materials, tools and platforms.

We are Arm Education Media: Unleashing Potential

Arm Education Media Online Courses

Our online courses have been developed to help students learn about state of the art technologies from the Arm partner ecosystem. Each online course contains 10-14 modules, and each module comprises lecture slides with notes, interactive quizzes, hands-on labs and lab solutions.

The courses will give your students an understanding of Arm architecture and the principles of software and hardware system design on Arm-based platforms, skills essential for today's computer engineering workplace.

Available Now:

- Efficient Embedded Systems Design and Programming
- Rapid Embedded Systems Design and Programming
- Digital Signal Processing
- Internet of Things
- Graphics and Mobile Gaming
- Real-Time Operating Systems Design and Programming
- Introduction to System-on-Chip Design
- Advanced System-on-Chip Design
- Embedded Linux
- Mechatronics and Robotics

Digital Signal Processing Online Course

The explosion of digital data in today's world means it is crucial for learners to understand and practice how to manage and process digital signals that come in from a wide variety of sources. The Digital Signal Processing (DSP) Online Course addresses this need. The course is powered by Arm Cortex-M4 based microcontrollers, which enable high performance yet energy-efficient digital signal processing at a very affordable price. By reducing the barrier of entry with the introduction of these low-cost development boards, this course will allow students to practice theory with advanced hardware.

Learning Outcomes

Knowledge and understanding of
- DSP basic concepts such as sampling, reconstruction and aliasing
- Fundamental filtering algorithms such as FIR, IIR, FFT
- Arm-based microcontrollers as low-power DSP computing platforms
- Software programming basics and principles

Intellectual
- Ability to choose between different DSP algorithms for different applications
- Ability to use different design methods to achieve better results
- Ability to evaluate experimental results (e.g. quality, speed, power) and correlate them with the corresponding designing and programming techniques

Practical
- Ability to implement DSP algorithms and design methods on Arm-based microcontrollers
- Ability to use commercial hardware and software tools to develop real time DSP application

Course Syllabus

Prerequisites: Basic C programming and elementary mathematics

Modules
1. Discrete Time Signals and Systems
2. Sampling, Reconstruction and Aliasing: Complex Exponentials and Fourier Analysis
3. Sampling, Reconstruction and Aliasing: Time and Frequency Domains
4. Z-Transform: Time and Frequency Domains
5. FIR Filters: Moving Average Filters
6. FIR Filters: Window Method of Design
7. IIR Filters: Impulse Invariant and Bilinear Transform Methods of Design
8. IIR Filters: Simple Design Example
9. Fast Fourier Transform: Review of Fourier Transformation
10. Fast Fourier Transform: Derivation of Radix-2 FFT
11. Adaptive Filters: Prediction and System Identification
12. Adaptive Filters: Equalization and Noise Cancellation
13. Adaptive Filters: Adaptive FIR Filter

Arm Education Media Books

The Arm Education books program aims to take learners from foundational knowledge and skills covered by its textbooks to expert-level mastery of Arm-based technologies through its reference books. Textbooks are suitable for classroom adoption in Electrical Engineering, Computer Engineering and related areas. Reference books are suitable for graduate students, researchers, aspiring and practising engineers.

Available now, in print and ePub formats:

Embedded Systems Fundamentals with Arm
Cortex-M based Microcontrollers:
A Practical Approach
by Dr Alexander G. Dean
ISBN 978-1-911531-03-6

Digital Signal Processing using Arm Cortex-M
based Microcontrollers: Theory and Practice
By Cem Ünsalan, M. Erkin Yücel, H. Deniz Gürhan
ISBN 978-191153116-6

System-on-Chip with Arm Cortex-M Processors
By: Joseph Yiu, Distinguished Arm Engineer
ISBN 978-1-911531-19-7

Operating Systems Foundations with Linux
on the Raspberry Pi
By Wim Vanderbauwhede, and Jeremy Singer
ISBN 978-1-911531-21-0

Digital Signal Processing using Arm Cortex-M based Microcontrollers: Theory and Practice

By Cem Ünsalan, M. Erkin Yücel, H. Deniz Gürhan
ISBN 978-191153116-6

The Arm Digital Signal Processing (DSP) textbook introduces readers to DSP fundamentals using low-cost, high-performance Arm Cortex-M based microcontrollers as demonstrator platforms. To help readers understand DSP, it covers foundational concepts, principles and techniques, such as signals and systems, sampling, reconstruction and anti-aliasing, FIR and IIR filter design, transforms, and adaptive signal processing. Key features for those learning DSP include a set of hands-on labs that highlight the practical side, end-of-chapter exercises that reinforce the theoretical concepts presented (with answers available online), and online instructor resources.

The textbook is suitable for use in Electronic and Computer Engineering (ECE), Electrical Engineering (EE) and Computer Science (CS) university departments. The labs in this textbook edition target the low-cost Arm Cortex M4-based STM32F4 Discovery micro-controller board.

Cem Ünsalan, Marmara University

Dr. Cem Ünsalan has worked on signal and image processing for 18 years. After receiving a Ph.D. degree from The Ohio State University, USA in 2003, he began working at Yeditepe University, Turkey. He now works at Marmara University, Turkey. He has been teaching microprocessor and digital signal processing courses for 10 years. He has published 20 articles in refereed journals. He has published five international books and holds one patent.

M. Erkin Yucel, Yeditepe University

M. Erkin Yücel received his B.Sc. and M.Sc. degrees from Yeditepe University. He is pursuing a Ph.D. degree on embedded systems at the same university. He has guided microprocessor and digital signal processing laboratory sessions for three years. Currently, he is working in research and development in industry.

H. Deniz Gürhan, Yeditepe University

H. Deniz Gürhan received his B.Sc. degree from Yeditepe University. He is pursuing a Ph.D. degree on embedded systems at the same university. For six years, he has been guiding microprocessor and digital signal processing laboratory sessions. He has published books internationally on microcontrollers.

Table of Contents

arm Education Media

Digital Signal Processing using Arm® Cortex®-M based Microcontrollers

Theory and Practice

Cem Ünsalan, M. Erkin Yücel, H. Deniz Gürhan

Digital Signal Processing

Discover more at **www.arm.com/education**